Experts from Around the World Welcome
The Global Marketing Imperative

In their impressive work, *The Global Marketing Imperative*, Czinkota, Ronkainen, and Tarrant have constructed a veritable handbook for companies with international ambitions. Their descriptions of why progressive firms are moving *now* to take advantage of international markets are complemented with essential information on how to implement international strategies—and how to do so successfully. Recommended reading for those who recognize that opportunity knows no international boundaries.

Toon H. Woltman
Vice President/Area Manager, North America & Mexico
KLM Royal Dutch Airlines
New York, NY

The Global Marketing Imperative might have been called the gospel according to Michael, Ilkka, and John. Authors Czinkota, Ronkainen, and Tarrant make a first-rate team for practice and strategy know-how in international marketing. The strategy is global, the practice is venue- and boundary-specific. The theme: think globally but market locally.

Robert K. Mueller
Former Chairman
Arthur D. Little, Inc.
Cambridge, MA

Global marketing is the key success strategy for Japanese corporations. More than 10 years have passed since we heard the word globalization, yet even major Japanese firms are still lacking the basic skills of international marketing, explained so well in this book. *The Global Marketing Imperative* is a must for every business that wants to succeed in the coming decade.

Toshiyuki Watanabe
Director, Retail System Department
Mitsubishi Electric Corporation
Tokyo, Japan

Finally, a global book on global marketing issues. *The Global Marketing Imperative* is not written for the North American market alone, but can serve as an important tool for the world marketplace, namely practitioners, policy makers, and academics around the globe.

Professor Dr. Tevfik Dalgic
Henley Management College–Nederland
The Netherlands

A comprehensive, no-nonsense primer that can guide managers to success—
and keep them from failure—in a world where customers, channels, and markets
are going global.

Franklin R. Root
Emeritus Professor of International Management
The Wharton School, University of Pennsylvania
Philadelphia, PA

Opportunities abound in the global marketplace, but the perils are many. From
financing to marketing, this book offers a thoughtful, step-by-step guide to going
global—successfully.

Alexander H. Stanton, APR
President and Chief Executive Officer
Dorf & Stanton Communications, Inc.
New York, NY

A highly sophisticated and useful primer. If you want to succeed in international
markets, you need this book.

J. E. Harl
Director of Equity Sales and Trading
Vereinsbank Group
Munich, Germany

There are few guarantees for success in international marketing. Reading this
book comes pretty close.

Lew Cramer
Director General (ret.)
U.S. and Foreign Commercial Service
Washington, DC

The reader gets an excellent, clear and vital view of marketing by reading this
outstanding book. I only wish it had been there when I started the international
marketing adventure.

Birgit Kammerer, Manager
GfK Testmarktforschung GmbH
Nürnberg, Germany

An excellent portrayal of the new global marketplace. Timely information,
guidance, and "how to" recommendations. Valuable for veterans as well as
neophytes to international business.

Donald R. Nicholson II
Director
Profit Project, Deloitte & Touche
Arlington, VA

The Global Marketing Imperative is an outstanding and an important book. It is also timely, as many Japanese companies are rapidly expanding the scope of their globalization.

Masao Yukawa
General Manager, Corporate Business Design Office
Mitsubishi Corporation
Tokyo, Japan

Spot-on material, lively writing style and excellent examples. *The Global Marketing Imperative* drives the message home with a punch! Read it!

Professor A. Diamantopoulos
Chair of International Marketing
European Business Management School, University of Wales
Swansea, UK

The Global Marketing Imperative provides insights that are critical—both for companies in the earliest stages of expanding their geographic scope as well as those of us striving to do it better.

Robert F. Clark
President
Great Salt Lake Minerals Corporation
Overland Park, KS

As a controller of a global company I welcome *The Global Marketing Imperative*. For my job it gives a useful overview as well as many important details of how to control global activities.

Manfred Luessmann
Manager Controlling
AUDI Ag
Inqolstadt, Germany

Miss this book at your own risk. It matters little whether you're running a small or a large enterprise. This work is the window to the future survival of your company.

Martimer R. Feinberg
Chairman of the Board
BFS Psychological Associates, Inc.
New York, NY

In these times of rapid change, the marketing function lies at the crossroads of customers, products, competitors, and technologies. A change in any one of these has an immediate impact on marketing, thus affecting the profitability and survival of a firm. *The Global Marketing Imperative* deals with a broad spectrum of marketing issues that will be of critical importance to the success of every company in the coming years. It represents the best of marketing thinking and practice.

M. H. Battaille, Ph.D.
President
International Public Affairs Centre
Brussels, Belgium

Czinkota, Ronkainen, and Tarrant have written a comprehensive book on making it and surviving in the vast international desert. This book is the true divining rod all executives should put their hands on.

Douglas E. McMahon
Vice President/Account Director
J. Walter Thompson
New York, NY

After having read *The Global Marketing Imperative* it became obvious that the authors had captured the essence of what is driving, and what will drive, global competition. They have substituted elegant theory with pragmatics like countertrade and non-cash transactions in the marketplace. It is a must read for every manager focused on how to compete in a global arena.

Roy Herberger
President
Thunderbird
American Graduate School of International Management
Glendale, AZ

If you plan to make the world your playing field, this book will show you how to use the rules of the game to your benefit.

Wirt Cook
Assistant General Manager
IBM US
White Plains, NY

A true and practical overview from hands-on experience. This book can lead you to successful ventures in the new world of business.

Pieter Pagel
Marketing Manager—Export
DuPont Pharma GmbH
Hamburg, Germany

For the new exporter or experienced trader who thinks he has heard it all, *The Global Marketing Imperative* offers both good tuition and compelling insights.

Steven R. Saunders
Former Assistant US Trade Representative

THE GLOBAL MARKETING IMPERATIVE

Michael R. Czinkota
Ilkka A. Ronkainen • John J. Tarrant

NTC Business Books
a division of NTC *Publishing Group* • Lincolnwood, Illinois USA

Much of the material in *The Global Marketing Imperative* is based on an earlier work by Michael R. Czinkota and Ilkka A. Ronkainen, *International Marketing*, © by The Dryden Press.

Library of Congress Cataloging-in-Publication Data

Czinkota, Michael R.
    The global marketing imperative : positioning your company for the new world of business / Michael Czinkota, Ilkka Ronkainen, John Tarrant.
        p.   cm.
    Includes bibliographical references and index.
    ISBN 0-8442-3550-4
    1. Export marketing—Management.   2. International business enterprises—Management.   I. Ronkainen, Ilkka A.   II. Tarrant, John J.   III. Title.
HF1416.C95   1995
658.8′48—dc20

                                                           CIP

1995 Printing

Published by NTC Business Books, a division of NTC Publishing Group.
4255 West Touhy Avenue, Lincolnwood (Chicago), Illinois 60646-1975, U.S.A.
© 1995 by Michael R. Czinkota, Ilkka A. Ronkainen, and John J. Tarrant.
All rights reserved. No part of this book may be reproduced, stored
in a retrieval system, or transmitted in any form or by any means,
electronic, mechanical, photocopying, recording or otherwise, without
the prior permission of NTC Publishing Group.
Manufactured in the United States of America.

     4 5 6 7 8 9 BC 9 8 7 6 5 4 3 2

ABOUT THE AUTHORS

Dr. Michael R. Czinkota is one of the nation's top international business and marketing experts. Serving as Deputy Assistant Secretary of Commerce during the Reagan Administration, Dr. Czinkota continues to advise government bodies and corporations on international trade, financing, and investment. A faculty member at Georgetown University, Dr. Czinkota publishes and is interviewed extensively in the trade press. He is a frequent and dynamic speaker on international issues.

Dr. Ilkka A. Ronkainen serves on the faculty of Georgetown University, directs Georgetown's program in Hong Kong, and holds an appointment of docent in international marketing at the Helsinki School of Economics in Finland. Dr. Ronkainen teaches in executive programs around the world and has served as a consultant to a wide range of U.S. and international institutions, including IBM, the Rank Organization, and the Organization of American States.

John J. Tarrant, a veteran writer and consultant, has held executive positions at the Research Institute of America and Benton & Bowles Advertising. Mr. Tarrant has authored or coauthored more than 15 books, including *Drucker: The Man Who Invented the Corporate Society* and *Perks and Parachutes.*

DEDICATION

To Ilona, my greatest international marketing success. (MRC)

To Sanna and Susan, my partners in global endeavors. (IAR)

To Dot, my professional partner and beloved companion. (JJT)

We thank the hundreds of executives and professionals in Europe, Asia, the Americas, and Australia who contributed ideas and insights and who, by working with us, permitted us to learn from them.

—The Authors

CONTENTS

THE GLOBAL IMPERATIVE
The World Is Your Marketplace

The global imperative is upon us! No longer merely an inspiring exhortation, thinking and acting globally is the key principle for business success. Both the willing and the unwilling are becoming participants in global business affairs. No matter how large or how small your business, ready or not, here comes the world.

The U.S. home appliance market is a sign of the times. This $11 billion industry has gone global. At the beginning of the 1990s, U.S. manufacturers were locked in a mounting battle with foreign companies, from Electrolux, the world's largest appliance maker, to new entrants from the Pacific Rim. To add to the gloom, industry fundamentals in the United States were and continue to be grim: stagnating sales, rising raw materials costs, and fierce price wars. In contrast, the European market has been growing fast. The onset of the European Union (EU), with all its birth pains, makes the picture even more attractive.

Smaller companies, too, are in the international picture. While conventional wisdom holds true that the 2,500 largest multinational corporations dominate U.S. exports, a rising tide of small and medium-sized firms is coming ·to the fore.

Syntellect, Inc., a manufacturer of automated voice-response systems based in Phoenix, Arizona, increased its export shipments from one percent of total revenue to 21 percent in the 1988–1991 period. The company's sole product is a machine that can answer telephone calls in several different languages and direct the calls to the appropriate recipient. Syntellect commits considerable resources to engineering the product to understand new languages. These efforts have paid off. The automated voice-response machines now respond to 18 languages and

Appliance Manufacturers Go Global[1]

Maytag moved to globalize. It acquired Chicago Pacific Corporation, best known for the Hoover vacuum cleaner in the United States and Europe. Chicago Pacific also makes washers, dryers, and other appliances carrying the Hoover name, selling them not in the United States, but exclusively in Europe and Australia.

Hoover boasts a strong presence in the United Kingdom, but it is not a major European player. So Maytag, in targeting Europe, was essentially introducing new products into new markets. Hoover's name recognition in the United Kingdom offered Maytag the chance to exploit some synergies there, and in Australia. Its strength allowed the expansion of the Hoover line to include Maytag's washers and dryers.

Other appliance manufacturers have kept the same pace. General Electric entered into a joint venture with Britain's General Electric PLC. Whirlpool took a 53 percent stake in the appliance business of Dutch giant N.V. Philips. Whirlpool's move gave it 10 plants on the European continent and some popular appliance lines—a major asset in a region characterized by fierce loyalty to domestic brands.

The U.S. companies confront many new challenges as they venture abroad. The political union of the EU, has of course, not resulted in a convergence of consumer tastes and preferences. The British favor front-loading washing machines, while the French swear by top loaders. The French prefer to cook at high temperatures, causing grease to splatter on oven walls, which calls for self-cleaning ovens. This feature is in less demand in Germany, where cooks prefer lower temperatures.

The heat of the competition matches the size of the opportunity abroad. The appliance companies see their margins suffering as more than 300 manufacturers in Europe alone jockey for position. Nevertheless, the major players are committed to competing in all major world markets. As one Whirlpool executive puts it, "Becoming a global appliance player is clearly the best use of our management expertise and well-established brand line-up."

are sold in 37 global markets, including the Middle East, Central and South America, Asia, and Europe.

From Maytag to Syntellect, companies large and small are facing the fact that they cannot survive by concentrating solely on the domestic market. And while, for smaller companies, exporting is still the most logical way to go global, large-scale concerns seeking a permanent presence abroad must go beyond exporting into more challenging strategic alliances.

The potential rewards are great, and they are matched by high risks. There is fierce competition from all corners of the world. Different world markets have their own peculiarities, their own preferences, their own regulations, and their own problems for those who aspire to sell there. Failure at the global level can ignite a backfire that consumes existing brands and business relationships. But, holding back almost inevitably will mean losing out permanently to competitors who *are* ready to act.

Marketers have no choice. Globalization is an inevitable process. The world is becoming more homogeneous, and distinctions between national markets are not only fading but, for some products, will disappear altogether. This means that marketing is now a world-encompassing discipline. To survive, we have to understand *every* market open to our companies and to our competitors. Without this knowledge, we're doomed.

It's not that until now marketers have been insular or blind to the broader world; they have just not had to think about it. Typically, a company gets a few orders from abroad, or sees other companies generating some export business, and executives think, "Yes, doing business in other countries might be a possibility someday . . . down the road." "Down the road" is here. The window of opportunity is now wide open. But the strategies we've used in the past to reach out into world markets will not carry us much further. Historically, businesses have entered the international market gradually, introducing new products first in highly industrialized nations and subsequently expanding sales to other countries. For consumer goods, the argument was that demand in other countries had not caught up to the more industrialized nations. In this way, corporate planners have seen international markets primarily as a way of giving products a few more years of life after they are moribund domestically. That strategy is now obsolete. Products and innovations speed around the globe. International marketing can no longer be gradual. Products must be introduced into multiple markets simultaneously.

The vastly accelerated rate of information flow, enhanced by tighter international communications links, is a paramount factor in this transformation. Furthermore, the increased level of wealth in emerging nations makes it easier—and more desirable—for consumers to buy *new* products.

Another feature of the transitional world market is the frequent unavailability of exchangeable currency. Even when a marketer identifies a need and comes up with a product to fill that need, nothing happens because there's no way the customers can pay. The new world entrepreneur must adjust to this situation by somehow making use of the "soft currency" available or by using countertrade or barter. These approaches impose great burdens on international marketers, who must not only sell to the original customers but also contrive to market the products received in return to other customers.

World competitors . . . unknown markets . . . instant information . . . collapsed currencies. The world is rudely bursting through corporate castle walls. Executives must figure out—and quickly—the labyrinthine nuances of markets in countries that, a short while ago, they did not even know existed. The stake is survival.

Globalization Drivers

In general, the principles of successful marketing apply universally. However, the application of those principles undergoes a sea change when the company ventures abroad. Marketers have to know the new rules of the game: referees call different infractions, opponents get away with moves that would be fouls on home ground, and certain victory can suddenly slip away because a seemingly minor point was overlooked.

Globalization is taking place against a backdrop of change, clearly evidenced in the three critical ingredients of effective marketing: customers, channels, and the marketplace.

Customers Are Global

A new world customer is taking shape. As just one example, a new group of consumers is seen as emerging in the triad of North America, Europe, and the Far East. Approximately 600 million in number, these consumers have similar educational backgrounds, income levels, aspirations, and use of leisure time. Today's marketers can sell to consumers who, though dispersed throughout the world, are similar enough to each other that they form viable market segments.

Channels Are Global

As customer segments are becoming global, so are channels of distribution. A growing number of retailers are showing great flexibility and resourcefulness in entering new geographic markets. Some are already world powers (such as Bennetton and McDonald's), and others are pursuing aggressive policies of world growth (Toys 'R' Us and IKEA). The availability of worldwide and regional channels makes it imperative for marketers to think globally, if only because if you don't, the competition will.

The Marketplace Is Global

Global marketing is an issue for all companies, even very small ones. This is true even for companies that do not envision selling abroad; now or for decades to come. The world is a marketplace, difficult, and dangerous, but a marketplace nevertheless. And what happens in that global marketplace reverberates to all corners of the world. The sheltered company, working away happily in what seems to be a protected industry feels the rumblings. The "safe" market is no longer safe, because competitors from astonishingly faraway places are suddenly on the scene. The fundamentals of doing business domestically change so radically that the firm must find new markets, or go under.

Those new markets exist; they have to be located. Once located, they have to be assessed. And then they have to be sold, in spite of language barriers, cultural anomalies, government difficulties, fierce competition from all directions, strange distribution arrangements, peculiar legalities, logistical mazes, currency differences, unfamiliar compensation arrangements, and a host of other exotic elements that make the world bazaar an exciting but nerve-wracking place.

The Race Is On

Fear of the unknown is inherent in the human psyche. Until now, many marketers have enjoyed the comfort of home markets. When a corporation got big enough, of course, it went multinational. But for most, there was no reason to think seriously about selling in other countries.

That comfort zone is gone forever. There are still plenty of companies, and plenty of managers., who, blindfolded, choose to go on ignoring the world. But the world will not be ignored any longer. Those who try to do so are ranking themselves with the Jurassics.

Businesses in other industrialized nations have moved faster than those in the United States. As an example, the group of German companies commonly called the Mittelstand has combined forces to get to grips with international markets. Companies in developed nations must now vie for business in the new world markets with the highly developed apparatus the Germans have been building for decades through the Mittelstand. A small but growing number of U.S. executives are starting to watch Germany's small to mid-sized companies closely. In fact,

The Mittelstand: A Role Model for Exporters[2]

The Mittelstand has more than 300,000 members and collectively generates 30 percent of German exports. With fewer than 500 employees each, the Mittelstand companies produce more than two-thirds of Germany's gross national product, train nine of every ten apprentices, and employ four of every five workers.

One reason for the Mittelstand's success is a superior export infrastructure that greatly assists smaller companies. Germany started its export drive in the 1950s. Other countries—the United States among them—are just now building export assistance networks.

Principal benefits of the German export network for small businesses are financial and technical assistance. Small companies are eligible for up to $6 million in inexpensive funding from the government and may also receive substantial research grants. Industry associations provide standard contracts translated into different languages and offer legal assistance. A centralized embassy information network provides expert advice. And local banks go out of their way to help the Mittelstand. For example, many provide their customers the use of an office in their foreign branches and a secretary while they prospect abroad for business.

Mittelstand companies are able to excel even though they compete at a labor cost disadvantage. Take the Wilhelm Zuleeg company, an 85-person, $18 million textile manufacturer. Pressured by low-cost Asian rivals, Zuleeg still manages to churn out high-fashion fabrics for designers such as Anne Klein, Cerruti, and George Resch. The company increased exports from zero to 20 percent in three years.

---

the Mittelstand is being viewed as a more appropriate model for U.S. companies to follow than the often-praised Japanese model.

Global Marketing Literacy

For marketers, global marketing literacy is as important as computer literacy. A command of the elements of international marketing will be essential in the decades to come.

Some aspects of global marketing literacy involve new ways of doing familiar tasks. You need to study the market to find out what customers want and how much they'll pay for it. You need distribution and promotion. You need to get the product to the customer. And you need to get paid. The questions that arise are the same globally as they are domestically, but the answers are different.

Other aspects of international marketing are stranger; some even seem to depart altogether from accepted business practices. But like Alice's experiences when she stepped through the looking glass, they become less strange as soon as you begin to understand the underlying realities and discern the new rules of the game. Until then, if you are not prepared for it, culture shock can be traumatic—and damaging to the bottom line.

Stepping through the Looking Glass with International Research

One major challenge for marketers headed for the new world markets is a lack of information about consumers. The entire marketing discipline is founded on the basic objective of understanding and satisfying customer needs. That's the marketing concept that has pulsed like a dynamo at the center of Western business dominance.

What happens to the marketing concept when you don't know what the buyer wants? As we will see throughout this book, it is dangerous and short-sighted to project our own buying patterns onto substantially different cultures. But, while we know these cultures are different, we don't know *how* they differ. The only way to find out and to know what levers to use in moving buyers is through research.

Although international market research is growing and improving, it is still, by and large, substantially below Western standards. What to do? First entrepreneurs tempted by the new world markets should remember that life existed before the market research industry. Great enterprises were built by founders who used a mixture of observation, hearsay, expert opinion, educated guesses, and gut feeling to learn what customers wanted. This was risky, but risk is ever-present in any venture.

Market research may reduce risk but will never eliminate it. Starting a business in Russia or any other new world market is in a way a return to the higher-risk days of, say, a half-century ago. But the reversion is not complete. There are ways for business people to get a good idea of what end-users in a foreign market will respond to. We will describe these techniques, some of them easily available and inexpensive.

Entrepreneurship Grows from the Ashes of Socialism[3]

Jeffrey Zeiger, age 25, of Trenton, New Jersey, plunged into the newly opened Russian market by opening a restaurant on Komsomolsky Street in the center of Moscow. Zeiger's idea was simple: offer U.S.-style steak and potatoes, followed by apple pie. Expatriates and well-to-do locals, ambassadors, government ministers, and prominent business executives made the eating place, called Tren-Mos, a favorite hangout.

The success of Tren-Mos is not the norm among the new ventures started in Russia. Many hopeful foreign investors fail to get off the ground. Russia is the Klondike for many prospectors, but most fail to strike gold. It will not be any different in any of the other markets opening up around the world.

Two key strategies have made Tren-Mos successful. One is the personal attention provided by Zeiger, who welcomes every guest and asks diners whether they are enjoying their meals. If the entrepreneur had tried to accommodate the venture to local customs and attitudes, he would not have done this. Restaurant patrons in the old Soviet Union were used to much rougher treatment.

The second key is the use of the ruble. The restaurant generates enough profit in rubles to cover almost all expenses. About 80 percent of the lunch customers pay for their meals in rubles; the rest pay in hard currency, with a typical tab being about $21–50. At dinner time, the situation reverses: 80 percent pay hard currency, an average of $30 per meal.

The restaurant buys many staples, such as sugar, flour, and cream, at cheap state prices. With most costs covered by rubles, the dollar profit margin is about 65 cents on every dollar taken in. Zeiger and his partner, the Lenin District Food and Catering Trust, are clearing a solid profit and looking forward to doing even better.

The Tren-Mos story touches on a few aspects of the world's tumultuous transition. The potential is vast. The opportunities for success appear glittering. The surging entrepreneurial spirit always rushes into new openings. Consumers in many parts of the world will respond to approaches that are different from the dreariness and indifference that marked the socialist approach to captive customers. And it is all-important for the new venture to work out a way of capitalizing on the local currency situation as well as the culture of the market.

Sometimes the Flow Is in the Other Direction

Inevitably, Western businesses tend to look at the emerging Central European democracies as potential markets, never dreaming that entrepreneurs in those countries are casting hungry glances westward. We wholeheartedly support democracy and free markets, but increasingly we will be startled to find that the enterprises fostered in the region intend to compete with us in our home markets.

Take the case of the Czech clothing company OP Prostejov. After losing its market in Russia, which used to buy half the firm's output, the company found new customers in Germany, the Netherlands, Belgium, Luxembourg, and the United States. But when a ship loaded with woolen coats and suits arrived in New York, the company ran into import quotas designed to shield the U.S. clothing manufacturers from overseas competition.

Or consider the Russian MI-26 helicopters made by Mil Design Bureau. The MI-26 is the Godzilla of world helicopters, able to lift 40,000 pounds, twice as much as any U.S. heavy-lift chopper. When Mil Design tried to lease its helicopters to Alaskan loggers, the U.S. industry fought back. A spokesperson for Columbia Helicopters said the MI-26 would be dumped on the U.S. market: "They don't know what costing is, so they just give them away. How can we compete when we have banks and interest and principal and things like that?"

As Eastern European officials see it, the very industries that hold their best prospects for success correspond to sectors in the West that possess great political clout, which has paid off in protection from imports. They are finding that Western trade policy is most generous in sectors that don't matter much. For example, the United States signed an agreement allowing U.S. imports of small firearms from the Czech Republic. This was all well and good, said the Czechs, but it's a drop in the bucket compared to what would happen if the West opened its textile and clothing markets.

Production Downshift

A fundamental truth of astrophysics is the "red shift," the tendency of light from remote galaxies to shift toward the lower frequencies in the color spectrum. The red shift is one of the prime indicators of an expanding universe.

A fundamental truth of international business is what we might call "production downshift." Its principle can be stated this way: Production gravitates down the scale of national development. Countries at the high end of the scale—the U.S., Japan, Germany, Canada—become the global equivalent of corporate home offices, sites of management, planning, financial operations, and research and development. In these highly industrialized centers, knowledge is collected, analyzed, and deployed around the world.

However, the "plants" are somewhere else. It is more economical for the industrial entities centered in these countries to manufacture elsewhere. Proximity of home office to plant is no longer a factor. So, as countries move up the scale of business sophistication, they tend naturally to shift production downward to nations with lower cost production capability.

Production downshift foments political and economic storms. People are thrown out of work. Communities are stricken. Powerful forces battle to maintain the status quo. But production downshift, for better or worse, is a fact of world business life. It operates in every part of the globe.

Asia is no exception. There is still a tendency in some Western quarters to think of the Pacific Rim as a kind of monolith. This assumption can skew the thinking of marketers when they begin to plan for doing business in the East.

Entrepreneurship Leaps over Borders

While protectionism and tariff barriers are likely to persist for a considerable time as vestiges of the old order, the new type of world marketer will, increasingly, go over and around those borders to do business.

Anders Dege, a young Norwegian, happened upon the Jalypso filter, a smoke protection device invented by a Missouri man and manufactured in Corona, California. Dege found out that there was a healthy market potential for the device in Norway. The conventional course would have been for Dege to try to work out a way to become the Norwegian representative for the filter. Instead, he moved to the United States, became a distributor for the fledgling product, and now sells an impressive number of filters in his native land by fax and phone.

Increasingly, entrepreneurial thinking will cast off the implicit limits imposed by country of origin. People with good business ideas will try to go to the optimum place in the world to put those ideas into practice. The choice, of course, will be heavily influenced by considerations of lifestyle. Anders Dege moved to Colorado. No matter how well it might have fitted his strategy, he would probably not have moved to, say, Beirut.

International entrepreneurship is generating a new class of adventurers who range the world seeking opportunities. When they spot opportunities, they go for them, ignoring borders. They are tremendous

Daewoo Downshifts Toward the Third World

In the 1980s, South Korea was hailed as the "next Japan," meaning that the country was headed toward a leading place among the world's industrial giants.

It didn't happen that way. Consumers in the developed countries balked. Some Korean goods acquired a reputation for poor quality and poor service.

A couple of decades ago, that might have brought Korea up against an economic brick wall, with no place else in the world to turn. However, today Korean industry is betting that it's possible to make a major shift in direction.

For example, Daewoo Group, the fourth largest of Korea's conglomerates (called *chaebols*), is still making cars, electronic equipment, and home appliances, but it is now targeting developing countries like Colombia, Pakistan, and the Philippines. In 1993 alone, Daewoo had committed some $8 billion to Eastern Europe, Central Asia, and Latin America.[4]

Nor is the commitment just to selling. Daewoo's strategy involves making and selling goods in these places, where the company intends to take advantage of cheap labor *and* find new consumers.

So South Korea may still become the "new Japan." Though Korean companies are gradually building markets in the United States and Europe, their major focus is in the Third World. Everything is relative. Goods spurned by the most developed countries can find other rewarding markets.

---

risk-takers, willing to bet on their skill and drive in markets where information about buying patterns is far from complete, competition is fierce and comes from all directions, and cultural differences and political shifts make for a climate of great uncertainty.

Asian countries and businesses are already stratified and sharply differentiated and are becoming more so. Japan is in a class by itself as an industrial giant. Just as the United States sees manufacturing processes relocating to Mexico because of lower cost, Japan has long since seen a shift of production facilities to technologically less developed Pacific locations. South Korea and Taiwan are complex and sophisticated countries.

Hong Kong, while moving politically under the Chinese umbrella, remains a powerhouse of finance and information technology. And Malaysia has leapt to the fore as a major player.

Production downshift is in full force in the Pacific, as in other parts of the globe. Here's an illustration: a U.S. company sells digitized tablets used in creating computer graphics. The units are bought complete from a company in Malaysia. But they are not made in Malaysia. The Malaysian producer, which has for a long time obtained components made in other Asian countries, has now set up its own manufacturing plants in China.

China, with its vast resources and workforce, will be the scene of an explosion of manufacturing as we approach the year 2000. China is the optimum beneficiary of the production downshift in action and it has the population and willingness to take full advantage of it.

Selling to the World: A Necessary Adventure

Maybe the whole idea of international marketing is enough to give you a headache. Language barriers! Cultural differences! Government regulations! Conflicting buying patterns! *Who needs it?*

We *all* need it. The global marketplace is here. That's where the action is. And the money. And the future.

It can be intimidating, because it's new and strange. But when you see how it happens—and recognize the ways in which basic principles of marketing work worldwide, albeit in different ways and wearing different costumes—you begin to see the gold shining within the dark cave of the unknown.

Going global requires some rethinking and relearning. Is it worth it? Well, if you want to succeed and survive, it is more than worth it—it's a lifeline to the future.

Check Points

✓ Markets today are world markets.

✓ Continued reliance on domestic markets is a losing strategy.

✓ Products and innovations spread around the globe with increasing velocity.

✓ Businesses in other countries have, on the whole, moved faster than those in the United States in adapting to the global imperative.

✓ The basic principles of marketing are valid worldwide—but with vital differences in application.

 ✓ New groups of consumers with similar spending habits are emerging in North America, the Far East, and Europe.

 ✓ Lack of information about consumers is a major obstacle to successful international marketing—but it can be overcome.

 ✓ The worldwide downshift of production to lower-cost regions will continue.

FAMILIARITY BREEDS SUCCESS

International Research: The Broad-Brush Approach

Insufficient knowledge is the most frequent reason for failure in the international marketplace. When we analyze global failures, we often find that critical errors could have been avoided if only the firm and its managers had known more about the business environment they were entering. Why didn't the marketers do the necessary research? The answer is usually simple. They thought it would be too expensive, or they didn't know how to do it.

Don't sail into the treacherous waters of the global market without a chart. You can build a low-cost research program that will assess potential target markets, spot the pitfalls, and lay the groundwork for an effective marketing effort.

The key to creating a cost-effective way of surveying foreign markets is to climb on the shoulders of those who have gone before: make intelligent use of secondary research. In many cases the information you need is there for the taking. You just have to know where to look.

Here are the nine steps in the preliminary research process:

1. Understand the need for research.

2. Overcome objections and win support for research.

3. Determine research objectives.

4. Determine information requirements.

5. Identify sources of information.

6. Evaluate information source, quality, and compatibility.

7. Obtain the information.

8. Interpret and analyze the information.

9. Present research results.

After completing these nine steps, you'll have a broad base of information from which to make the major decisions involved in going global.

Why Do You Need Research?

Many companies neglect to conduct adequate research before entering the global marketing arena. This neglect exposes the firm to serious business risks, such as:

- Loss of market penetration effectiveness

- Incitement of ill will that precludes further efforts

- Damage to the company's overall image

- Erosion of confidence in the financial markets

There is another risk, one that is not likely to be spelled out in block letters on an easel chart: If the international marketing effort fails, the reputations and careers of all those involved in it will take some direct hits. A well-thought-out research program will not be as expensive and difficult as the doom-sayers predict. Nevertheless, it will take money, time, and resources. If management honestly considers the costs of *not* conducting decent research, it will pay the price.

Some managers are misled into skimping on the research function because they are already selling overseas. They carry on a certain amount of export business—not through any planned undertaking, but because it "just happened." Some international orders came in over the transom, so the firm has continued to sell there. Or the firm was contacted by a distributor abroad and has maintained the relationship without really thinking much about it.

The fact that you're doing some business in a particular foreign market doesn't necessarily mean that this is the only or the best foreign market for your products or services. A logical research program lets you evaluate what you're doing now as well as figure out what you *should* be doing.

The objectives of international marketing research are the same as

those of domestic marketing research. However, the following environmental factors mean that the research might have to be executed quite
differently: new parameters, new cultures, the risk of overload, and a
broader definition of competition.

New Parameters

We become so used to the parameters of doing business in our own
country that we take them for granted, like the walls of the office. We
may chafe at regulations. We may protest, with good reason, various
reporting requirements. But we are accustomed to these things. They
may shift as the political winds blow, but their general outlines remain
the same.

When we start to do business in another country, we're prepared to
cope with different requirements and other forms of paperwork. But
we may be unprepared for the ways in which these rules are imposed,
for their seeming lack of fairness, and for the sometimes unpredictable
ways in which they change.

New Cultures

What we sometimes call "culture shock" is a reaction to radical change
in some area of our accustomed cultural pattern. When we start looking
into marketing abroad, we must be prepared for "cultural megashock."
We must learn about the culture of the host country, understand its
political systems, and grasp the differences in societal structure. The
assumptions on which the firm was founded and on which it runs may
not hold true internationally. They must be reevaluated. This is often
tough to grasp for managers who have been born and bred in the constraints and opportunities of the domestic marketplace. When these
managers enter a different part of the world, they must, in effect, learn
a new marketing language, culturally as well as linguistically. The
research process should be geared to helping them do that.

The Risk of Overload

Going international often means entering more than one new market.
As a result, the number of changing dimensions increases geometri-
cally. Management must not only understand all these factors, but also
understand the interaction between them. Coordination becomes increasingly difficult because of the sheer number of factors.

The international marketing effort may fail because the company
tries to do too much, for example, by entering too many markets too
soon. The research process should provide an accurate picture of the
network of dimensions as well as a framework for dealing with them.

A Broader Definition of Competition

A manufacturer, weary and battered by the cut and thrust of a ferociously competitive industry, might mistakenly think that his or her new international division will provide a respite. But things might be even tougher abroad. The competition in the new arena will be difficult to master because, for openers, the marketer does not even know who the competitors are.

Your definition of competition may have to be totally revised when you go international. For example, fishery products may have to compete not only with other fishery products, but also with certain meats or vegetables that scarcely exist in the domestic market. A labor-saving device prized in your home market might run into terrific competition abroad, not from a similar device, but from the existence of cheap manual labor.

Domestic market research usually identifies and evaluates competitors in the same or allied businesses, because those are the only competitors who count. But market research in a foreign country that covers only entities resembling domestic competitors may be wildly off the mark. International market research must do more than cover "competitors" in the conventional sense. It must provide information about all of the possible competitive pressures that might confront the company.

Get Agreement about the Benefits of Research

Here are some of the attitudes that the proponent of research might encounter.

It's hard to do, so let's not bother.   As this chapter will demonstrate, it's not that hard at all.

This will cost a bundle; do we really need it?   Whatever the research program costs—and it's likely to be a lot less than you think—Compared to the cost of failure of the international marketing effort, it's cheap.

We have good information on Mexico; let's apply it to Argentina.   It is the facile assumption that foreign markets are essentially similar that has led so many promising efforts to ruin.

Why can't we start exporting into the market and pick up information as we go along?   The product, price, promotion, etc., might be wrong for the market. A botched export program is likely to destroy the potential market, making the information acquired during the process useless.

As you can see, the key objections can easily be overcome once the issues and stakes are understood.

Determining Research Objectives

The objectives of the research program will vary widely from firm to firm because of such factors as the corporate mission, the nature of the product or service, the domestic marketing situation, and the company's financial status.

It is essential that the firm discuss what the program is expected to accomplish. Although the specific research objectives will be unique to the firm, the effort is designed, in general, to find out where in the world the company should be doing business, to discover as much as possible about the environment, to pinpoint problems, and to assess the profit possibilities. The more precise the objectives, the better the researcher will be able to get the necessary information while conserving time and money.

Determining market potential breaks down into three stages: preliminary screening, assessing the industry market potential, and analyzing company sales potential. The progress is from macro economic data, through broad market measurements, to readings on specific products. Here is a summary of the stages.

STAGES OF MARKET POTENTIAL[1]

1

PRELIMINARY SCREENING FOR ATTRACTIVE COUNTRY MARKETS

Key Question:

Which foreign markets warrant detailed investigation?

2

ASSESSMENT OF INDUSTRY MARKET POTENTIAL

Key Question:

What is the aggregate demand in each of the selected markets?

3

COMPANY SALES POTENTIAL ANALYSIS

Key Question:

How attractive is the potential demand for company products and services?

Researchers' Ruses in Russia[2]

Western businesses want to know how Ivan shaves and Olga washes her hair. Marketers are finding that research in Eastern Europe calls for creativity and resourcefulness.

One U.S. researcher has developed a novel system for dispersing questionnaires to distantly located interviewers: finding a willing traveler, perhaps a train conductor or Aeroflot stewardess, to deliver the package and then calling ahead with a description of the ad hoc courier. Sometimes it works, sometimes it flops.

Eastman Kodak joined other firms in a multiclient survey conducted by SRG International Ltd. in nine republics of the former USSR. The questionnaire had to be translated into nine languages. Kodak couldn't follow its customary practice of using photos to find out what kind of cameras people use; they were unable to scrounge up adequate pictures of Soviet cameras.

Training local interviewers can be an adventure. One researcher recalls a Moscow woman being groomed as a focus group moderator: in strident drill sergeant fashion she would browbeat panelists: "I just asked you a question and you have to respond!"

Discussion groups often work well, but, contrary to Western practice, discussions must be held on the same day as recruitment, because, as a researcher comments, "They can't predict what they'll be doing in two days. They may have to stand in some line."

Problems do not end when the data have been collected. Interpretation has its own adventures. PepsiCola International received results from a survey in Hungary which said drugstores were an outlet for soft drinks. Drugstores don't exist in Hungary; the information was forced into a structure developed in the West.

Some skeptics question the value of consumer studies in markets where the problem is often a lack of products, not consumer preference. Since habits have been shaped by what's available, say critics, surveys are not a good indicator of how people would behave when confronted with a choice of brands. However, researchers continue to plow ahead, insisting that these are necessary first steps.

The job is tough and full of surprises. But not all the surprises are unpleasant. Researchers are gratified at how willing Eastern

Europeans are to answer questions. Indeed, the subjects are flattered to be asked their opinions. A Gallup researcher recalls an old Hungarian woman who said, "It was such a wonderful experience to have a chance to talk to you for so long. How much do I pay you?"

Because of time pressure and budget constraints, you might be tempted to curtail or omit stage three, especially if the answers from stage two are positive. This is a mistake, possibly a fatal one. The aggregate industry data collected in stage two are a necessary step in the process, but they are too general as a basis for product-specific decisions. For example, the market demand for medical equipment should not be confused with the potential demand for a specific brand.

Domestic market research is aimed at answering the question, "How attractive is the potential demand for company products and services?" It's even more important that this question be answered before going into a foreign market.

Determining Information Requirements

The researchers are now prepared to pinpoint the types of information needed. Often the first requirement is macro data, such as population statistics. If it is relevant to identify market restraints, it may be necessary to acquire information about international accords, GATT guidelines, "voluntary" agreements, and the like. At certain milestones it will be appropriate to look at the results so far and decide whether to discontinue the project or to collect more detailed information.

Just ahead you'll find a checklist of research questions on broad strategic issues, foreign market assessment and selection, and the marketing mix. The list of information requirements should be detailed and complete. It's better to include a few headings that turn out to be unimportant or impractical than to overlook an information category that might be sorely needed later.

Where Can You Go for Information?

The cost-effective approach to getting answers to the questions listed here is to make maximum use of secondary research: information collected by other entities. You can collect a remarkable amount of useful information from readily accessible, low-cost (or free) secondary sources. (The more expensive alternative, primary research, in which the company undertakes a new data-gathering project, will be discussed in the next chapter.)

International Marketing Questions and Information Requirements[3]

Broad Strategic Issues

What objectives should be pursued in the foreign market?

Which foreign market segments should the firm strive to satisfy?

Which are the best product, place-distribution, pricing, and promotion strategies for the foreign market?

What should be the product-market-company mix to take advantage of the available foreign marketing opportunities?

Foreign Market Assessment and Selection

Do opportunities exist in a foreign market for the firm's products and services?

What is the market potential abroad?

Are there foreign markets that the firm can serve?

What new markets are likely to open up abroad?

What are the major economic, political, legal, social, technological, and other environmental facts and trends in a foreign country?

What impact do these environmental dimensions have on the specific foreign market for the firm's products and services?

Who are the firm's present and potential customers abroad?

What are their needs and desires?

What are their demographic and psychographic characteristics— disposable income, occupation, age, sex, opinions, interests, activities, tastes, values, etc.?

What is their life-style?

Who makes the purchase decisions?

Who influences the purchase decisions?

How are the purchase decisions made?

Where are the products purchased?

How are the products used?

What are the purchase and consumption patterns and behaviors?

What is the nature of competition in the foreign market?

Who are major direct and indirect competitors?

What are the major characteristics of the competitors?

What are the firm's competitive strengths and weaknesses in reference to such factors as product quality, product lines, warranties, services, brands, packaging, distribution, sales force, advertising, prices, experience, technology, capital and human resources, and market share?

What attitudes do different governments (domestic and foreign) have toward foreign trade?

Are there any foreign trade incentives and barriers?

Is there any prejudice against imports or exports?

What are different governments doing specifically to encourage or discourage international trade?

What specific requirements—for example, import or export licenses—have to be met to conduct international trade?

How difficult are certain government regulations for the firm?

How well developed are the foreign mass communication media?

Are the print and electronics media abroad efficient and effective?

Are there adequate transportation and storage or warehouse facilities in the foreign market?

Does the foreign market offer efficient channels of distribution for the firm's products?

What are the characteristics of the existing domestic and foreign distributors?

How effectively can the distributors perform specific marketing functions?

What is the state of the retailing institutions?

Marketing Mix Assessment and Selection
Product

Which product should the firm offer abroad?

What specific features—design, color, size, packaging, brand, warranty, etc.—should the product have?

What foreign needs does the product satisfy?

Should the firm adapt or modify its domestic market product and sell it abroad?

Should it develop a new product for the foreign market?

Should the firm make or buy the product for the foreign market?

How competitive is or will be the product abroad?

Is there a need to withdraw the product from the foreign market?

At which stage in its life cycle is the product in the foreign market?

What specific services are necessary abroad at the presale and postsale stages?

Are the firm's service and repair facilities adequate?

What is the firm's product and service image abroad?

What patents or trademarks does the firm have that can benefit it abroad?

How much legal protection does the firm have concerning patents, trademarks, etc.?

What should be the firm's product mission philosophy in the foreign market?

Are the firm's products socially responsible?

Do the products create a good corporate image?

Price

At what price should the firm sell its product in the foreign market?

Does the foreign price reflect the product quality?

Is the price competitive?

Should the firm pursue market penetration or market-skimming pricing objectives abroad?

What type of discounts (trade, cash, quantity) and allowances (advertising, trade-off) should the firm offer its foreign customers?

Should prices differ according to market segment?

What should the firm do about product line pricing?

What pricing options are available if costs or exchange rates increase or decrease?

Is the demand in the foreign market elastic or inelastic?

How are prices going to be viewed by the foreign government— reasonable, exploitative?

Place-Distribution

Which channels of distribution should the firm use to market its products abroad?

Where should the firm produce its products, and how should it distribute them in the foreign market?

What types of agents, brokers, wholesalers, dealers, distributors, retailers, etc. should the firm use?

What are the characteristics and capabilities of the available intermediaries?

Should the assistance of EMCs (export management companies) be acquired?

What forms of transportation should the firm use?
Where should the product be stored?
What is the cost of distribution by channel?
What are the costs of physical distribution?
What type of incentives and assistance should the firm provide its intermediaries to achieve its foreign distribution objectives?
Which channels of distribution are used by the firm's competitors, and how effective are these channels?
What collaborative opportunities exist in international logistics?

Promotion—Nonpersonal (Advertising and Sales Promotion)
How should the firm promote its products in the foreign market? Should it advertise? Should it participate in international trade fairs and exhibits?
What are the communication needs of the foreign market?
What communication or promotion objectives should the firm pursue abroad? What should be the total foreign promotion budget?
What advertising media are available in the foreign market? What are their strengths and limitations? How effective are different domestic and foreign advertising media?
Should the firm use an advertising agency?
How should it be selected?
How effective and competitive are the firm's existing advertising and promotion programs concerning the foreign market?
What are the legal requirements?
Are there foreign laws against competitive advertising?

Promotion—Personal Selling
Is there a need for personal selling to promote the product abroad?
What assistance or services do foreign customers need from the sales force?
What should be the nature of personal selling abroad?
How many salespeople should the firm have?
How should the sales personnel be trained, motivated, compensated, assigned sales goals, quotas, and foreign territories?
What should the nature of foreign sales efforts be?
How does the firm's sales force compare with its competitors?
What criteria should the firm use to evaluate sales performance?
How should the firm perform sales analysis?

Government Sources

Governments of industrial countries offer a wealth of useful information to companies interested in international trade. For example, the U.S. government provides thousands of up-to-date publications each year. Many of these are produced both in print format and as electronic databases that can be searched using computer software.

U.S. government. Most of the data available from the U.S. government are collected by the departments of Commerce, Agriculture, State, and Treasury and U.S. embassies abroad.

Information provided by the U.S. government may bear on macro issues (the broad questions) or micro issues (very specific questions). For example, the annual *Statistical Abstract of the United States* (found in nearly every library) contains a section on comparative international statistics. This provides dozens of interesting tables: population totals and trends, population projections for 25 years into the future, age breakdowns, urban population and growth, life expectancy and health, education and literacy, GNP, GDP, source of imports and destination of exports for the EC and Japan, types of taxes and tax revenues, consumer prices and money supply, labor force by sex and age group, unemployment, time lost due to industrial disputes, manufacturing activity, energy production, transportation, communications, exchange rates, reserve assets and current account balances, public debt, and net flow of financial resources to developing countries.

You can find out how many murders take place in a country; how many people fly from the country to the United States and back again; and exports and imports of merchandise by continents, areas, and countries. What makes the *Statistical Abstract* even more useful is its source notes, which point the marketer to the complete, detailed data sources from which the tables are abstracted.

The U.S. government also offers customized data services responding to the detailed needs of a firm. The Trade Information Center is a one-stop information source providing export assistance based on data gathered by 19 federal agencies. Professional international trade specialists are available by phone to advise marketers on how to locate and use government programs and to guide them through the export process. The nationwide toll-free telephone number is 1-800-USA-TRADE (1-800-872-8723).

Other governments. Many countries make available a wide variety of national and international trade data available. This information is often published only in the native language of the country of origin, but embassies and consulates might be able to provide translations of relevant information from these sources. Keep in mind that most of the information is provided in the form of numbers and tables—you won't need a translator. Virtually all countries today are trade-conscious. They are trying to enhance their economies by increasing international commerce. So more and more countries, even smaller ones, are making it a point to provide useful research to potential trading partners.

Once you have narrowed down the list of possible countries in which to do business, a few days spent in the nation's capital can be most profitable. The various "country desks" at the Department of Commerce are excellent sources. Foreign embassies usually have more complete data than do their offices in other parts of the country.

The visitor to embassies (and even to some U.S. government offices) may be targeted for a sales talk on the benefits of doing business in a particular country. The idea is to winnow out the hard facts from the optimistic claims.

International Organizations

Some international organizations provide useful information for the researcher. The *Statistical Yearbook,* produced by the United Nations, contains international trade data on products and information on exports and imports by country. The *World Atlas,* published by the World Bank, provides useful general data on population, growth trends, and GNP. The Organization for Economic Cooperation and Development (OECD) publishes quarterly and annual trade data on its member countries. Organizations like the International Monetary Fund (IMF) and the World Bank publish occasional staff papers that discuss regional or country-specific issues in depth.

Service Organizations

Useful data can be acquired from organizations that are familiar in other contexts but that are not usually regarded as data sources. Banks, accounting firms, airlines, and freight forwarders can provide information on business practices, legislative or regulatory requirements, and political stability as well as basic trade data. A consulting firm retained for domestic assignments might have useful international data. Firms sometimes offer such general information as an "appetizer." The "full-course meal" of detailed answers will cost money.

State Governments

It makes sense for state governments to encourage firms within the state to export. Any company considering a first venture into international marketing needs as much useful information as it can get. The state government might have data and services to complement the assistance available from the federal government and other sources. The state's export-related services may be particularly useful because they reflect specific local viewpoints.

The ways of tapping these resources vary from state to state. Usually a call to the office of the Secretary of State (or the equivalent) will generate general information and a list of services. The state legislators representing the district in which the business is located should be helpful, too. Too many firms fail to maintain productive contacts with their state representatives. They tend to get in touch only in a negative context, for example, to complain about taxes or regulations. The legislator's staff can be asked to help on a more positive level, in identifying and obtaining state assistance relevant to exporting. Also, state agencies might be able to put the company in touch with other companies that have coped with the same problems.

Trade Associations

Trade associations vary widely in the vigor and range of their activities. For example, world trade clubs and domestic and international chambers of commerce can provide information on local markets. Some maintain files on international trade flows and trends affecting international marketers. Some industry associations can supply valuable information, much of which they have collected from their members. While quite general, the information might stimulate some valuable insights. Ask at a public or university library for the Encyclopedia of Associations, which lists thousands of organizations and tells how to get in touch with them, what they are concerned with, and what information or services they might provide.

Directories and Newsletters

There are many industry directories available on local, national, and international levels. These directories identify firms and provide general background information—location, address, phone and fax number, name of the CEO, etc.—along with some information on products and services.

There are newsletters devoted to specific international issues such as international trade financing, bartering, countertrade, payment flows, and customs. Some newsletters are published by banks or accounting firms to keep their clientele up to date. Newsletters usually cover narrow subject areas in great depth. They can provide important information on specific topics. Most newsletters maintain an index, allowing the researcher to obtain back issues relevant to the project.

Databases

Increasingly, international marketing information is available in the form of electronic databases, ranging from the latest news on product developments to new writings in the academic and trade press and the latest updates in international trade statistics. Online data services can provide information like the following:

American Express, Time Warner, and the National Basketball Association are taking steps to protect their trademarks in Eastern Europe.

700 U.S. CEOs, surveyed by KPMG Peat Marwick, indicated that 58 percent of their companies were planning to merge, acquire, or enter a joint venture with a European partner.

Westinghouse will sell an $11 million air traffic system to Poland.

Well over 6,000 databases are available worldwide, with almost 5,000 available online. The United States is the largest participant in this database growth, producing and consuming more than 50 percent. These services are available for a subscription fee and often require payment on an as-used basis. Because of their rapid updates, their convenience of access, and their extensive research capabilities, these services can be well worth the price. As we progress toward a worldwide network of "fiber optic highways," the use of such databases will increase, becoming a key information source.

Other Firms

Occasionally, useful information on international marketing can be obtained from other firms. A firm that is guarded about revealing any facts concerning its domestic activities is sometimes more open about international activities.

A firm will not hand useful data to an actual or potential competitor. But in noncompetitive or, better yet, mutually helpful situations, there may be useful cooperation. Let's say, for example, a medium-sized company buys components from a very large company engaged in international trade. The smaller firm, thinking of going international, asks for certain information. Because it is to the bigger company's advantage to increase the business of its customer, the information is passed along.

Evaluating Information Source, Quality, and Compatibility

Let's pause a moment before we plunge into gathering the information. You might spend a lot of time and money mining sources that produce the fool's gold of unreliable data. Or you can amass a great deal of sound information that does not answer the key questions. So before starting to obtain the data, it makes sense to check out the reliability of the sources and the relevance of the information to be gathered.

Source Quality

Following are three important questions about a data source:

- Who collected the data?

- What was the purpose of the original data collection?

- How were the data collected?

In some cases, such as U.S. Census information, the answers will be fairly obvious. However, in other cases it's essential to understand the origins and methods of the source.

Ideally, the researcher would obtain the initial research specifications drawn up for the data collection. Any legitimate research project starts with some general specifications, which might include questions like those listed under previous steps in this section.

Of course, if the data are being provided at little or no cost to the researcher, it might be somewhat awkward to ask a lot of questions. A courteous request will often persuade the source to send along a copy of the specs, which should help the researcher to determine the purpose and method of the original data collection.

It's important to check the quality of the source because some research is slanted. The slant might be conscious, or it might be an unconscious bias that creeps in because the originators of the project are trying to please the sponsor by proving a point.

For example, many countries attempt to attract foreign investment by demonstrating that their economies are improving. They don't exactly falsify the data, but certain factors are overstated, making the economic picture look better than it is. We also find countries that *understate* certain factors, making their economic situation appear worse. Why? Because they are trying to indicate a need for more foreign aid.

Finally, there is the problem that many countries simply do not have sophisticated data collection systems. When asked for data, they tend to supply numbers that are estimates rather than precise readings. Such information may reflect wishes or goals rather than reality. This is not necessarily done out of a cynical desire to deceive, but rather out of a cultural inclination toward pleasing the inquiring party.

Inexact information from various countries may be collected—without

rigorous checking—by international organizations, which then disseminate it. Researchers should not assume that all the data being put out
by highly regarded organizations is sacrosanct. It is useful to scrutinize
introductory remarks and footnotes to studies to spot unusual methods
of data collection.

Data Quality

Bad information can come from good sources. Or the information might
be reliable but of limited use in answering the questions. Information
from a certain source may contain a higher margin of error than the
researchers are used to or find acceptable; the margin of error of some
international statistics can be as high as 25 percent.

There are several questions important to the researcher in evaluating
data quality.

Primary or secondary source? A primary source is the originator
of the data; a secondary source is a processor of the data removed one
or more steps from the original data collection. The researcher should
always try to get information from the primary source, because this
permits an evaluation of source credibility.

How was the information collected? The researcher knows proper
research procedures and definitions. When the procedures and definitions used in collecting the foreign data stray from the norm, the data
themselves are suspect.

How recent is it? Things can change fast in the world today. Information collected a year ago may be totally out of date. In many nations,
the most recent data available may be three to five years old. The age
of the data may not be clear. The researcher should find out when the
information was collected.

How relevant is it? Unless controls are imposed, researchers can be
buried under an avalanche of data. For one thing, a country interested
in promoting itself may obligingly supply enormous amounts of facts,
some ranging pretty far afield from the purpose of the project.

Here is where some researchers are misled. Gratified by a glut of
information, they study each individual bit, asking, "What does this
mean to us?" After precious time has been consumed, the answer appears: "Nothing!"

At this stage, the researcher should concentrate on spotting the kinds
of information the job needs, rather than trying to fit disparate pieces of
data to the job. Otherwise, the project will suffer information overload.

Compatibility: Are we comparing apples and oranges? Researchers dealing with data from different countries often find the data more or less useful in describing what is happening within each of the countries, especially if trend lines are drawn. But these same data may be misleading when trying to compare the countries. Great care must therefore be taken to make sure that identical or at least similar units of measurement and definitions are used. Facts assumed to be compatible may not be compatible at all. For example, an "engineer" may have different qualifications in an industrial country than in a developing nation.

An objective assessment of source quality, data quality, and relevance need not take much time. It can save a lot of time and money. It can keep the project from wandering down dead ends. And it can help to make sure that the facts amassed are really facts, not fiction, and that these facts bear upon the tasks to be accomplished. Only when this has been done should the project move to the next step: obtaining the data.

Obtaining Information

The existence of data does not guarantee their availability. Researchers may find out that certain information exists and is probably relevant. But the job of getting the information turns out to be more complicated than anybody thought.

This is a danger point. The researchers can devote more and more of their energies to obtaining these data. It becomes a challenge; almost an obsession. Finally, when the material becomes available, it's too late to do much good.

For information to be useful, it has to be obtained in a timely manner and with relative ease. Furthermore, the cost of getting the information must be weighed against its importance. If it turns out that a certain part of the research job will cost substantially more than was anticipated, the researchers might tend to plunge ahead anyway. It's up to senior management to maintain control, asking: Considering the real cost, do we still need this? Can we get it from some other source?

Time Constraints

Time can be a bigger cost than money. The U.S. Department of Commerce is a treasure-trove, amassing all kinds of detailed information. The information is reliable and current; furthermore, you can get it for a modest user fee. However, sometimes several weeks go by before the information comes through. If you are asking for individual data runs, it can take a lot longer. If there is time pressure on the project, this must be considered.

Sometimes you can speed the process by working with a local Department of Commerce district office that maintains substantial library holdings of department materials. Also, many universities are designated as official depositories of government documents. Many public libraries maintain holdings of data from international organizations, offering a shortcut in getting data from these organizations.

A Warning against the "Funnel Principle"

Some research efforts work on the funnel principle: collect everything within reach and sort it out later. It is time-consuming and expensive to discard data after they have been obtained. This approach also leads to confusion, as pertinent data can get mixed up with irrelevancies. It's far better to reduce the amount of information to be handled. Use questions like those in the foregoing sections to precisely determine the information requirements, carefully match the sources of data with these requirements, and select the data with the best fit.

Data Privacy

As the capability of obtaining data has increased dramatically, society has become increasingly sensitive to data privacy issues. For example, there are growing protests about the use of certain statistics on individuals for market research purposes. Even when there has been no objection to furnishing the data for one purpose, there is strenuous objection when it is used for another. Readily accessible large-scale databases contain information valuable to marketers that is considered privileged by the individuals who have provided the data.

The international marketer must study the privacy laws in different nations. It's important, also, to look beyond the laws themselves, to media practices and societal attitudes. Take, for example, an emerging country from the old Eastern Bloc, which offers a potential market to an American manufacturer of a particular consumer product. The manufacturer wants to know as much as possible about the market. The research effort stays within the privacy laws of the country. There is, however, in the country—and especially among its intellectuals and journalists—a generalized resentment of the United States. An influential newspaper in the target country reports that a U.S. company is nosing into the private lives of citizens in order to sell its goods. Other media take up the cry. The company has done nothing wrong, but the nature of the research effort has raised barriers to selling the product long before the project starts.

The Triplecast Fiasco

In the summer of 1992, Cablevision and NBC got together to offer coverage of the Olympics on a pay-per-view basis. Television viewers just did not go for the packages. Cablevision and NBC kept cutting the price, but sales still lagged. The losses were high.

Afterward, some people asked why the companies had not done the kind of market research that would detect public resistance to the idea. The answer is that the sponsoring companies had conducted extensive and sophisticated research.

When the results of the research came in, well before the projected launch date, the TV executives looked at them with dismay. The numbers showed that only one percent (or less) of the total possible market would "definitely" buy the Triplecast. Logic dictated that the companies bite the bullet and abandon the project. Another possibility would have been to revise the project extensively and test again.

NBC and Cablevision took a third course. They adjusted the test results. By adding the "probables" to the "definites," they were able to upgrade the projected sales to an acceptable level. This was like a doctor finding a patient to have a temperature of 105° and then sticking the thermometer under cold water to make the patient look healthier.

Interpretation and Analysis

The information has been collected. Now the challenge is to make the "fit." Companies are called upon to be creative in making the best use of the data. Just squirreling away facts is not enough.

It is vital that the research team be thoroughly briefed on the company's policies, strategy, and style. If outside researchers are used, they should ask the questions that will give them a good feel for the mission. Otherwise they will be less likely to use the data in the most effective way.

At the same time, the researchers should be independent enough to be objective in interpreting the facts. Many marketing ventures have been doomed because executives who were already committed to the venture turned negative data into positive encouragement.

Obviously, any company that starts an investigation into a foreign marketing venture is hoping to find out that the venture can be

launched and carried on successfully. The hope for good news can communicate itself to those who are interpreting the data. Nobody wants
to be the bearer of bad news to the boss, especially if there is any likelihood that the messenger's head will roll. Therefore, it is absolutely
critical at this stage that researchers be supported and encouraged to
come up with completely objective findings.

Compromising on Data Precision

Secondary data, having been collected to serve some other purpose,
must be compared and combined to fit into the new project. Often the
facts will be close to what is needed, but not match exactly. So researchers use *proxy variables*—pieces of information that can be interpreted
to provide answers to other questions. For example, it might not be
possible to measure demand for video recorders in a particular market,
but the market penetration of TV sets can be used as a proxy variable.
Similarly, in an industrial setting, information about plans for new
port facilities can be used to determine future containerization requirements. The degree to which a society is becoming computerized can
shed light on the need for software. And so on.

The researcher must go beyond the scope of the data and use creative
inferences to arrive at knowledge useful to the firm. Of course, this is
not just a seat-of-the-pants exercise. It is based on cross-tabulation and
extrapolation of data. Nevertheless, it is an application of creativity,
and as such it departs from the realm of exact science.

Top management should understand that this is what is happening
and not expect 100 percent precision where it is not possible. There is
risk here, as at all other stages of the enterprise.

Reducing the Risk of Inaccurate Analysis

The risk can be reduced in various ways. Researchers ought not to be
subjected to pressure—conscious or unconscious—from managers hoping
for rosy results. However, the researchers need not toil in a total vacuum
either. They can, at this stage, be given some input from marketing
people who are not necessarily at the policy level, but who can help to
fit the available data to the new questions.

Once the interpretations and analyses have been made, they should be
checked for consistency. Researchers should always cross-check results
with other possible sources of information or with experts. A couple of
useful questions follow:

- Is this the only reasonable interpretation?

- If there are several possible interpretations, what is the worst-case
  scenario?

Where data are suggestive without being conclusive, researchers should be encouraged to point this out, and discuss the various possibilities.

In addition, researchers should take another look at the research methods employed and think about any modifications necessary for future projects. This enables the corporation to learn from experience. If, for example, the research signals a "no-go" on the proposed international venture, it can have served the additional purpose of sharpening the research machinery.

There are many conflicting impulses during the interpretation phase. Different members of management might want the findings to come out in different ways and might "lobby" for the desired result. There is sometimes an increasingly impatient message to "get on with it" communicated from the top. Some executives, not tuned in to the importance and delicacy of this stage, may say, "You've got all the numbers, let's see them. What's holding it up?"

The data must be analyzed thoroughly, without pressure to force them into certain channels. Everyone must acknowledge that interpretation is not exactitude. The purpose is the best possible readings on the shape the venture should take and its chances for success.

Presenting Research Results

Now comes the time to communicate the research results to management. This is a crucial point. Many worthwhile research efforts have been damaged, and occasionally derailed, by bad presentations. Here are some of the key issues in the presentation.

Nature of the Presentation

Are the results to be presented initially to one or two senior managers? A larger group? Does the corporate style run to fairly elaborate meetings, with high-powered graphics? Or is the prevailing style simpler?

Perhaps the results are to be disseminated in writing. Often the best method of presenting the findings is to circulate a memo with the principal conclusions, then hold a meeting for elaboration and answers to questions. Whatever the form chosen, it should be picked to suit the audience and the message, not the researchers.

Researchers should think about the best ways to make the presentation in terms of:

• Making the results clear to everyone

• Answering the questions relevant to the project

• Alerting people to particular problems or opportunities

Some research professionals, though very good at gathering and analyzing information, are very bad at making presentations. They put out a massive document containing pounds of details and minutiae. They speak at great length about how the data were amassed, rather than what they are or what they mean. They tend too far toward the extreme of making extravagant claims of accuracy or toward the extreme of hedging everything.

Managers usually don't know much about the intricacies of research. The presentation is not the time to educate them. The fact is that they probably do not want to be taken into the kitchen to see how the meal is prepared.

Format of the Presentation

Whether the results are being presented orally or in writing, the major findings should be presented first. The researcher should, right up front, give the answers to the important questions:

• Can we enter this market successfully?

• What should we sell?

• How should we sell it?

It is not unreasonable to ask that the memo giving the major findings be limited to one page. By presenting the material briefly, researchers acknowledge that management time is a precious commodity.

And a crisp, concise presentation does something else: It *sells*. Granted, this is not a sales presentation in the sense that the researchers are urging a particular course of action. However, an incisive, well-handled presentation helps to sell the validity of the research process and the professionalism of the researchers. There are bound to be many difficult moments as the findings are thrashed over and their implications are debated. This will go better if all members of management have confidence in the report and those who created it.

Relevant supporting material follows the main conclusions. Among the purposes of the supporting material are these:

• Point out significant connections between facts.

• Clarify difficult points.

• Call attention to areas requiring more investigation.

• Show how estimates and extrapolations were done.

• Alert management to places where the margin for error is high.

Detailed information should be placed in appendices, which can be consulted if needed but do not clutter the report.

Follow Up the Initial Presentation

No matter how clear and concise the initial presentation, there will remain misunderstandings and blank spots. For one thing, it is a human tendency to filter data through the screen of our desires. An individual who urgently supports a particular international venture may read a key section through rose-colored glasses. Another party, who opposes the venture or feels threatened by it, will see the worst.

So the initial presentation must be followed up quickly. The optimum way to do this is through a meeting or meetings at which managers are urged to ask questions and to express doubts. This is not a matter of "Speak now or forever hold your peace." Managers should be reassured that for a reasonable time, as questions come up, they can talk with researchers about what the report means and how much it can be relied on.

The report shapes the perception of the entire research. Therefore, it is a crucial component in the research process. This is not always understood. Certain dedicated professionals think the process has ended successfully when the facts have been gathered. These researchers think of the dissemination of the information as a minor matter.

A slipshod presentation of good research is like serving an excellent meal on chipped and not-quite-clean dishes. It spoils the appetite and wastes the cook's efforts. The presentation stage is the point at which the stream of research flows into the main stream of management action. Any damming or diversion can affect the mix for the worse.

Moreover, the presentation phase cannot be allowed to deteriorate into nit-picking over details and questions that are asked ostensibly to get more information, but that are actually intended to impede the project. Make every reasonable effort to see, first, that all managers understand the findings, whether or not they like them or agree with them. Then make reasonable efforts to win consensus on the implications of the facts. When everybody is on the same page—even though some may be on different paragraphs, and some may not like what they're reading—it's time to make the go/no-go decisions and move ahead.

Don't Skimp on Research

"Look before you leap" is even better advice in going international than in launching a new domestic marketing venture. The secondary research phase that precedes the international effort is tricky. There are traps to be avoided if the research is to provide information that leads to the right decisions. Here's a brief recap of problems and objections.

It Costs Too Much

Some line executives have a built-in antipathy to research. It seems like a peripheral activity. Sales staffs with products to sell have to sit around while a bunch of ivory-tower theorists play with their computers, producing overpriced reports.

The answer.   If you know what you're doing, you can accomplish a great deal with relatively low-cost research data. The trick is to find them and apply them.

It's Not Relevant to Our Business

Secondary research involves trade-offs. The basic trade-off is that you pay less for the information because you're using data that have already been collected.

The answer.   Obtain information that comes as close as possible to answering the important questions. Then use such devices as proxy variables to come up with reasoned inferences.

It's Not as Accurate as Domestic Research

True. In most cases the research done on foreign markets is likely to be less reliable than research done close to home. The margin for error increases as the researchers probe deeper into uncharted territory, going farther afield for data and using information from less standard sources.

In other words, there is risk in research, as there is in every other aspect of business. To expect research to be pristine in its total accuracy is to be blind to reality. Secondary research should be viewed realistically, with healthy skepticism. Researchers should always figure out the degree to which the facts may be off target and account for that margin of error in their findings and conclusions. Even more important, researchers must emphasize the margin of error in presenting results to management. And line managers should make sure to ask about, and understand, the possible inaccuracies.

The answer.   Acknowledge that international secondary research is apt to be less reliable than domestic research. Allow for this fact of life. If anything, overemphasize it.

We Already Know How To Sell

Naturally, marketers who have worked hard to come up with the best selling strategies are reluctant to loosen their grip on those strategies when the time comes to sell abroad. So the information coming in from the research arm is shaped to fit certain preconceptions or ignored if it doesn't square with established patterns.

The answer. Clinton's campaign headquarters in 1992 featured the sign, "It's the Economy, Stupid!" The research effort should hoist a banner reading, "It's the Environment, Stupid!" The environmental factors influencing marketing in a foreign country affect and distort every aspect of the campaign. The environmental differences encompass cultural, legal, technological, political, social, and language differences. The international environment affects distribution, product, price, and promotion.

So, while researchers must not explain every discrepancy away with vague references to environmental factors, line managers must resist the tendency to "dance with the one that brung you." International marketing is a different party; you must learn different steps and different tunes.

Let's Get More Information

In domestic research there is always the option of gathering more facts. Sometimes this is beneficial (e.g., when previous research has raised some new questions). All too often, though, the call for further research is heard when people don't know what else to do. It's a stall and a cry for help. The "more research" people cherish the hope that they will find one magic fact that will make everything clear and assure that all the decisions are made correctly.

This effect can be even more pronounced in dealing with international research. The data are farther from the bull's-eye of direct relevance. The sources are more questionable. So it is understandable that management will say, "This is not adequate. Let's get more information."

The answer. All hands should accept the truth; international research is not likely to answer all questions to everybody's satisfaction. It's good to ask, "What are the possibilities of finding out more in this particular area?" But the questioner should be prepared for the answer that there are no more lodes of information to be mined. The company must make do with what is available, drawing conclusions from the data which, admittedly, were not originally gathered for this purpose.

You need charts of the international waters before you embark on them. For the most part, the charts already exist. During the preliminary research phase, do a thorough job of exploring all the possible sources. If you do it right, you will collect a lot of pertinent, valuable data at modest cost.

And you will have amassed the essential information you need to support the crucial decisions that will launch your international marketing venture.

What Happens When Secondary Research Is Not Enough?

It is crucial that marketers be able to recognize when the benefits and usefulness of secondary data are exhausted.

The cost of obtaining this information will be considerably less than the cost of mounting a primary research project that addresses precise questions about the company's product or services. However, if the information thus gathered is off the target, or simply repeats information already gathered, then it is a waste of money. At this point, researchers must be prepared to explore the primary research option, the subject of Chapter 3.

Check Points

✔ Insufficient knowledge is the key reason for failure in the international marketplace.

✔ You can conduct a cost-effective preliminary research program by using information that has already been collected.

✔ The preliminary research process has nine steps:

1. Understand the need for research.

2. Get agreement about the benefits of research.

3. Determine research objectives.

4. Determine information requirements.

5. Identify sources of information.

6. Evaluate information source, quality, and compatibility.

7. Obtain the information.

8. Interpret and analyze the information.

9. Present research results.

THE CLOSER, THE BETTER
In-Depth International Research

A group of people in London sit around a table discussing in great depth what they like and dislike about a consumer product. At the same time, a group of consumers in New York are doing the same thing. This is nothing new. Focus groups are a staple of modern marketing. What's different about this example is that the consumers in London and New York are connected by videoconferencing technology and are talking to each other.

Global focus groups *are* new. The day is fast approaching when they will become the backbone of international marketing. The *Wall Street Journal* quotes an advertising executive who talks about target audiences "separated by the miles and cultural differences but they inhabit similar worlds and have similar needs."[1]

Focus groups comprising consumers half a world away from each other is just one instance of the resources being mustered to support international marketing campaigns. As companies begin to do a substantial volume of business abroad, and as they cope with increasingly sophisticated and aggressive competition for foreign markets, they are recognizing the need to conduct primary research internationally. This recognition of need is often grudging.

Primary research is used internationally far less than it should be. The reason is cost. A basic cost-benefit analysis dictates that spending a lot of money on consumer research in a distant market of dubious value is unwise. Besides, even if you wanted to perform research in the foreign market, who would you get to do it? There is widespread skepticism about the competence and reliability of foreign research companies.

So, typically, when a company spots what might be an opening in a foreign market, the temptation is to use secondary data to serve *all* research functions. The secondary data may have supported the decision to move into the foreign market. But now the questions get to be specific, such as:

- What is the market potential for our furniture in Indonesia?

- How much does the typical Nigerian consumer spend on soft drinks?

- What will happen to demand in Brazil if we raise our prices along monthly inflation levels?

- What effect will a new type of packaging have on green-conscious consumers in Germany?

Secondary data only rarely shed much light on such questions. Resourceful professionals may be able to do some creative extrapolation. But the basic truth must be faced. If you want to know how to sell to consumers, whether in Kansas or Kenya, you will get better results if you have reliable insights into the makeup and reactions of those consumers.

Before the growth of today's tremendous consumer research apparatus, companies were, of course, obliged to rely more on experience and intuition in gauging whether a product or service would sell. Some marketing executives look back wistfully on the good old days, lamenting the present-day trend toward hyper-analysis of every tic in a shopper's eyebrow. Nevertheless, these executives use the fruits of modern research even while deriding the excesses of the discipline.

In foreign marketing, companies have been able to avoid making the hard choices on research expenditures because there did not seem to be enough potential profit in it; because the agencies available to carry on the research were dubious or nonexistent; because nobody else was doing much real research; or for all of these reasons.

Bad data sometimes get used as good data because marketers want them to be good, want it so much that they override their critical faculties. They persuade themselves that the secondary research is valuable because they think they can't afford primary research.

When the time comes to decide whether to do primary research, marketing research professionals should be encouraged to give their

---

Grass-Roots Marketing Intelligence in Mexico[2]

Peter Johns wanted to distribute mail-order catalogs from upscale U.S. companies to consumers in Mexico. Johns suspected that there was a rich market there, waiting to be tapped.

With 30 years of international marketing behind him, Johns knew that instinct was not enough. But when he tried to test his theory against hard data, he ran into a blank wall. He could not find a useful marketing study for Mexico City. Census reports were not much help because, in Mexico, they stop breaking down income levels at about $35,000, and they give ranges, rather than precise numbers, on family size.

So Johns embarked on some primary research. He went into the affluent neighborhoods and found just what he had suspected: satellite dishes, imported sports cars, women carrying Louis Vuitton handbags.

Having decided that there was, indeed, a market for upscale catalogs in Mexico City, Johns needed mailing lists. He couldn't buy the kind he needed. So he started to build his own lists. He asked local investors for membership lists of the city's exclusive golf clubs. He obtained directories of the parents of students at some of the city's exclusive private schools. Out of necessity, Johns was engaging in what he called "grass-roots marketing intelligence."

---

unvarnished opinions, about the likelihood of the necessary answers being reached through secondary data.

Peter Johns's story above points up the paucity of research facilities around the globe. The vacuum is being filled. In response to the growing need, research services of various kinds are springing up in various places. The situation is still uncertain enough to make the do-it-yourself approach a serious possibility.

Buy It or Do It Yourself?

One problem for companies that must decide whether to undertake international primary research in-house is overconfidence. Firms often estimate their internal research strengths to be greater than they actually are. Take, for example, the job of putting together prospect lists. List-building is such a sophisticated discipline in the United States, Canada, and Great Britain that marketers tend to take it for granted. True, you can make big mistakes by choosing the wrong lists for the campaign, choosing the wrong appeals to make to a particular list, and so forth. But, for most purposes, the lists exist. There are not many situations in which the firm must build its own list.

So, when faced with the need to run some primary research in a foreign country, the marketer might say, "There's nothing complicated about this. We'll do it ourselves." This conclusion is based on the fact that the process has *seemed* easy, but only because the company had been hiring professionals to do it. It's all too easy for marketers to fall into the trap of assuming that certain functions are easy, even though they have no firsthand experience in performing the functions in question.

Here's an example of an inflated estimate of internal capacity for primary research. A company has decided to mount an intensive effort in Spain. A sales manager who is a native of Spain happens to be on the payroll. He is deemed the best person to entrust with the task of conducting research in that country. But his knowledge of the market is outdated. He makes certain unfounded assumptions.

Even though the sales manager's Spanish is good, some of the terminology used in Spain is different from the terms he has picked up in the United States. He taps into various contacts in Spain, but although they are eager to help, some of the help they offer is not particularly useful, and the ad hoc research director does not have the experience or the perspective to see this. The cost figures the sales manager obtains are dangerously out of date. Remember that the cost of in-house research that generates misleading results is catastrophically high.

Be Realistic about In-House Strengths

Corporate management should not reject out of hand the possibility of using its own staff to conduct international marketing research. However, the step should not be taken without a realistic assessment of in-house capabilities.

Cost projections are especially tricky. Cost savings is the biggest reason for handling the job in-house. Proponents will tend to estimate costs as if the corporate research facility is an established entity, whereas it might not even exist, except on paper. Estimates of cost and time should be increased generously to reflect reality.

No matter how big a firm is, it is unlikely to have specialized expertise in international marketing research for each market it currently serves or is planning to serve. Rather than overstretch the capabilities of its staff, or assume a degree of expertise that does not exist, the company will have strong reasons to think about farming out the research job.

If the firm has a successful department handling market research domestically, that department will have powerful credentials to offer for the overseas assignment. Top management will be tempted to reward success, but it should be conscious of the danger of turning a good domestic market research department into a mediocre global operation.

So the firm moving into a foreign market will want to check out the current availability of primary research agencies in the target market. *Current* is the operative term. Relying on anecdotal evidence is misleading. Somebody says, "Oh, there is absolutely nothing there in the way of professional research. The only two outfits that even claim to do it are a joke." And the negative assessment is probably accurate— as of, say, two years ago. But things are changing fast in this area. Find out what's available now. For one thing, some very reputable market research firms are starting to provide international research. A.C. Nielsen is one of the better-known companies in this category.

Experience Is the Keystone

In investigating the capabilities of an outside organization, the prime criterion should be experience in the target country and the relevant industry. General technical capabilities are important, of course, and some experience is transferable from one industry or country to another. However, the better the agency's past research accomplishments overlap the firm's present research needs, the more likely it is that the job will be done well.

In the domestic arena, there are research agencies (and advertising agencies with research arms) that sell the benefits of "one-stop shopping." This option might seem easier, but marketers should consider subcontracting each international marketing research task to specialists in that function, even if research within one country is carried out by several agencies. Although the research may be more difficult to administer, it's better to have experts working on every phase of a problem than to centralize all research activities with one provider, who may be only marginally familiar with key aspects of the research.

There's the trade-off. The company commits sufficient corporate resources to the arduous chores of administration and coordination in order to get expertise for each aspect of the research job. It isn't easy. The marketing team may be working with research agencies from various countries and trying to resolve conflicts across borders and cultures.

Managing Research Techniques

Good marketing strategists don't *do* the research, but they know how to run it. An important part of administration is knowing the research techniques and how they can be blended into the optimum mix.

Hard Data versus Soft Data

European managers have developed a tolerance for "soft" data. North American marketers, used to "hard" data, often have to make a big adjustment to the realities of international research.

In the hard data approach, the research team gathers large quantities of numeric data through surveys, amassing numbers that can be manipulated statistically. In Japan, market research relies heavily on two kinds of information: soft data obtained from visits to dealers and other channel members and hard data about shipments, inventory levels, and retail sales. The head of Matsushita's videocassette recorder division is reported to have said, "Why do Americans do so much marketing research? You can find out what you need by traveling around and visiting the retailers who carry your product."[3]

"Hard-liners" scorn this approach as "anecdotal." They maintain that soft data lead to subjective interpretations. Those who dissent from the hard-line position point out that the statistical manipulation of masses of hard data can be subjective in ways that are less obvious and more insidious than the acknowledged reliance on soft data.

Worldwide Variations in Research

The basic techniques of market research—interviews, focus groups, surveys, observation—are used in all corners of the globe. However, the application and interpretation of these techniques will vary to fit the parameters of languages, cultural styles, technological levels, etc.

Focus groups.   When conducting international research via focus groups, the researcher must be aware of the importance of culture in the discussion process. Not all societies encourage frank and open exchange and disagreement among individuals. Status consciousness, which has little effect on a U.S. focus group, might have a much more potent effect in another culture, where the opinion of an "influential" member is adopted by all other participants. Some people see disagreement as discourtesy and shy away from it, thus negating the whole point of the focus group. And then there are topics that can be discussed frankly in one society but are taboo in another.

Observation. This technique is often undervalued by researchers who lean toward heavy use of statistical analysis. Observation can be especially valuable for marketers who are entering a totally unfamiliar situation. The technique can be a great help in clarifying phenomena that are difficult to assess with other techniques. For example, Toyota sent a group of engineers and designers to Southern California to observe how women get into and operate their cars. The observers found that women with long fingernails have trouble opening the door and operating knobs on the dashboard. Based on their understanding of the woman driver's plight, Toyota engineers and designers redrew some of the automobile's exterior and interior designs.

Observation can have its pitfalls. For example, people in different cultures will react differently to the discovery that their behavior is being observed. It may be necessary to deal with several languages, and this can complicate the task considerably. This difficulty can be seen in Europe, where in-store research is still fairly new. Although most executives speak English, store employees, especially in France and Spain, often do not. Sometimes multiple languages are spoken in a single country. In Belgium, for example, researchers must deal with four different languages.

Surveys. Usually conducted via questionnaires administered personally, by mail, or by telephone, the basic assumption of the survey is that the population under study is able to comprehend and respond to the questions posed. Given recent histories of government control and repression, people in many countries are not comfortable with being asked questions by a stranger.

When surveys are done by mail, the postal system has to work. Telephone surveys depend on the widespread availability of telephones and the reasonably efficient functioning of the system. These systems, which can be taken for granted in some countries, are doubtful propositions in others.

The Russian telephone system, for instance, is a shambles. In 1991 the *Economist*'s Moscow office logged 786 attempts at international calls, most to the *Economist*'s London headquarters. Of these, 754 resulted in no connection at all. Among the remaining 32 calls, two were wrong numbers and six were cut off halfway through. About one call in every 33 tries was a success. Things are not much better on calls within the city and country. At the time of the survey, Moscow still did not have a phone book. In Russia, it is often impossible to call Moscow direct from other cities.

Mail has its perils as well. In many countries, only limited information is available about dwellings, their location, and their occupants. In

Venezuela, for example, most houses are not numbered, but rather are given individual names like "Casa Rosa" or "El Retiro." In some countries, street maps are unavailable.

In other places, it may be possible to obtain correct addresses, but getting mail delivered there is a different matter entirely. The Italian postal service, for instance, has been buffeted by repeated scandals exposing such practices as selling undelivered mail to paper mills. (We might call this premature recycling.) In Hong Kong, one researcher mailed out surveys with a dollar bill as a cash incentive. The response was zero. The researcher concluded that either he had run into a fascinating cultural aversion to incentives, or—however unlikely it might seem—post office personnel had pocketed the money.

Surveys can be hampered by social and cultural constraints. Recipients of letters might be illiterate or reluctant to respond in writing. In some nations, entire segments of the population (e.g., women) might be totally inaccessible to interviewers.

In quite a few countries, one can learn something from studying consumer behavior but not by asking consumers questions. One reason for this is absence of responsibility: the consumer is sincere when spending but not when talking. Another factor is vanity: the universal human tendency to exaggerate might be intensified in the society, and the researcher might be mislead.

In spite of all these difficulties, the survey approach remains a useful one because it allows the marketer to accumulate a large amount of information amenable to statistical research. International comparative research is not easy, given all the obstacles, but it has been carried out quite successfully, especially when the environments studied are sufficiently similar to limit the impact of variables. Even in dissimilar environments, in-depth comparative research can be carried out. The techniques for effective use of the survey technique are improving and will continue to improve as the growing international marketplace increases the need.

Mix and Match

Companies are likely to get the best results internationally by using a mix of techniques; for example, by augmenting surveys with interviews. Interviews with knowledgeable people can be most useful when the marketer is seeking, not a wide variety of data, but rather specific answers to narrow questions.

Government may be of some help. For example, the U.S. federal government offers assistance through programs like the "comparison shopping service," part of the U.S. Foreign and Commercial Service of the Department of Commerce. This service provides, for a set fee, the answers to nine company-specific questions. The questions are sent to the service in Washington, which relays them to its commercial outpost in the country under study. A foreign commercial officer then gathers facts to provide the response. Such information, added to broader-scale research, supports important decisions in international marketing.

When in Rome . . . Adapting Techniques To Suit International Markets

Whether the research is domestic or foreign, researchers try to construct questions that are easy for respondents to understand and easy for data collectors to administer. There are some particular points to be considered in devising international questionnaires.

Who Is Surveyed?

To obtain valid results, researchers must sample representative members of the population under study. Methods that work superbly to do this in industrialized countries may be useless abroad. Phone books and address directories are not available. Multiple families live in what seems like a single-family dwelling. Differences between population groups living, for example, in highlands and lowlands, may make it imperative to differentiate these segments. Lack of basic demographics can make it impossible to design a sampling frame.

Such circumstances need not make it impossible to conduct useful research. But they add to the uncertainty and, perhaps, the cost. It's important that marketers encourage research experts to discuss such problems openly. Otherwise, there may be a tendency to sweep them under the rug. This can warp the results and trap marketers into making very expensive mistakes.

Researchers cannot change the environments in which they seek information. They must play the hand as it is dealt, be creative in looking for the right research mix, and be candid about the limitations and uncertainties.

Question Format

Structured questions (e.g., multiple choice), cut down the effect of bias. However, in carrying out research abroad, researchers find that open-ended questions are useful, even at the price of some bias, because they help to identify respondents' frame of reference. In an unfamiliar culture, the frame of reference is often startlingly different; therefore, it makes sense to use the open-ended technique to help draw the outlines of the reference framework.

People in some cultures are extremely averse to answering direct questions about income, age, or other personal data. Also, the categories used in certain kinds of questions are often appropriate in one environment but not in another. For example, in a developed country a white-collar worker is usually part of the middle class, whereas in a less-developed country the same job would put a person in the upper class. This is particularly important for questions that attempt to collect attitudinal, psychographic, or life-style data, because cultural variations are most pronounced in those areas.

Question Content

In some places, people are absolutely unwilling to answer certain kinds of questions, however adroitly they are structured. Or they might be willing to answer but unable to do so accurately. And then there are the places where people are strongly motivated to give inaccurate answers. For example, in countries where taxpayers routinely evade the tax collection system, questions about income level are doomed to fail.

The subjects of research in a place like the United States are sometimes annoyed when they are asked a lot of questions, but they don't think of the questioners as a kind of Gestapo. In some places, though, people are afraid that their answers will be passed on to the government, with unpleasant results. Because of government restrictions in Brazil, for instance, individuals will rarely admit to owning an imported car. So a survey in Rio de Janeiro might elicit the information that foreign cars are a great rarity, whereas a stroll through the streets of Rio will reveal a great many foreign automobiles.

Question Wording

Language and culture differences open up yawning possibilities for misunderstandings and misinterpretations. To reduce problems of question wording, it is helpful to use a translation-retranslation approach. The researcher formulates the questions, has a translator put them into the relevant language, then has a second translator render them back into the original language. This way the researcher can spot ambiguities and downright distortions. One frequently cited example of this technique concerns a translation of the Bible quotation "the spirit is willing but the flesh is weak." It was translated into English as "the bourbon is good, but the steak leaves a lot to be desired."

An additional safeguard is the use of alternative wordings. Here the researcher uses a number of questions that address the same issue but are worded differently and scattered through the questionnaire.

How Reliable Is the Data Collector?

In some cultures, questionnaires are viewed as useless, a strange exercise undertaken by odd people. When the data collectors, the people asking the questions, share that feeling, they are unlikely to be overly rigorous in feeding back accurate answers to the researcher. In fact, the data collector—far from actually collecting data—is more likely to rig the returns to humor the researcher.

This is frustrating. Professional researchers throw up their hands in despair over such irresponsibility. Marketers grit their teeth at the difficulty of finding out useful facts about consumers in the society.

What can be done? The marketer could abandon the market, but irreverence for questionnaires does not equate with lack of sales potential. Therefore, the move might mean turning one's back on profits. The marketers could try to penetrate the market without the benefit of primary research.

Or the research process can go forward, building in whatever safeguards are possible and making allowances for the inevitable fudging in data collection. Spot checks should be made as frequently as necessary to curtail interviewer cheating on a large scale. This adds to cost, but the added cost has to be accepted as the price of useable information.

Another device is the *reality check*. For example, if marketing research in a part of Italy reports that very little spaghetti is consumed, the researcher should consider whether individuals responded based on their use of purchased spaghetti rather than homemade spaghetti. The collected data should therefore be compared with secondary information and with analogous information from a similar market in order to make an estimate of data quality. In other words, use common sense.

Interpreting and Analyzing Data

Analytical tools used in international marketing research are often quite shallow; sketchy evidence suggests that analytical techniques, particularly quantitative ones, are not widely used by international marketing managers. The researcher should, of course, use the best tools available and appropriate for analysis. The fact that a market is in a less-developed country does not preclude collecting good data and subjecting those data to rigorous analysis.

However, international researchers should be careful about using overly sophisticated tools for unsophisticated data. If the data quality is bad, even the best tools will not improve the quality. When overly sophisticated analysis is applied to mediocre information, the analysis tends to package the results in a way that the information looks better than it actually is.

The Proof of the Pudding: Presenting Research Results

A research team completes its study of buying patterns in the newly emerging South African market and presents the results to top management. The presentation, orchestrated thoroughly and clarified by good graphics, goes over well. Managers are able to ask pertinent questions, and those questions are answered.

The campaign based on the findings is kicked off—and it flops. One reason for the failure is that the benefits of the research did not reach the company's managers in South Africa in useable form. The findings were masticated at headquarters and then processed to the provinces in the form of policies and instructions.

In multinational marketing research, it is as important to communicate thoroughly with managers in the local operations as it is with managers at headquarters. Indeed, the politics of the situation aside, it may be more important to brief the front-line troops.

When local managers don't get a full-fledged presentation of research results, the synergistic benefits of a multinational operation are largely lost. Not that line managers in the home office or in the target markets abroad should be covered with an avalanche of information and analysis. That is not a presentation, it is a snow job. Researchers, working with marketers, should translate the analyzed results into useful information, prioritizing it in terms of what is most important to the people who actually do the marketing, and presenting it in a crisp, useful fashion. Top management can contribute by ensuring that the research team does this and that the presentations are carried out in the best way possible.

Because application of research is the proof of the pudding, marketers and researchers ought to use interesting and creative ways of developing applications and seeing that those applications are used wherever they will help. Here's one way such a program can be carried out. Top marketers and researchers visit local operations and sit down with the people there, talking about problems and how the research can be turned into solutions. When an application is found to work, it is passed along to other operations around the world. A monthly newsletter is a useful format.

Follow-Up and Review

When the research process is finished and presented, there is still one more important stage. The organization must absorb the research and make appropriate managerial decisions based on it. For example, if it has been found that a product needs to have certain attributes to sell well in Latin America, management must make sure that the product development area is aware of the finding. Furthermore, management should follow up to see that product development is cranking the findings into its work. Sending a memo is not enough.

Without such follow-up, research becomes a mere "staff" function, increasingly isolated from "line" activity and failing to influence corporate decision making. Thus critical research findings are ignored. The lack of connection between research results and line application is always a potential problem. It can be a greater problem in international marketing, because there are more line entities to be apprised of key findings, impressed with their importance, and assisted in turning them into successful marketing tools.

Building and Maintaining the Decision Support System

Most of the time, marketers have to make daily decisions for which there is neither time nor money for special research. To provide the decision maker with data to support ongoing decisions, there must be an information system already in place. Information and data management for international markets is more complex than for the domestic market because of separation in time and space as well as wide differences in cultural and technological environments.

Qualities of Useful Decision Support Systems

Corporations have responded by developing marketing decision support systems like those of Corning and Digital Equipment. To be truly useful to the decision maker, the system must be relevant, timely, flexible, accurate, exhaustive, and convenient.

Relevant. The data gathered must have meaning for the decision-making process. Few companies can spend a lot of money collecting facts that are "nice to know." So the system can't be an electronic grapevine or Christmas tree on which to hang anything that comes to mind. There must be a well-understood and widely disseminated set of guidelines about what goes in, as well as a gatekeeper controlling the supply.

Networking Information Systems

Corning started its global system, called the Business Information Exchange Network, with a pilot program. One key feature is a news-search service that automatically clips articles and places them in the interested user's electronic mailbox.

Digital Equipment launched its Competitive Information System (CIS) at first to collect and disseminate information about domestic competitors. After four years it became truly global. CIS contains product descriptions, announcements, internal and external competitive analyses, company strategies, policies, and a direct feed from an external news wire. Digital's analysts use data from CIS for strategic decision making and planning. Its sales reps use CIS data to formulate sales tactics. The system generates more than 100,000 log-ins each day worldwide.

Timely.   When managers need to know something right away, it might be acceptable if the answers arrive in a couple of days, but not if the decision maker has to wait a month. Conversely, when information becomes outdated it should be replaced, deleted, or at least clearly labeled as being possibly erroneous.

Flexible.   Information must be available in the forms needed by management. A marketing decision support system should, therefore, permit manipulation of the format and combination of the data.

Accurate.   Accuracy is particularly important in the international field. Information that is valid one day may be invalid the next because of major changes taking place in the world.

Exhaustive.   The system's data bank should be reasonably exhaustive. Because of the interrelationships among variables, all the factors that can influence a particular decision ought to be appropriately represented in the system. Because international marketing can be affected by many issues that don't come into play domestically, the necessity for an ample reservoir of pertinent data is apparent.

Convenient.   Finally, the system must be convenient to access and use. Cumbersome, time-consuming systems will not be used enough to justify their cost.

Contributing Factors in Decision Support

There are various reasons why international marketing decision support systems are being developed successfully. These include technological advances in hardware and software, managers' increased familiarity with technology, and acknowledgement by managers that flying by the seat of the pants is potentially disastrous.

To build a marketing decision support system, corporations use the internal data available from such divisions as accounting and finance as well as from various subsidiaries. In addition, many organizations have developed new approaches to enrich the basic data flow. Three such approaches are environmental scanning, Delphi studies, and scenario building.

Environmental Scanning

Any change in the environment can have serious repercussions. Environmental scanning is an early warning system for the marketer. Environmental scanning models are used for a variety of purposes:

- Providing a mind-stretching experience for management

- Developing broad strategies and long-term policies

- Formulating action plans and operating programs

- Creating a frame of reference for the annual budget

Basically, environmental scanning is what the term suggests: an instrument for observing the marketing environment. When it's working well, the marketing decision makers continuously receive information on international political, social, and economic affairs; on changes of attitudes held by public institutions and private citizens; and on possible upcoming alterations in international markets.

One method of environmental scanning consists of obtaining factual input regarding pertinent variables. For example, the International Data Base (IDB) of the U.S. Census Bureau collects, evaluates, and adjusts a wide variety of demographic, social, and economic characteristics of foreign countries. IDB provides estimates for all countries of the world on such economic variables as labor-force statistics, GNP, and income statistics, and also on health and nutrition variables. Similar factual information can be obtained from international organizations like the World Bank and the United Nations. This is another example of highly useful information that can be gotten from government sources at a small fraction of what it would cost if the company gathered the material on its own. Far too few companies know what's available to them for the asking.

Factual information, however, often doesn't tell the whole story about what is actually happening—and what will happen—in a foreign market. Corporations are developing ways of measuring the underlying dimensions of social change. One significant method is content analysis.

Content analysis investigates the content of communications in a society. It entails literally counting the number of times designated words, themes, symbols, or pictures appear in a given medium. The use of content analysis is made easier by the emergence of new tools like optical scanners and specially designed software. For example, the Apple PC can analyze texts in Chinese, Japanese, Hebrew, Korean, and Arabic.

Companies can use content analysis to pinpoint upcoming changes and to spot new opportunities by identifying trendsetting events. For example, the Alaskan oil spill by the tanker *Valdez* set in motion a surge in concern about environmental protection and safety around the world, far beyond the dimensions of the event itself.

Many firms set up small staffs at headquarters to coordinate the information flow. Subsidiary staff can be used to provide occasional intelligence reports. Groups of volunteers gather and analyze information worldwide and feed back reports to headquarters, where they can be used to form the "big picture."

One key to making content analysis work is to limit the extent to which subjectivity can influence results. Paid staff and volunteers must be trained and motivated to count and record the times the agreed-on items appear in the media, not to put their own spin on the reporting.

Some large corporations that have set up environmental scanning operations are turning the function into a profit center by offering it to outsiders on a fee basis. Bank of America, for example, set up World Information Services to offer such services as Country Outlook, Country Data Forecasts, and Country Risk Monitor.

Environmental scanning is a strategic rather than a tactical tool, focusing on the long term. Although many corporations see it as valuable, there are dissenting voices. For example, certain researchers note that "in those constructs and frameworks where the environment has been given primary consideration, there has been a tendency for the approach to become so global that studies tend to become shallow and diffuse, or impractical if pursued in sufficient depth."[4] This assessment points up a major challenge faced by companies in trying to do a good job of environmental scanning. Like many techniques and disciplines, it can become bloated with jargon and costly frills. The approach is far from perfect, but the need to sound the environmental waters of foreign markets will continue to impel companies to pursue environmental scanning.

Delphi Studies

Delphi studies are used to enrich the information obtained from factual data. They are creative and highly qualitative data gathering methods.

Typically, Delphi studies are carried out with groups of about 30 well-chosen participants who possess particular in-depth expertise in an area of concern, such as future developments in the international trade environment. These participants are asked, most frequently by mail, to identify the major issues in the area of concern. They are also asked to rank their statements according to importance and explain the rationale behind the order.

Next, the aggregated information is returned to all participants, who are encouraged to clearly state their agreements or disagreements. Statements can be challenged, and, in another round, participants can respond to the challenges. After several rounds of challenge and response a reasonably coherent consensus takes shape. The Delphi technique uses mail, including electronic mail, to bridge great distances and bring together individuals who would otherwise not meet to exchange views.

The key to successful use of the Delphi study approach is to select the right participants and to motivate them to participate and keep on participating through all the steps. It takes time—several months— to do it right, because of the process of response and counter-response. When it's obtained regularly, Delphi information can be a crucial supplement to the facts gathered by the marketing information system.

Scenario Building

Some companies use scenario building to flesh out the facts amassed by the system. Scenario builders take the facts and weave them into projections of possible things to come. Variables like economic growth rates, import penetration, population growth, and political stability are the building blocks for the possible versions of the future.

A wide variety of scenarios should be built to expose executives to a range of potential occurrences. Ideally, even far-fetched variables deserve some consideration. A scenario for Union Carbide, for example, might have included the possibility of a disaster such as occurred in Bhopal. Similarly, oil companies need to work with scenarios that factor in dramatic shifts in the supply situation, precipitated by, for example, regional conflict in the Middle East, and that consider major alterations in the demand picture, due to, say, technological developments or government policies.

Scenario building is speculation. You might call it fantasizing within the bounds of reality. The scenario builder cannot just extrapolate from current situations and compose buttoned-up narratives that string together likely events with a linear plot. Unlikely things happen. Anybody can manage when the expected thing always occurs. Good managers expect the unexpected, and good scenarios—although they can't predict the future—give managers a workout on the possiblities, good and bad.

Scenarios should recognize that occurrences might not be confined to one market, but rather spread over wide regions. One example of this is the debt crisis that hit Latin America. The inability of any one or two countries to pay their debts would not have presented a major problem for the international banking community; large and simultaneous defaults presented a severe problem indeed.

So scenario builders should be encouraged to think big. They should consider what might happen if, for instance, a massive cornerstone of current technology were to suddenly become obsolete. Quantum leaps in computer development and new generations of computers can render obsolete the technological investment of a corporation or even a country.

Scenarios are not just narratives to be enjoyed and then kicked around conversationally. The payoff for scenario building is when effective contingency plans are developed from them. A rigorous application to the job of forging contingency plans stretches managerial muscles, hones response capability, shortens response times, and enhances performance under changed circumstances.

The trick, of course, is to devise scenarios that are unusual enough to trigger new thinking yet sufficiently realistic to be taken seriously by management. Corporations that commit themselves seriously to scenario building as a tool often turn to outside experts.

The information and insight provided by consulting firms is usually worth what it costs—*if* it is accurate and insightful, *if* it addresses issues relevant to the company's concerns, and *if* it is used properly. The first qualities, accuracy and insight, are the consultant's responsibility. The second, relevance, is a responsibility shared by consultant and client. The client must, first of all, know what it wants, and must be able to communicate those wants. The consultant has to facilitate the process by asking the right questions. The job of using the projections falls on the shoulders of the client. If a company does not have a clear idea of what it will do with consulting input, it should not sign the contract.

Scenario building, Delphi studies, environmental scanning, and the other techniques discussed here are components of a decision support system that gathers, reports, and analyzes data that are the raw materials of management excellence.

High-Powered Help with Scenario Building

One well-known resource in creating international scenarios, as well as advising clients on a whole panoply of global issues, is Kissinger Associates, the New York–based firm established in 1982 by former Secretary of State Henry Kissinger, former Undersecretary of State Lawrence S. Eagleburger, and former National Security Advisor Brent Scowcraft.

For its corporate clients, Kissinger Associates offers broad-brush pictures of political and economic conditions in particular countries or regions, along with analyses of political and economic trends.

Some have argued that pointing out political trends is not, in itself, a consulting service worth big fees. Kissinger himself seems to agree, saying that to provide only abstract information on the political situation in a foreign country is not fair to the client. The firm's principals believe that by correctly assessing, for example, the political outlook in Greece for the next five years, they can help a client decide whether to make new investments there or to prepare to pull out in anticipation of a hostile socialist government. Similarly, the firm might help a U.S. oil company with limited Middle East experience in its first attempts to negotiate and work with a government in the region.

Although this kind of work does not deeply involve Kissinger Associates in specific business decisions, it does require (as is true with any good consultant) a firm grasp of clients' businesses and goals.

Kissinger Associates commands high fees for its services. There can be various reasons for paying large amounts for consultants, not all of them having to do with the superlative practicality of the advice, useful though it might be. One pragmatic reason for getting high-powered consulting input was explained by a former member of Kissinger Associates: "These days, in case an investment goes sour, it is useful for (management) to be able to say, 'We got this expert advice and acted on that basis.' They have to show due diligence in exercising their fiduciary duties."[5]

Check Points

✔ Management must fully formulate the questions it wants answered before undertaking primary research.

✔ Cultural differences, variant attitudes, and unreliable research methods can make primary research difficult.

✔ Language is a stumbling block. Marketers should use techniques like retranslation to cut down chances of misunderstanding.

✔ Once the information is collected, researchers and marketers should make sure that it is processed with tools appropriate to its quality.

✔ International marketing research is still, in many cases, unsophisticated, but it is gaining in sophistication.

✔ A marketing decision support system provides ongoing information to management and hones decision-making abilities.

✔ Among the most crucial variables to be tracked in a decision support system are the following:

1. Legal requirements in exporting and importing, regulation, taxation, employment and labor costs.

2. Economic trends: GNP growth, level of industrialization, inflation, and savings rate

3. Political trends

4. Technological trends and innovations

TAKING YOUR FIRST STEPS
Local Guides and Shipping the Goods

You have to hunt where the ducks are. The markets are all over the world today, but, as Professor Harold Hill sings in *The Music Man,* "You've got to know the territory!"

Global territories are, all too often, as baffling as they are potentially lucrative. When you export—and exporting is the way most firms start going global—you must be able to rely on someone who knows the territory.

The first step is to get a grasp on international channels of distribution: how they work and how you can get the right intermediaries for your product or service. Manufacturers battling in the domestic market know the importance of having the right distributor. The wrong distributor can doom you, even if you have a superior product at a good price.

Why Do You Need an International Distributor?

Finding the right distribution channel is just as important internationally as domestically. If anything, it is more important. As a new market entrant, you know little about the market and thus must depend on the distributor not only to get the goods into the stores and do business honestly, but also to serve as a guide, interpreter, and mentor in the ways of the foreign country.

Export or Perish!

For companies big and small, going global is now more a matter of survival than of choice. That was the case with South Carolina-based Greenville Machinery Corporation (GMC). Unlike most U.S. firms, GMC, a manufacturer of denim dyeing and finishing machines, was already selling abroad; export accounted for 20 percent of its sales. But GMC was seeing its primary customer base, U.S. textile mills, forced out of business as a result of lower costs in other countries. So GMC went global—aggressively. It wouldn't be easy.

The firm's strong points were technological superiority and customer service. The technology was far less of a problem than the service. The company went to exceptional lengths to choose the right people to represent it abroad. Selling through carefully screened agents, GMC built export business to 60 percent of total sales, selling in 30 countries in Africa, Latin America, and Asia.

It took patience. For years, despite repeated attempts, GMC had not made a single sale in China. Then the company landed three multimillion-dollar projects. Similarly, it took two years of repeated sales pitches in Turkey to close a deal. Venezuela and Mexico were hard nuts to crack as well, but GMC was at last able to win profitable business in those lands.

GMC's experience embodies a number of key facts of life in business today. The company had to mount a strong, coherent drive to sell into foreign markets. The task was sometimes frustrating; the company had to be willing to commit years of hard effort to bridge the cultural, political, and economic gaps.

And the firm made sure of good representation abroad.

When Distributors Approach You, Listen!

A legitimate foreign distributor contacts a firm, suggesting there may be a market for the company's products in the distributor's country. One response that many companies are inclined to make is to say, "We're not ready to consider exporting, but we'd be glad to talk to you when we are ready."

That's a waste of a good opportunity to learn from an expert about global marketing and about an overseas market. Even if you are

Coals to Newcastle

With the right distributor, amazing things are possible. Timberland Shoes was looking for new markets for its rugged footgear.

Timberland's first choice was an astonishing one: Italy. Italy, after all, is a center of shoe manufacture, home to many of the world's best-known and highest-priced brands of leather footwear. Ignoring the scoffers, Timberland went ahead. Today Italy is one of the most profitable of the company's dozens of export markets.

What happened was that Timberland found the right distributors. Or, more accurately, the distributors found Timberland. Italian distributors approached the U.S. company, saying they saw an opportunity in Italy. This was a time when many U.S. companies were being solicited by foreign distributors and were brushing them off. Timberland paid attention.

The company's president said, "We were discovered by people in Europe who saw an opportunity for us to export at a time we did not believe we could. The good news is that once we realized there was an opportunity, we went after it."

Timberland's approach is unconventional. The company does not scout for markets in which it thinks it can gain a foothold. It responds only to distributors that approach it. "We have talented distributors who understand the market better than we ever could," says a spokesperson. Timberland looks at the line of footwear the distributor carries and how it is marketed. If the line is high quality and the distributor has a successful track record, then Timberland will go into the market.

Not that many companies are lucky enough to be pursued by first-class distributors around the world. Nevertheless, the Timberland case illustrates a few points about the selection of channels in international marketing.

---

not about to go international, treat this as a useful learning experience. As Timberland observes, the foreign distributor knows more about the market than the company is ever likely to know. When selling abroad, there is a great advantage in having a distributor who acts as consultant and facilitator and can channel the goods to the best outlets.

Welcome any approaches of the foreign distributors, ask questions, and find out all you can about the market.

Make Distribution a Major Issue in the Decision

Would-be exporters have come to regret overlooking the importance of distribution channels. After conducting good and lengthy research that indicates a demand, many just assume that proper channels can be found. This assumption can be costly. The availability of a suitable distributor is likely to be much more important in marketing abroad than it is at home.

Let the Distributor Be Your Guide

Some companies are used to keeping a tight rein on domestic distributors. They value the channel above the expertise. They provide detailed instructions about how the marketing should be done.

This approach is less likely to work well abroad. In international marketing, the key to success lies in teaming up with a savvy, reliable distributor and relying on the distributor to deal with various cultural and government issues.

Finding Top Representatives in Foreign Countries

How do you locate good representatives in foreign countries? Finding high-quality distributors abroad is as important as recruiting and hiring the best people for top jobs within the company. Experts know that an ineffective foreign distributor can set you back years; it is almost better to have no distributor than a bad one in a major market.

Teaming up with distributors can be active or passive. For many, like Timberland, it starts with a distributor's approach. Distributors are always on the lookout for products they can sell profitably.

However, even if the initial contact is made by the distributor, the company should not remain passive, simply settling for the first intermediary to approach the firm. Once the contact has been made, however it is made, the final choice should result from a logical process. Learn enough about the foreign market to understand what should be expected of an intermediary. As we have discussed, the intermediary can be a primary source of information. However, always verify the statements of the distributor through independent research. Then check out other available representatives. This does not imply discounting the enthusiasm and interest shown by the initial distributor. Value the distributor's initiative, but also maintain a healthy measure of skepticism.

Learning about possible representatives abroad need not be a cumbersome or expensive process. Government agencies can be of considerable help.

Government Assistance

The U.S. Department of Commerce can be a valuable resource in locating foreign representatives.

All of the following services are available for relatively small fees. Various publications give more information about these programs and other guidance on international marketing. Two titles of interest are *A Basic Guide to Exporting* and *Commerce Export Assistance Programs.*

The World Traders Data Report (WTDR) is particularly useful in the screening of candidates. WTDRs provide a trade profile of specific foreign firms. A typical report covers the firm's location, history, size, area of operation, assets, financial references, etc. It rates the company's reputation and offers informed comment on its strengths and weaknesses. WTDRs can be obtained for all kinds of companies, including manufacturers as well as distributors.

The Agent/Distributor Service (A/DS) locates foreign firms that are interested in export proposals submitted by U.S. firms and determines their willingness to correspond with the U.S. firm. Both U.S. and foreign service posts abroad supply information on up to six representatives who meet these requirements. As of 1993, the cost for an A/DS application is $125 per country.

The New Product Information Service (NPIS) provides worldwide publicity for new U.S. products available for export. This exposure enables foreign firms to identify and contact U.S. firms, and gives the U.S. firm a direct indication of market interest. It also reduces wasted time by making sure the first contact comes from a representative with some interest.

Firms can subscribe to the Trade Opportunities Program (TOP), which matches the product interests of foreign buyers with those of U.S. subscribers.

The department also collects data on foreign firms for the Foreign Traders Index (FTI). Covering more than 140 countries, the file contains information on more than 140,000 importing firms, agents, representatives, distributors, manufacturers, service organizations, retailers, and potential end users.

Private Sources

A good place to look for intermediaries abroad is in trade directories. Country and regional business directories such as *Kompass* (Europe),

Bottin International (worldwide), *Nordisk Handelskalendar* (Scandinavia), and the *Japan Trade Directory* should be checked. Company lists by country and line of business can be ordered from Dun & Bradstreet, Reuben H. Donnelley, Kelly's Directory, and Johnston Publishing. Telephone directories, especially the yellow pages sections or editions, can provide lists of distributors. The *Jaeger and Waldman International Telex Directory* can also be consulted. Although not detailed, these listings will give addresses and an indication of the products sold.

If you have a bank with connections in foreign countries, this can be helpful in seeking representation. Banks usually have very extensive networks through their affiliates and correspondent banks, so they are a good place to check early in the process. Useful also are organizations like advertising agencies, airlines, and shipping lines. Such agencies have substantial international information networks and can put them to work for their clients by making a preliminary list of possible distributors and screening candidates. Some major airlines (e.g., Northwest Airlines and KLM) have special staffs for this purpose in their cargo operations.

Advertisements

Marketers who want to take a more direct approach to finding representation can buy space in appropriate publications in target countries or areas. Such advertisements typically indicate the type of support the marketer will be able to give to the distributor. Here is an example of this kind of ad, from the Finnish *Kauppalehti:*

> Real Business Opportunity
> Agent is wanted in Finland for a well known European Mail Order company.
>   The agent, who will become part of a newly established Scandinavia group of franchise agents, will be supported with marketing material, catalogues and computer system from our office in Copenhagen.
>   This is an ideal opportunity for someone looking for easy expansion into new business.
>   All applications will be handled confidentially, and all will receive a reply.

This ad might be worded in rather odd English, but it gets the job done, laying out the basics of the proposition in a brief space.

Trade Fairs and Other Means

Trade fairs are a useful forum for finding out about intermediaries in the industry and meeting potential distributors. You can also deal

directly with contacts from previous applications, launch new mail solic-
itations, use your own sales organization for the search, or ask companies in similar but noncompetitive businesses.

Yet another interesting way of finding out about distributors is to go
directly to customers, both current or potential. If, for example, you
have made a few unsolicited sales to a market, the customers could be
approached on the basis that you may want to enter the market on a
more formal basis. Or a good potential customer can simply be asked
about capable and reliable distributions.

You will use these information sources to generate a list of prospective
representatives for the next step: screening.

Separating the Wheat from the Chaff

Screening criteria vary by industry and by product and service. Here's
a useful summary list of criteria used across the board:

- Goals and strategies

- Size of the firm

- Financial strength

- Reputation

- Trading areas covered

- Compatibility

- Experience

- Sales organization

- Physical facilities

- Willingness to carry inventories

- Service capability

- Use of promotion

- Sales performance

- Relations with local government

- Communications

- Overall attitude

To a large extent, these characteristics parallel those used to screen
domestic distributors. There are notable exceptions. For example, in

certain environments, the intermediary's relationship with government may be of paramount importance, overshadowing all the other dimensions.

Evaluating a domestic distributor is comparatively easy. The domestic intermediary's reputation is known in the trade; the firm's size, facilities, and area of operation are relatively accessible; and you know where to go to get information on the firm's financial condition.

Screening is a lot harder abroad. Because selecting the right foreign representative can mean life or death for any venture it is essential that it be done with the utmost care.

Fortunately, there are ways for marketers to obtain practical help. For example, the U.S. Department of Commerce World Traders Data Report mentioned earlier is a highly useful tool. Your bank can also be of great help.

Financial Standing

The candidate's financial standing is a good starting point. Is the distributor making money? Is the distributor in good enough financial shape to absorb risk and extend adequate credit to customers? Financial reports may not be complete, in which case the candidate ought to be ready to supply more information. Where possible, the reports should be checked via third-party opinion, for example, a local bank. If the candidate deliberately supplies false information, then end your investigation right there.

What Are They Selling?

Sales are an excellent indicator. What is the distributor doing for its current list of marketers? Get the list and ask.

The most desirable distributors may already be handling competitive products. Occasionally such a distributor may be tempted to switch lines, but it does not happen often. If you are trying to lure these top distributors away from your competitors, be very wary of giving them information that will help their current client.

When the best distributors in an area are unavailable it's tempting to take the best available candidate, even if that candidate offers dubious credentials. Eagerness and availability are not enough. If you cannot find a distributor with experience in your product category, you're probably better off looking for an equally qualified distributor handling related products. The complementary nature of products may be of interest to both parties, especially in industrial markets, where ultimate customers may seek one-stop shopping or be in the market for complete systems.

The quality of the other products handled by the distributor is important. A high-level product might suffer from being carried alongside lower-quality products, even when they are entirely different lines. How many lines is the distributor handling now? This is a sensitive question. First-class distributors are offered many lines to sell. But when the representative has too many products, anything additional may receive short shrift. Some distributors like to carry as many products as possible to enhance their reputations and cut down competition, but they put real effort only into lines that provide the best payoff.

Facilities

The candidate's physical facilities (e.g., refrigerated storage in the case of food), market coverage, and service capability must be checked by people who are qualified to judge. How does the sales force work? Does it call on executives, engineers, and operating people, or does it concentrate mainly on purchasing agents? If distributors in adjoining areas will be used, do their territories overlap?

Comfort

Above all, you must feel comfortable with the distributor and be able to rely on the distributor's energy, professionalism, and ethics. This means talking with the distributor's customers, suppliers, bankers, competitors, and other members of the business community. This effort will shed light on certain less tangible, but exceedingly important, variables. One key variable, particularly important in developing countries, is political clout. Is the representative well connected? Or out of favor? Don't take the representative's word for it.

Nurturing a Relationship

To a greater degree than is usually the case in domestic operations, you must acknowledge the distributor as an independent entity with its own goals. What is the distributor's business strategy? What does the distributor expect to get out of the relationship? What does the distributor hope this arrangement will lead to? How does the distributor see the long-range prospects for your products?

The relationship is like a partnership; the distributor should be chosen with the same care as a partner. A mistake may not be correctable any time soon. Channel relationships are long-term arrangements, so the distributor's view on future expansion of the product line or its distribution should be clarified. At this stage, too, you must find out if there are any limitations on the representative's capacity to take on other lines.

Communication

Because global communication is likely to be more complicated than that with a domestic distributor, now is the time to determine just how much help the distributor needs in terms of price, credit, terms, delivery, sales training, merchandising, service, warranty, product modification, warehousing, technical support, and personal visits. The foreign representative should be raising all these questions and seeking clear answers. If the questions don't come up, you should see that as a warning signal. Do these people really understand what's required? Or are they just eager to sign an agreement?

Get everything spelled out so the relationship will run as smoothly as possible. There will be plenty of bumps in the road, but on these foreseeable issues the way can be paved to some extent.

Finally, you have to judge the distributor's overall commitment and willingness to cooperate. One effective way to do this is to ask the distributor to assist in developing a local marketing plan—or even to come up with one on its own. This endeavor will bring out potential problems. If the representative brushes off the request, or does a lackluster job, then maybe you should look at a smaller but more eager candidate. Size and strength alone are not enough. They have to be energized by commitment.

The Distribution Agreement

Once you have chosen an intermediary, it's time to draw up the agreement. In the domestic sphere, distribution agreements tend to be standardized. Everyone concerned understands the terms and the frame of reference. However, it's worthwhile to take a little more time to review an agreement with a foreign intermediary. Although the basics are the same as in any domestic agreement, there will be differences in emphasis and interpretation. You should find some typical agreements in the foreign market and study them with the help of someone who is familiar with the market.

One important issue is the duration of the contract. In general, distribution agreements should be for a specified, relatively long period. However, the initial contract should specify a trial period of six months or a year, possibly with minimum purchase requirements.

These are desirable provisions of most contracts with new distributors. There will be exceptions. The higher the distributor's standing, the greater its ability to call the shots. When several marketers are competing for a leading distributor, it may be necessary to make some concessions. However, the trial period makes great sense from the point of view of either party. If a distributor resists this idea or holds out for an exceptionally long term, you should ask why and scrutinize the answer.

The competitive situation—present and future—influences the decision about the term of the contract. Let's say, for instance, that a marketer is first in getting into a foreign market but knows (or has a strong idea) that other competitors will follow soon. The need to sew up the distributor will loom larger in this scenario.

The Importance of Boundaries

Firms, especially smaller firms, will want to be particularly careful in agreeing on geographical boundaries. If the distributor is granted rights for too broad an area; or if the distributor has potential or optional rights on the larger area; or if the agreement is ambiguous in this regard; then there could be problems ahead when you want to expand. The initial distributor might claim the right to the new territories or the right to distribute other products manufactured by your firm, even though you would prefer to use another channel.

You should retain the right to distribute products independently and to certain customers and in general specify that the intermediary work within well-defined limits. For example, Parker Pen maintains a dual distribution system, dealing directly with certain large accounts. Such arrangements are common in the domestic arena; the danger is that lack of familiarity might induce you to overlook the need for them abroad.

The operation must be spelled out clearly in terms of territory, products, and customers. If things go well, of course, the distributor can be given broader scope later.

Payments

The payment section of the contract should stipulate the methods of payment as well as how the distributor or agent is to draw compensation. Distributors get their compensation from discounts, whereas agents receive a specific percentage of net sales, such as 15 percent.

In what currency will the intermediary be paid? With the volatility of currency markets, this provision must be pinned down. It isn't necessary to prognosticate the movements of, say, dinars against dollars, but it is necessary to be precise about the medium of payment so there is no room for argument.

You need to make sure that none of the compensation sent to the distributor violates the Foreign Corrupt Practices Act. A violation occurs if a payment is made to influence a foreign official in exchange for business favors, depending on the nature of the action sought.

There is a school of thought that says, basically, "In doing business abroad, anything goes." This cynical view, which used to be more prevalent than it is today, suggests that all officials are corrupt and all business runs on bribery.

Now, it would be naive to deny the reality that, in various cultures, casual off-the-books payments are the lubricant of commerce. But this should not be confused with the out-and-out buying of government officials, purchasing agents, or contracts. And, indeed, the Foreign Corrupt Practices Act makes practical distinctions. For instance, so-called "grease" or facilitating payments, such as paying a small fee to expedite paperwork through customs, is not considered a violation. Some of what gets paid to the foreign distributor may be grease, but there had better not be larger, unaccounted-for amounts of money passing from you to the intermediary.

Products

The products or product lines included in the deal should be stipulated. If there is any chance of confusion, the contract should also list products that are *not* included. The agreement must pin down the functions and responsibilities of the intermediary in terms of carrying the goods in inventory, promoting them, and providing service. If anything, the contract should err on the side of overspecificity. The sales operation is far removed from the home office by distance and language. It will be hard enough to keep everything on track. The agreement should provide a clear track on which to run.

Communication

How will you and the distributor communicate with each other? The answer might be obvious at home, but not so clear abroad. One issue is to agree on the kind and amount of information to which you are entitled. You should have total access to all information concerning the marketing of your products, including past records, present situation assessments, and market research. There should be a formal channel for the distributor to voice grievances. (And distributors should be encouraged to vent their complaints, rather than letting them fester.)

The agreement should state the confidentiality of the information provided by both parties. And it must protect intellectual property rights, such as patents. You should not neglect to obtain adequate legal counsel, in both countries if necessary, to see that this is done and that the agreement is a good one.

Working Together: Managing the Distribution Channel

A channel relationship, like a marriage, brings together two independent entities with shared goals. Marriage counselors say that for a

Multinational? With 13 Employees?[2]

Mirus Industries of California makes digital film recorders which "print" onto 35mm film. Before it had a single customer, Mirus knew it had a product with global appeal. In two years, the company recruited ten distributors in Europe, the Far East, and the Middle East. Export accounts for 60 percent of its production.

This worldwide company has a mere 13 employees. When asked about the ability of such a small firm to perform internationally, Mirus's president, Bruce MacKay replies, "The answer is that you must want to export and have the courage to do it. You must approach the export market with a passionate commitment, and you must have a well-thought-out plan."

Relationships with distributors are central to Mirus's success. Skeptical international distributors have to be made comfortable. MacKay says that they need to know the company will be around in six months: "You cannot expect instant results—you must remain patient and consistent in your dealings and distributors."

MacKay learns about foreign markets firsthand. In 18 months he has traveled to Japan four times, Southeast Asia twice, and Europe three times. He believes that communication, quality, and collaboration are the keys to success: "You must keep in mind that international distributors are very savvy people who know what is going on in this high-tech world. Fax machines, magazines, and fast travel keep everyone up-to-date. Your international distributors are your local partners, and they represent your reputation. Never forget that."

---

marriage to work, each party must be open about its needs, expectations, and problems. Each party must communicate. Each party must be willing to sit down and talk about its own problems, the other party's problems, and shared hopes and fears. Each party has to communicate, factually and objectively, about perceived changes in the other's behavior that might jeopardize or violate the agreement.

Marriages between partners from different cultures usually require additional care because of the built-in chances for misunderstanding. Here are some key points about maintaining a good "marriage" between a marketer and a foreign intermediary.

Manage for the Long Term

Even if the initial agreement is only for two years, the success of the venture depends on how well the relationship works over the long haul. You may be in a seller's market, and be able to pressure the representative for heavy concessions. If this pressure is too great, the intermediary may bow temporarily, only to turn on you later when the situation becomes more competitive.

Anticipate Conflict

Conflicts will arise, ranging from small grievances (such as billing errors) to major ones (disputes over territory). In some cases, the conflict will be caused by outside forces, in which unauthorized intermediaries compete with legitimate exporters and exclusive distributors.

Although such conflicts are not caused by the parties to the agreement, they will nevertheless have to solve them. You should take the lead. At the outset, you and your intermediary should list the foreseeable causes of friction. You can role-play the situations, feeling your way toward mechanisms that will come into play when the actual problems arise. Even when the problems are difficult to deal with, the fact that they have been discussed in advance will be helpful.

Be Flexible

From the beginning, it should be assumed that the initial agreement is not carved in stone. It will require adjusting. Change is a normal part of the relationship, not an admission of failure.

Channel adjustment can take a number of forms:

- **Channel shift:** Eliminating a particular type of channel

- **Channel modification:** Changing individual members while leaving channel structure intact

- **Role or relationship modification:** Changing the functions performed or the reward structure

Evaluate

The machinery for evaluating the relationship should be set up at the start and understood and accepted by both parties. Evaluation ought not to be a one-way street; the distributor should participate in discussions of performance and problems. Most of the criteria used in selecting intermediaries can be used for evaluation as well.

Check Out the Laws

Working with a foreign intermediary involves not just a different culture but also a different body of laws. For example, in the European Community, you cannot keep a distributor from transporting products to customers in another member country, even if you have another distributor in that market. The only remedy for this is to spell out in the distributor agreement the desired situation—in this case, perhaps, a clause prohibiting transshipments.

A foreign distributor who uses differences in laws to gain advantage over the marketer is not a desirable partner. So, although the agreement should reflect the laws of the country and the regulations of the community, there must be a good-faith assumption that neither party will use loopholes to the other's disadvantage.

Allow for the Gap in Distance and Culture

Distance, whether it is geographic, psychological, or a combination of both, can be bridged by going beyond routine business communication to find innovative ways of sharing pertinent information. You might place one person in charge of distributor-related communication. Another way to handle it is through an interpenetration strategy, that is, an exchange of personnel so that each organization can gain insight into the workings of the other.

Whatever the organizational setup regarding communications, the exchange of personnel is a good idea. The cultural chasm narrows as people come to know each other better.

Channel management must acknowledge cross-cultural differences. Belief systems and behavioral patterns affect operations in ways that may startle marketers. For example, in markets where individualism is stressed, local channel partners may seek arrangements that foster their own self-interest and may expect their counterparts to watch out for themselves. Conflict is seen as a natural phenomenon. By contrast, in societies of low individualism, a common purpose is fostered between the partners. These days marketers have to be practical ethnologists.

Terminating the Relationship

When savvy executives negotiate employment contracts, they pay particular attention to the provisions covering termination. Not that anybody thinks premature termination is likely; both parties hope and assume the relationship will be happy and prosperous. Nevertheless, it makes sense to look at the worst case, so the contract will spell out causes for termination and procedures to be followed.

There are many reasons to terminate a channel relationship. The most typical are changes in your distribution approach (e.g., the establishment of a sales office) or a (perceived) lack of performance by the intermediary.

If the arrangement is terminated because of a structural change, the situation has to be handled carefully. You can't just say, "We've decided to put in our own people here, so thanks for your help, and good luck." If the intermediary is hurt by the termination, then the intermediary may be able to make life difficult for you. This is especially true in countries where a distributor is chosen partly because of its clout with the government. You should think carefully about what could happen if that clout is exerted in the other direction.

Then, too, a messy breakup with an intermediary is likely to make it difficult to reach an agreement with other representatives in the region. A marketer with a reputation for playing hardball with distributors is vulnerable to competitors vying for the best representation.

How will the termination affect major customers? This question requires good answers and adroit handling, especially if a scorned intermediary decides to go after those customers.

Just causes for termination include fraud or deceit, damage to the other party's interest, or failure to comply with contract obligations (e.g., minimum inventory requirements or minimum sales levels). These must be spelled out carefully in the agreement. A legal action fought in the foreign country will often find courts that are favorably disposed toward local businesses.

In the EU and Latin America, terminating an ineffective intermediary is time-consuming and expensive. A notice of termination must be given three to six months in advance. The penalty on the marketer for termination without justification is, typically, one year's average commissions. In Austria, termination without just cause or failure to give proper notice of termination can result in damages amounting to average commissions for 1–15 years.

Clearly, an acrimonious breakup with a distributor will be costly and possibly disastrous. The time to think about the issue is before the distribution agreement is signed. It is especially prudent to find out what kind of experience other firms have had in the particular country.

From the moment that the relationship begins, you should keep careful records in order to supply documentation in the event a dispute arises.

But the overriding consideration is to keep a dispute from emerging. Build clearly defined and easily measurable performance benchmarks into the agreement. Talk to the intermediary beforehand. Ask, "Have you been terminated by other manufacturers? What happened?" Get a sense of the reasonableness of the intermediary.

Discuss the possibility of serious disagreements. Set up procedures to handle them. The best procedure resembles a good executive performance review system. Both parties sit down periodically to talk about performance. When questions are raised, the other party gets a chance to respond. The two parties talk over the problems as partners looking for solutions rather than adversaries spreading the blame.

The arrangement between you and your intermediary should provide such clear benefits to both if it works out right that each does everything possible to keep it going, rather than looking for an escape hatch. You ought to think about this in setting up the terms. If the agent bargains for, say, more advantageous terms or territories, you might allow these in exchange for precise language covering causes for termination.

A Special Problem: Gray Markets

Gray markets (also known as *parallel importation*) are profoundly important in international marketing. Gray markets emerge when authentic and legitimately manufactured trademarked items are traded by bypassing designated (or even legal) channels.

The value of gray markets in the United States has been estimated at $6–10 billion at retail. The products may be as expensive as automobiles or as inexpensive as chewing gum.

The gray market is spreading around the globe. Japan, for example, has seen the growth of gray markets because of the high value of the yen and high local taxes. Japanese marketers often find it cheaper to go to Los Angeles to buy export versions of Japanese-made products.

Just about any product carrying a well-known trademark is a candidate for the gray market. Seiko is a good example. Unauthorized importers buy Seiko watches around the world at advantageous prices and then bring them to the United States to sell at substantial discounts over authorized Seiko dealers. Seiko has fought back by warning consumers against buying gray market watches because they may be obsolete or worn-out models and noting that consumers might have problems with warranties.

However, many gray marketers provide their own warranties and their own service. These gray marketers by no means fit the stereotype of a furtive hustler working out of the back of a truck. Some of the importers and retailers handling Seiko watches boast highly respected names.

Conditions Causing Gray Markets

Various conditions make gray markets possible—and profitable. The most important are price segmentation and exchange-rate fluctuations. Competitive conditions often require the international marketer to sell

Chiclets from Lebanon[3]

The distance between an upscale grocery on New York's Park Avenue and Zouk-Mikhail, a shattered suburb located seven miles north of Beirut, can be measured in miles—or in money.

The money comes from peppermint Chiclets. Many of New York's Korean greengrocers have begun to use alternative sources to supply packaged goods. One of the most unusual gray goods they are currently stocking is Chiclets, manufactured not by Warner-Lambert Inc. in Morris Plains, New Jersey, but at a company-owned plant in Zouk-Mikhail in Lebanon. The 20-year-old plant has continued to operate even as Beirut has been transformed from "the Paris of the Mideast" to a battle zone.

Warner-Lambert is pleased that the facility has miraculously remained intact, but it is not happy that the plant's product has made its way to U.S. stores. The company has brought several lawsuits against importers of the Chiclets and continues to try to stop the goods from coming into the country. But, as company officials say, despite slight flavor differences in the foreign and U.S. gums, consumers do not really notice where the particular packages come from.

The gray-market Chiclets trade is part of the thriving underground marketplace that has come to dominate Lebanon. Products ranging from television sets to truffles are often smuggled in and out of the country by taxicab owners who have seen their tourist trade dry up. Many are loaded onto boats from Cairo or Greek ports and sent to Paris, London, or New York.

essentially the same product in different markets or to different customers. A gray marketer can buy products in one country and offer them between 10 and 40 percent below list price when reselling them back into the country of manufacture. Exchange rate fluctuations give gray marketers openings for arbitrage. For example, when the dollar was high in 1984 and 1985, gray marketers imported Caterpillar excavators and loaders built in Scotland, Belgium, and Japan into the United States at prices 15 percent lower than the same equipment built in Caterpillar's domestic plants.

In some cases, gray markets emerge as a result of product shortages.

In 1988, U.S. computer manufacturers would have seen their production lines grind to a halt if they had not been able to turn to gray marketers to secure their supply of memory chips. In these cases, though, the gray market goods typically cost more than those usually available through authorized suppliers.

Benefits and Drawbacks for Consumers

The gray market has marched steadily toward legitimacy. Once it had practically the connotation of bootlegging. But proponents have supported it on the basis of "free trade." They point to manufacturers who are both overproducing and overpricing in some markets. The main beneficiaries of the gray market are consumers, who enjoy lower prices, and discount distributors, who were shunned by manufacturers but now find a profitable marketing niche.

Gray market goods sometimes also disappoint consumers. They are not always what they seem to be. They can severely undercut local marketing plans, erode long-term brand images, and eat up promotion dollars. For example, Lever Brothers had to cope with the parallel importation of Shield deodorant soap, made in Great Britain. The soap was formulated for the hard water of the United Kingdom. It dissolved quickly in American showers. The company took a bath in dollars and image.

Legal Responses

Court rulings, notably a decision by the U.S. Supreme Court in 1988, have served to legitimate gray markets in the United States. But that does not mean manufacturers cannot fight. Nor does it preclude action by other branches of government. In January 1991, the U.S. Customs Service enacted a new rule whereby trademarked goods that have been authorized for manufacture and sale abroad by U.S. trademark holders will no longer be allowed into the United States through parallel channels. Parallel channels bringing in the goods of overseas manufacturers are not affected.

What Can You Do about It?

The effects of the gray market must be considered by any marketer who is planning to go global. Will products find their way back into the domestic market? How badly can the company be hurt, abroad and at home? In a perfect world (from the point of view of international marketers), there would be no leaks in the pipeline. All the goods committed to the foreign channels would proceed through the system all the way. After all, the gray market can't function if it has no merchandise to sell.

The world is not perfect. In almost all cases of gray marketing, someone in the authorized channel commits a diversion. This violates the signed agreements. One standard response is to disenfranchise violators. However, tracking down offenders can be time-consuming and expensive, and it is not by any means guaranteed to be effective.

Before signing agreements, you should try to check out the reputations of candidates as they relate to gray market diversions. In all too many cases, the answer may be, "They all do it."

Then what? The adage "If you can't lick 'em, join 'em" comes into play. Some of the gray marketers can be added to the authorized dealer network if mutually acceptable terms can be reached.

A one-price policy can eliminate one of the main factors that drive the gray market. This means choosing the most efficient of the distribution channels. But then you have to think about your partners. A meaningful one-price strategy must also include a way to reward the providers of other services, such as warranty repair, in the channel.

Another strategy is to produce different versions of products for different markets. For example, Minolta markets an identical camera in the United States and Japan but gives it different names and warranties. Some companies have introduced price incentives to consumers. Hasselblad, the Swedish camera manufacturer, offers rebates to legally imported, serial-numbered camera bodies, lenses, and roll-fill magazines.

It's best to assume that the gray market will continue to flourish and to incorporate that knowledge into the decision-making process preceding the foreign venture. If gray market activities would seriously damage the company, then maybe the move abroad carries too high a price tag.

In fact, we should probably discard the term "gray market," with its implication of illegality or at least shady dealing. Let's face it; as the world becomes one big marketplace, the practice is becoming commonplace. Think of it as parallel importation and consider it as another way that goods get to market.

The International Shipment

With a channel system in place, your next challenge is getting the product to the distributor.

In domestic operations, this is a relatively simple process. It involves three basic entities: shipper, carrier, and receiver. The paperwork is also relatively simple. International shipments are more complicated in both dimensions. The shipment must first be routed from the plant to the port of export, where it is transferred to another mode of transportation (e.g., from truck or rail to an air carrier or ocean vessel).

In domestic business, the marketing department is able to remain blithely ignorant of the nitty-gritty of shipping. When the company goes international, it is unlikely to have a shipping department geared to the vicissitudes of global trade. So somebody at a higher level has to pay attention to such matters.

Paper Shock

Perhaps the first unpleasant revelation about international shipment is the paperwork. Domestic shipping may seem complex, but it is child's play compared to what happens when the company ventures abroad. Some marketers suffer "paper shock," equivalent to the sticker shock induced by an exceptionally high and unexpected price.

Documentation for international shipments can be so complicated that it becomes a trade barrier, especially for smaller firms. There is hope, however. As the result of recent efforts toward standardization, most of the documents needed are now aligned through a system called the U.S. Standard Master for International Trade. Certain standard entries, such as export carrier and document number, are placed in the same position on all of the forms. Such seemingly small changes as this can make a big difference in reducing the time, cost, and aggravation of the paperwork.

The EU has made dramatic strides in cutting paperwork. Before 1992, a driver taking a load from Amsterdam to Lisbon needed two pounds of documents; now drivers on this route require only a single sheet of paper. There has also been dramatic change at the once-notorious Spanish border town of La Jonquera. Paperwork that took ten minutes in Germany would take a day here.

The town's economy was built on the delay. Truckers would hire middlemen to fill out forms and get them stamped. The drivers themselves passed the time in the town's shops, taverns, and brothels. According to the *Wall Street Journal,* "even clerks could earn 300,000 pesetas (about $2,500) a month—not counting rake-offs." Now the trucks whiz through. La Jonquera's paperwork-based businesses are silent. The mayor says, "Paperwork is finished as a career."[4]

The savings from the European elimination of red tape are substantial. As electronic data transfer replaces paper, the flow will be even smoother.

The rest of the world lags behind Europe in this respect. Few international marketers, especially small or medium-sized firms and those new to exporting, have a full grasp of the many and varied details involved in transportation. Because these details are a considerable cost factor, they should be understood beforehand and factored in.

Documentation

The two basic documents in exporting are the bill of lading and the export declaration. The bill of lading represents the basic contract between the shipper and the carrier and serves as evidence of title to the goods for collection by the purchaser. The export declaration states the authorization for export and serves as a means for the government to collect data, which are compiled into sources that can be of great help to business.

The following list provides a summary of the main documents used in an international shipment:

A. *Documents required by the U.S. government*
   1. Export declaration
   2. Export license

B. *Commercial documents*
   1. Commercial invoice
   2. Packing list
   3. Inland bill of lading
   4. Dock receipt
   5. Bill of lading or airway bill
   6. Insurance policies or certificates
   7. Shipper's declaration for dangerous goods

C. *Import documents*
   1. Import license
   2. Foreign exchange license
   3. Certificate of origin
   4. Consular invoice
   5. Customs invoice

Not all documents are required by all countries. But since improper or missing documents can lead to difficulties that delay payment or even prevent it, you are advised to check the requirements beforehand. Improper documents can cause problems with customs. Customs can inspect goods, damage them if it is necessary to the inspection, and, if the inspection raises questions, order the goods returned.

Shippers can fight customs in the courts, but disputes may last years. Meanwhile, the goods rot and the bottom line atrophies. If a customs

Bill of Lading

ACL   BILL OF LADING   ACL

SHIPPER/EXPORTER	DOCUMENT NO.	BOOKING NO.

| SHIPPER/EXPORTER | EXPORT REFERENCES
FORWARDER REF. NO.
SHIPPER'S REF. NO. | |

| CONSIGNEE | FORWARDING AGENT F.M.C. NO. | |

| | POINT AND COUNTRY OF ORIGIN | PLACE OF RECEIPT* |

| NOTIFY PARTY | DOMESTIC ROUTING/EXPORT INSTRUCTIONS | |

| PIER | | |

| EXPORTING CARRIER | PORT OF LOADING | PLACE OF DELIVERY* |

| PORT OF DISCHARGE | FOR TRANS-SHIPMENT TO | |

PARTICULARS FURNISHED BY SHIPPER

MARKS AND NUMBERS	NO. OF PKGS.	DESCRIPTION OF PACKAGES AND GOODS	GROSS WEIGHT	MEASUREMENT
		*APPLICABLE ONLY WHEN USED AS THROUGH BILL OF LADING AS PER CLAUSE 3 (III) ON REVERSE HEREOF.		

PREPAID	COLLECT	FREIGHT AND CHARGES PAYABLE AT _____
		ALL CHARGES EX SHIPS TACKLE FOR ACCOUNT OF CARGO

ACL
an affiliate of:
Cie Generale Maritime
The Cunard Steam Ship Company Ltd.
Intercontinental Transport (ICT) BV
Swedish American Line
Swedish Transatlantic Line
Wallenius Line

RECEIVED by ACL for shipment by ocean vessel, between port of loading and port of discharge, and for arrangement or procurement of precarriage from place of receipt and on-carriage to place of delivery where stated above, the goods as specified above in apparent good order and condition unless otherwise stated. The goods to be delivered at the above mentioned port of discharge or place of delivery, whichever applicable. Subject always to the exceptions, limitations, conditions and liberties set out on the reverse side hereof, to which the Merchant agrees by accepting the B/L.

In Witness whereof three (3) original Bs/L have been signed, if not otherwise stated above, one of which being accomplished the other(s) to be void.

B/L NUMBER   DATE

For ACL

Source: Seaschott.

Shipper's Export Declaration

U.S. DEPARTMENT OF COMMERCE—BUREAU OF THE CENSUS—INTERNATIONAL TRADE ADMINISTRATION
FORM 7525-V 11 1 88   SHIPPER'S EXPORT DECLARATION   OMB No. 0607 0018

1a. EXPORTER *(Name and address including ZIP code)*			
	ZIP CODE	2. DATE OF EXPORTATION	3. BILL OF LADING/AIR WAYBILL NO
b. EXPORTER'S EIN (IRS) NO	c. PARTIES TO TRANSACTION ☐ Related ☐ Non-related		
4a. ULTIMATE CONSIGNEE			
b. INTERMEDIATE CONSIGNEE			
5. FORWARDING AGENT		6. POINT (STATE) OF ORIGIN OR FTZ NO	7. COUNTRY OF ULTIMATE DESTINATION
8. LOADING PIER *(Vessel only)*	9. MODE OF TRANSPORT *(Specify)*		
10. EXPORTING CARRIER	11. PORT OF EXPORT		
12. PORT OF UNLOADING *(Vessel and air only)*	13. CONTAINERIZED *(Vessel only)* ☐ Yes ☐ No		

14. SCHEDULE B DESCRIPTION OF COMMODITIES *(Use columns 17–19)*
15. MARKS NOS AND KINDS OF PACKAGES

D/F reg.	SCHEDULE B NUMBER (17)	CHECK DIGIT	QUANTITY SCHEDULE B UNIT(S) (18)	SHIPPING WEIGHT (pounds) (19)	VALUE (U.S. dollars and cents) *(Selling price or cost if not sold)* (20)

21. VALIDATED LICENSE NO (GENERAL LICENSE SYMBOL)	22. ECCN (When required)
23. Duly authorized officer or employee	The exporter authorizes the forwarder named above to act as forwarding agent for export control and customs purposes

24. I certify that all statements made and all information contained herein are true and correct and that I have read and understand the instructions for preparation of this document set forth in the "Correct Way to Fill Out the Shipper's Export Declaration." I understand that civil and criminal penalties, including forfeiture and sale, may be imposed for making false or fraudulent statements herein, failing to provide the requested information or for violation of U.S. laws on exportation (13 U.S.C. Sec. 305, 22 U.S.C. Sec. 401, 18 U.S.C. Sec. 1001, 50 U.S.C. App. 2410)

Signature	Confidential—For use notify for official purposes authorized by the Secretary of Commerce (13 U.S.C. 301)
Title	*Export shipments are subject to inspection by U.S. Customs Service and/or Office of Export Enforcement*
Date	25. AUTHENTICATION *(When required)*

This form may be printed by private parties provided it conforms to the official form. For sale by the Superintendent of Documents. Government Printing Office. Washington, D.C. 20402, and local Customs District Directors The "Correct Way to Fill Out the Shipper's Export Declaration" is available from the Bureau of the Census, Washington, D.C. 20233.

Source: Seaschott.

service seizes the merchandise, delays can be measured in weeks and may result in a total financial loss of the particular shipment.

Agencies Providing Services for International Shipment

Given the high cost of delay, one crucial decision is the selection of an international freight forwarder, which acts as your agent in moving goods to the foreign destination. The forwarder can advise you on shipping documentation and packing costs and will prepare and review the documents to ensure they are in order. Forwarders book the necessary space aboard a carrier. They arrange to clear outbound goods with customs and, after clearance, forward the documents either to the customer or the paying bank.

In the United States, independent freight forwarders are regulated; they should be able to display certification by the Federal Maritime Commission.

A customs broker serves as an agent for an importer with authority to clear inbound goods through customs in the receiving country and ship them on to their destination.

Because the marketer depends heavily on—and delegates considerable authority to—the freight forwarder and customs broker, it's important to check out these agents. How long have they been in business? What references can they supply? The agent's reputation and *bona fides* are the primary factors, not cut-rate prices or insinuations of vast influence and vague assurances of being able to cut corners.

In addition, you should understand the functions of these agents well enough to talk with them, ask the right questions, and keep track of what is going on.

Check Points

✔ Going global is, for more and more firms, a matter of survival.

✔ Exporting is the predominant opening approach to global markets.

✔ Foreign distributors might make the first move.

✔ Government can be of great help in building a list of potential intermediaries.

✔ Other important sources include trade directories, trade publications, existing customers, and trade fairs.

✔ Careful screening of distributors is vital.

- ✔ At the outset of the relationship it's important to set up a mechanism for its termination.

- ✔ Manage the partnership for the long term.

- ✔ Gray markets may actually be appropriate channels.

- ✔ International shipments are complex; any slip along the way can break the chain.

CHAPTER

5

PRESENCE WITHOUT PROPRIETORSHIP
Easing into the Market through Licensing and Franchising

Anyone who doubts that we are becoming one huge global market need only look around. Wherever in the world you go, you're likely to spot familiar logos. Companies from the United States, Japan, Germany, France, Italy, and other developed economies reap profits around the world, not by exporting or by investing in foreign firms, but by allowing others to capitalize on their ideas and their corporate images.

Export is still the broadest avenue to international business. But export is not always feasible. For one thing, it can require considerable capital at the outset. A company might recognize the size of the international market but not have the capital to mount an adequate export program. Two key strategies are coming into increasing use as alternatives to exporting and direct foreign investment: licensing and franchising.

Licensing and franchising can be used by all kinds of firms, big and small. A small company can use licensing to enter a foreign market without making a heavy commitment of capital or resources. A multinational corporation can use the same strategy for the sake of its speed to exploit openings quickly and foreclose opportunities to the competition.

Licensing: Exploiting the Intangibles

Under a licensing agreement, one firm, the licensor, permits another, the licensee, to use its intellectual property in exchange for compensation, usually in the form of a royalty. The property might include products, patents, trademarks, copyrights, technology, or even technical know-how or specific marketing skills. For example, a British firm that has developed a new packaging proven for liquids permits firms in Spain, Nigeria, and Argentina to use the same process.

What Are the Advantages of Licensing?

For many firms, a licensing strategy is the optimal first step into the world. Foreign markets can be tested without major commitment of capital or management time. Similarly, licensing can be used to preempt a market before the competition has a chance to get a foothold. For example, a French company with limited resources can use licensing in, say, Italy to maintain a presence in that market while making a full-scale effort in Belgium and the Netherlands.

Another advantage of licensing is that it offers a point of entry to markets in which there is high exposure to government intervention. The licensee is, typically, a local company that may be able to exert leverage with the government. Then, too, licensing is at least a partial answer to local prejudice against goods made elsewhere.

With the increase of host-country regulation around the globe, licensing might also permit the company to penetrate a foreign market that is closed to imports or direct foreign investment. Having used licensing to get through the door, you may be able to make other deals and also provide for foreign purchases of materials and components, thereby expanding your participation in the particular market.

Some companies find that licensing enables them to get more mileage out of technology that is outmoded in the home country. Guinness Brewery, for example, in order to produce Guinness Stout in Nigeria, imported licensed equipment that had been used in Ireland at the turn of the century. Although obsolete by Western standards, this equipment took on new economic life because it made a good fit with Nigeria's needs.

Because developing countries are likely to need more labor-intensive techniques or machinery than highly developed countries, it would seem that there is sound logic in the idea of licensing older technology to such countries. Nevertheless, there is criticism of the practice by such organizations as the United Nations Conference on Trade and Development. The gist of the criticism is that multinationals are fobbing off their worn-out ideas and equipment on the poorer countries.

Actually, in some cases the opposite is the fact. Developing countries have been known to insist that they get up-to-the-minute technology in everything. Peter Drucker pointed out that this is often a matter of national pride.[1] He tells the story of a Latin American country where certain equipment was needed to run a new industry. A delegation from the country approached a large U.S. company. The Americans said, "The machinery we turn out is too big and too sophisticated for you. But there is a plant in Canada that makes what you need; you can adapt their equipment most easily." But this would not do. Stung by the implication that they should take "less than the best," says Drucker, the Latin Americans insisted on the larger, more expensive, less practical machinery.

Licensing Has Its Drawbacks, Too

To a large degree, licensing shifts the international marketing functions to the licensee. As a result, the licensor is hampered in gaining sufficient international marketing expertise to ready itself for subsequent world market penetration. This effect is usually more pronounced when the arrangement is highly profitable and runs smoothly. The licensor is tempted to sit back and let the royalty checks roll in.

A more serious drawback lies in the danger that the licensor will create its own competitor not only in the markets for which the agreement was made but also in other markets. As a result, some companies are reluctant to enter licensing agreements. For example, Japanese firms are delighted to sell goods to China but are unwilling to license the Chinese to produce the goods themselves. They fear that, because of the low wage structure in China, the licensing arrangements will create a powerful future competitor in markets now held by Japan.

Licensing agreements typically have time limits. Although terms may be extended one time after the start-up period, some countries do not readily permit additional extensions.

Negotiating the Licensing Agreement

The key issues in negotiating the licensing agreement are costs and compensation, the scope of the rights conveyed, licensee compliance, dispute resolution, and the term and termination of the agreement.

Analyzing the costs of licensing. Both licensors and licensees should go into the negotiation with a thorough grasp of the costs of licensing. This understanding will guide the decision to consider licensing and, when the time comes, it will enable the parties to bargain their way to a good agreement.

The costs the licensor should cover are (1) transfer costs, which are all variable costs incurred in transferring technology to a licensee and all ongoing costs of maintaining the agreement; (2) R&D costs incurred in developing the licensing technology; and (3) opportunity costs

Licensing Aircraft in Thailand

Assume that the government of Thailand wants to start producing F-20 Tigershark fighters under license from Northrop. The negotiations will first have to cover the scope of the rights to be conveyed. The product or patent rights to be negotiated would be the exact nature of the technology, the amount of training, the type of training, such as personnel and instruction manuals, and the guarantees of these rights.

The negotiations will cover the compensation that Northrop will receive. Compensation should cover the cost of transferring the technology to Thailand and the cost of maintaining the agreement. Some agreements also cover R&D costs associated with the licensed technology. The licensor often asks to be compensated for giving up the chance to export directly.

The agreement must also cover licensee compliance with U.S. export regulations, confidentiality of the technology, recordkeeping, and regularly scheduled audits by Northrop.

Which country's laws will cover contract disputes? Which type of forum will be used for conflict resolution? The agreement should cover these points. For example, the contact might specify that disputes will be resolved by an International Chamber of Commerce arbitrator. Finally, the negotiations must address the duration, termination, renewal, and survival of rights of the agreement.

---

incurred because the licensor gives up other sources of profit, such as exporting or direct investment. In return, the licensor asks for a share of the profits generated from the use of the license. Opportunity costs are often the most hotly argued cost issues. Licensees tend to resist including this relatively intangible factor. In addition, licensees often argue that R&D costs have already been covered by the licensor.

In theory, royalties can be seen as profit-sharing. In practice, royalties are a function of the licensor's minimum necessary return matched with the licensee's need for the license and the next-best alternative open to the licensee.

Compensation can take the form of ongoing royalties, such as five percent of sales made by the licensee, or up-front payments, service fees, and disclosure fees for allowing the licensee to use proprietary data.

Scope of the rights conveyed. The rights conveyed are product or patent rights. Defining their scope involves specifying the technology, know-how, or show-how to be included, the format, and guarantees. An example of format specification is an agreement on whether manuals will be translated into the licensee's language.

Assuring compliance. The agreement must stipulate what the licensee is obligated to do in such areas as recordkeeping, provision for licensor audits (usually conducted at least once a year), and confidentiality of the intellectual property and technology provided.

Dispute resolution. The key issues here are the choice of the laws that will govern interpretation of the contract and the choice of a forum for resolution of conflicts. Typically, the parties choose a third country's law to govern the agreement. Disputes would be argued under the third country's jurisdiction. If the parties cannot agree on an applicable legal system, the agreement should contain an arbitration clause. Following is the International Chamber of Commerce model clause:

> All disputes arising in connection with the present contract shall be finally settled under the Rules of Conciliation and Arbitration of the International Chamber of Commerce by one or more arbitrators appointed in accordance with the said rules.

Term and termination. How long shall the agreement run? The agreement should clearly state the term along with the procedures for termination. One paramount issue in termination is survival of rights, i.e., what the parties can do after the agreement ends, and what they are forbidden to do.

Trademark Licensing

For companies or brands that have established distinctive images, trademark licensing has become a substantial source of worldwide revenue. The names and logos of designers, sports teams, individual athletes, and movie and TV stars appear on clothing, shoes, games, foods and beverages, gifts and novelties, toys, and home furnishings. British designer Laura Ashley started the first major furniture program, licensing her name to Henredon Furniture Industries. Coca-Cola licensed its name to Murjani to be used on blue jeans, sweatshirts, and windbreakers.

Trademark licensors make millions with little effort. Licensees sell a branded product that consumers recognize instantly. Licensors and licensees ride the waves of the worldwide communications revolution, which dictates styles and fads to consumers, especially younger consumers, in every quarter of the globe.

The phenomenon feeds on itself. The more the logo gets around, the more people see it and buy products that it features. And the licensor enjoys the free services of hordes of walking advertisements.

There are dangers, too, to trademark licensing. The essence of the approach is the crossover of a trademark well known for one product onto another product. Licensor and licensee sometimes run into trouble if the reach is too far; that is, if the trademark is used in a context that is distant from the original success.

No sound marketer promotes a trademark primarily for the collateral benefits of licensing. However, worldwide licensing volume has soared toward the $100 billion mark in the 1990s; therefore, it is a potent consideration for companies analyzing a program to enhance logo recognition.

In licensing a trademark, it's important to anticipate what could happen if the brand's positioning changes. For example, when Löwenbräu was exported from Germany to the United States, it was the number-one imported beer in the market. Then the product name was licensed to Miller Brewing Company for domestic production. The beer's positioning (and subsequently its target audience) changed drastically in the minds of consumers, resulting in a major decline in sales.

The Löwenbräu case is an example of using a well-known logo on a product of the same category. The success stories in this genre tend to stem from cases in which the trademark is used on a different but congenial product category. The Laura Ashley name on furniture is designed to give the furniture the same aura of casual elegance as the clothing. You're not likely to see Laura Ashley on cheap dresses or Coca-Cola on cut-rate beverages.

Franchising

Although franchising originated in Germany, its greatest surge has come in the United States. In the early 1990s, franchising accounted for about 35 percent of all retail sales, and it was growing at about 10 percent per year. The growth rate is likely to diminish, but franchising in the United States has soared nearly to the trillion dollar mark.

International franchising has grown spectacularly as well. In 1990, more than 350 franchising companies in the United States operated more than 31,000 outlets in international markets. Franchisers were flourishing in other countries as well, for example, Holiday Rent-a-Car of Canada and Descamps, a French firm selling linens and tablecloths. International franchising can be an extremely effective way of establishing a beachhead

Maintaining Domino's Standards Abroad[2]

In 1991, *Marketing News* reported on the impressive strides taken overseas by Domino's Pizza. The $2.5 billion U.S. pizza-delivery giant had 450 restaurants in 25 countries outside the United States, with international sales of more than $150 million. With this as a springboard, Domino's was poised for further expansion.

Franchising is licensing with more strings than the basic licensing agreement. The franchiser grants the franchisee the right to do business in a specified manner. One major factor in franchising success is the adroitness with which the franchiser impels the far-flung franchisees to maintain the desired standards.

When Domino's—facing saturation domestically—looked abroad, the company found that the success of each franchise depends on foreign employees who uphold the standards of quality and service represented by the "mother church," but who at the same time accommodate cultural differences.

Domino's quizzes foreign applicants extensively. How many pizza establishments already exist in the market? Do they deliver? Do people accept home delivery? Does the country promote entrepreneurship? Does the concept of "hustle" (a prized element of Domino's domestic appeal) translate into the foreign culture?

The company found out the hard way that understanding cultural differences ranks very high among the traits necessary for success. Domino's, like other franchisers, looks for people who have been successful in the target country, even in quite different arenas from the pizza business.

---

in a foreign market. Domino's food chain is a phenomenal example of international expansion.

Foreign governments tend to look benignly on franchising. It does not replace exports or export jobs. There is little outflow of foreign exchange, and the bulk of the profit stays in the country.

There are, of course, problems. One difficulty is the need for a high degree of standardization. However, this cannot translate into rigid uniformity. Within the overall aura of recognizability, fast-food franchisers vary products and product lines to suit local conditions and tastes.

Another key issue is protection of the company's image. Some franchisers have been dismayed when they found that laws in other countries do not provide anything near the same level of protection as that enjoyed in the domestic market. The name can be protected, but competitions can, with impunity, copy the type of product or service and the general style of operation. Therefore, shortly after introduction, franchise operations might run into tough head-on competition from copycat rivals.

And, although governments might welcome franchises, that doesn't mean they will remain uninvolved. For example, government restrictions on the type of service to be offered or on royalty remissions can lead to a separation between a company and its franchisees. Hong Kong puts a limit on the repatriation of royalties. Taiwan requires that approval be sought for repatriation of profits or royalties. In some places, the government won't even let you get a foot in the door. Indonesia has been rejecting most franchises if they are not technology-related.

Controlling Franchises across the Globe

When the reins extend halfway around the world, it may be hard to control the horses. This fact can be most apparent in the critical area of selection and training of franchisees. Language and culture differences complicate further an issue that is already critical in the franchise industry. When a franchise goes sour in a foreign country, the result can be more than just loss of revenue. The company loses ground in the international race. The company image is sometimes tarnished. And the process of disentanglement from an unsatisfactory franchisee can be expensive and messy.

For example, in the 1980s, McDonald's biggest push was into France, because France was the only major European country where McDonald's lagged behind Burger King. The lag resulted from McDonald's suing to revoke the license of its largest franchise in France for failure to operate 14 stores according to McDonald's standards. McDonald's, boasting the stature of a 600-pound gorilla, can handle such setbacks better than most would-be franchisers.

The seeds of trouble are sowed right at the beginning if two failures in planning befall the company. First, insufficient attention is paid to the special problems of selecting and training franchisees in the foreign country. Management assumes they can be identified, recruited, trained, and controlled according to the same basic criteria used domestically. Second, the strategic emphasis is placed on rapid expansion, to the detriment of proper selection.

International marketing, through franchising or any other method, is a race. The marketer is vying to move faster than rivals for the same territory. So any suggestion that potential franchisees should be screened rigorously is often rejected. One reason for this is that the executive team responsible for the move is charged with expanding as fast as possible. Goals are set. If the desired number of franchisees is not reached by the target date, the venture is deemed to be in trouble.

Rapid expansion is certainly a key objective in building a franchise system abroad. If the effort does not reach critical mass within a reasonable time, it loses impetus. But the expansion goal must be balanced against the need to maintain standards. The marketers should be instructed to carry out an effective selection and training program. Furthermore, good selection and training should be prized and rewarded as highly as rapid expansion.

A delicate trade-off is embodied in this question: who is better qualified to make decisions about serving the local market—franchiser or franchisee? The local franchisee knows the market best. Too often, this fact of life translates into giving the franchisee more leeway than is necessary or desirable in hiring employees and running the operation. It's up to the franchiser to understand enough about the market to ask the right questions and to know when the answers are evasive or unsatisfactory. This goes for issues of product adaptation as well as operation. The franchiser should be the conductor of a coordinated effort by the individual franchisees, sharing ideas and engaging in joint marketing efforts like cooperative advertising.

Dealing with many individual franchisees in a foreign country is a tough, expensive business. The more individual units the company tries to work with, the greater the chance that there will be variations from the norm. To encourage organized and successful growth, companies are turning to the master franchising system, in which foreign partners are given the rights to a large territory within which they can subfranchise. The franchiser gains market savvy and a strong organization on the ground, which takes care of screening for new franchisees.

Franchising Is for Smaller Firms, Too

Is franchising strictly for the giants, the McDonald's and Domino's? It is often thought of as a strategy to be used for foreign market entry only by large firms, but it might be a mistake for smaller firms to write off the possibility too quickly. Franchising can be a valuable approach for a small firm if it is carried out in an undeveloped market where the firm can establish its reputation relatively unopposed. Of course, the number of undeveloped markets is shrinking. When the company does find an undeveloped market, it's eminently sensible to ask why it's undeveloped.

Although franchising might be the right way to begin an international marketing effort in a particular country, the franchiser should not assume that, in a subsequent phase of growth, the franchise system can be replaced with more direct involvement by the company. The government and culture of the country may not take kindly to abandonment of a program that has been good for the country. When a company elects to go the franchising route, that choice ought to be considered a long-range commitment.

Facilitating Intermediaries

A company is not in a position to undertake a full-scale export strategy. The firm's products don't lend themselves to licensing or franchising. Now what?

Companies that don't want to invest or export abroad can still participate in international marketing by making use of facilitating intermediaries. These entities exist already. They are an established part of the international marketing infrastructure.

The would-be international marketer often finds a facilitating intermediary right next door, so to speak, when it sells its products to another domestic firm that in turn sells them abroad. Typically, a smaller company turns to a larger one. Similarly, the government can be the "partner." Products sold to the Department of Defense are often ultimately shipped to military outposts abroad.

Why would a domestic company buy products from another company and then sell them overseas? One reason would be to round out a product line to make a bigger marketing impact in the foreign markets. Here are ten examples of "exporting in your own backyard."

1. Large companies purchasing goods for their own foreign affiliates

2. Large design and construction firms purchasing goods for foreign projects awarded to them

3. Branches of gigantic foreign trading companies purchasing goods for their affiliates

4. Export merchants buying for their own account

5. Large foreign companies purchasing goods through their own U.S. buying offices or agents

6. Exporters seeking goods to round out their own lines

7. United Nations members purchasing for development projects

8. Foreign governments purchasing U.S. goods

9. Foreign department stores purchasing U.S. goods through U.S. buying offices

10. Foreign buyers on purchasing trips

For most companies using this form of foreign penetration, the choice falls between two kinds of facilitating market intermediaries: export management companies (EMCs) and trading companies.

Export Management Companies

Export management companies (EMCs) are domestic firms specializing in international marketing. They work as commission agents or distributors. Most EMCs are quite small. They're often formed by one or two principals with experience in international marketing. EMCs usually focus on specific areas of the world. EMCs have two ways of operating. They take title to goods and operate internationally on their own account, or they act as agents.

EMCs serve a variety of clients. The nature of their services and their mode of operation varies from client to client and from transaction to transaction. For one client, the EMC will act as an agent; for another client, or even for the same client on a different occasion, the EMC will operate as a distributor.

When the EMC serves as an agent, its primary functions are to develop foreign marketing and sales strategies, to establish contacts abroad, and, generally, to facilitate the sale of the firm's products. EMCs charge a commission for these services. The higher the volume, the more commission. This creates a danger. The EMC might be tempted to take on as many clients and products as possible, stretching itself too thin to provide adequate representation. When this happens, the individual client's hopes of a bright international future fall victim to the EMC's need for income. So it is essential that the firm check out the EMC's total commitments and its ability to meet those commitments adequately. When an EMC is scuffling for commissions, one client can be replaced by another; but for the client who is shortchanged, the experience may be disastrous.

By and large, the most effective EMCs are those with specific expertise in the market because of previous exposure, language capability, and specialized contacts. By sticking to their areas of expertise and representing only a limited number of clients, such agents can be quite valuable.

When operating as a distributor, the EMC buys the firm's products and sells them abroad. This simplifies matters for the client and also reduces the client's risk dramatically. The other side of the coin is that the EMC, having assumed the risk, takes the lion's share of

Rescuing Foreign Orders from the Trash[3]

Business America quotes Carol Myers of Medical International Inc., an EMC based in Spring Lake, New Jersey, specializing in international marketing of health care supplies and equipment: "Small and medium-sized U.S. companies think it's great to have our expertise selling their products. Many of them wouldn't export at all on their own. Some get an unsolicited foreign order and it sits on their desk for a long time and ends up in the trash can. The smaller companies don't know about such matters as letters of credit. They just don't feel comfortable with international marketing."

Medical International's export services include market research and consulting, establishment of overseas sales outlets, product promotion and advertising, international trade show representation, handling of all correspondence and inquiries, financing arrangements and payment risks, export documentation and letters of credit, and shipping and consolidation services.

So the EMC, as Medical International demonstrates, can serve as the smaller firm's international marketing department, handling all the essential tasks of the operation. If and when the firm's international business flourishes, the company can set up its own department to take over these chores. Meanwhile, the EMC can be a viable alternative to just tossing unsolicited foreign orders in the wastebasket or trying to start a risky international marketing venture independently.

---

the profits. Then, too, such an arrangement gives the client little international marketing experience. The products may well be sold abroad, but for the client it is little different from doing business with a domestic jobber.

How EMCS get paid.   Before the EMC starts selling the firm's products abroad, products must be shown, visits arranged, and contacts established. One way to pay for these activities is through a fee or retainer, in addition to the commission on sales. The manufacturer is often expected to pay part or all of the direct expenses associated with foreign market penetration. Some of these expenses involve the production and translation of promotional product brochures. Others concern such items as rental for booth space at trade shows, provision of samples, or trade advertising.

Another approach is for the EMC to set the price for the product, with the price discounted to cover all these activities. In any case, the firm using the EMC must pay for the international marketing effort. If the firm declines to pay, or skimps excessively, the EMC might still take on the product line, but little or nothing will happen. The EMC simply adds the firm to its list and does nothing to achieve international market penetration.

Manufacturers should beware of EMCs that make glib promises and agree too readily to deals in which the costs of the marketing effort are exceptionally small. This probably means that there is no real marketing effort. The manufacturer winds up thinking that there is no market abroad, just because the EMC never really tried.

Power struggles between EMCs and clients. Many firms use an EMC just to test the international waters. If the venture goes well, the firm decides to become a direct exporter. EMCs, not surprisingly, resist this notion. For them, a long-term relationship is more profitable than a one-night stand. The EMC's principal weapon in the struggle to retain the client is information. The client needs international market information to export on its own. The conflict between the EMC and its client, with one side wanting to keep a monopoly on the power of information and the other side wanting to obtain that power, can lead to suspicion, friction, and a mutual lack of cooperation. If the firm is not getting adequate cooperation from the EMC, its short-term performance in the foreign arena may be damaged, and its long-term prospects are likely to be hurt.

It's vital that the agreement between client and EMC make a clear statement of the degree of information and cooperation that both parties will receive. On the manufacturer's side, the choice of an EMC should be made with as much care as the choice of a domestic channel. This requires a thorough investigation of the intermediary and the advisability of relying on its efforts, a willingness to reward successful effort, and a commitment to cooperate on a prolonged basis. Even if the manufacturer hopes the international venture will be so profitable that the firm will want to become a direct exporter, it is still wise to assume that the relationship with the EMC will run much longer than anticipated.

The EMC in turn must be willing to adopt a flexible approach. It must continue to upgrade the level of services offered and continually highlight the dimensions of post-sale service. Above all, the EMC must be willing to feed back relevant information to its supplier.

Trading Companies

Trading companies offer major benefits to many firms seeking to penetrate international markets. The concept is centuries old. Hoping to expand their imperial power and wealth, European monarchs chartered traders to form corporate bodies that enjoyed exclusive trading rights and government protection in exchange for tax payments. Early examples are the East India Company of the Netherlands, formed in 1602, followed by the British East India Company and the French East India Company. As the names indicate, these were companies formed under national auspices to exploit the wealth of the East for Europe.

Today the most famous trading companies are the *sogoshosha* of Japan. Names like Sumitomo, Mitsubishi, Mitsui, and C. Itoh have become household words around the world. In 1991, the nine trading company giants of Japan acted as intermediaries for about half of the country's exports and two-thirds of its imports. These general trading companies play a unique role in the world by importing, exporting, countertrading, investing, and manufacturing. Because of their vast size, they can benefit from economies of scale and perform their operations at profit margins that are generally less than 1.5 percent.

Four major reasons have been given for the success of the *sogoshosha*. First, by concentrating on obtaining and disseminating information about market opportunities and by investing huge funds in the development of information systems, these firms now have the mechanisms and organizations in place to gather, evaluate, and translate market information into business opportunities. Second, economies of scale enable them to use the leverage of their vast transaction volume to obtain preferential treatment by, for example, getting lower transportation rates or even opening up new routes. Third, these firms serve large internal markets, not only in Japan but also around the world, and can benefit from opportunities for barter. Finally, *sogoshosha* can draw from tremendous reservoirs of capital in Japan and on the international capital markets. They can therefore handle transactions that are too big and too risky for other firms.

For a long time, 20th century trading companies were considered to be peculiar to Japan. Because of the unique Japanese culture, it was reasoned, such intermediaries could operate successfully only from that country. Then trading companies were established in Korea. By 1981, the big Korean trading companies like Hyundai, Samsung, and Daewoo were handling 43 percent of Korea's total exports. It was still a Far Eastern phenomenon, though, until Brazil stimulated the creation of trading companies by offering preferential financing arrangements. Within a short time, these Brazilian firms were accounting for almost 20 percent of total Brazilian exports.

In 1982, U.S. export trading companies (ETCs) were given impetus by the passage of the Export Trading Company Act, which was designed to improve the export performance of small and medium-sized firms. To improve export performance, bank participation in trading companies was permitted. The antitrust threat to joint export efforts was reduced through precertification of planned activities by the U.S. Department of Commerce.

Under the act, the costs of developing and penetrating international markets can be shared. Firms can develop joint ventures more easily. For example, a single firm might not be able to afford a warehouse in a particular country; by sharing the warehouse with other firms, the effort becomes feasible. Joint financing of a service center by several companies makes the cost bearable for each. The trading company concept also offers a one-stop shopping center for the firm and its foreign customers. The firm can be assured that all international functions will be performed efficiently by the trading company. At the same time, the foreign customer will have to deal with fewer individual firms.

The legislation permits a wide variety of possible structures for an ETC. General trading companies handle many commodities, perform import and export services, countertrade, and work closely with foreign distributors. Regional trading companies handle commodities produced in only one region. Product-oriented trading companies concentrate on a limited number of products and offer their market penetration services only for these products. Trading companies also may be geographically oriented, targeting one particular region, or can be focused on certain types of projects, such as turnkey operations and joint ventures with foreign investors. Finally, trading companies sometimes develop an industry-oriented focus, handling only goods of specific industry groups, such as metals, chemicals, or pharmaceuticals.

Whatever its focus or form of operation, an ETC can deliver a wide variety of services. It can act as an agent. It can purchase products or act as a distributor abroad. It can provide information on distribution costs and even handle domestic and international transportation and distribution. This can range from identifying distribution costs to booking space on ocean or air carriers and handling shipping contracts.

American business neglects a useful approach to the world. Export trading companies offer major benefits to those who want to penetrate international markets. Nevertheless, they have not caught on very fast in the United States. By 1994, only 150 individual ETCs had been certified by the U.S. Department of Commerce. These certificates covered more than 5,000 firms. The total number of firms was swelled by the fact that various trade associations had applied for certification of all of their members.

Trade associations are natural starting points for ETCs. However, the concept is also worth serious consideration by banks and individual companies. It's easy to see why bankers might shy away from the idea. Traders tend to seize the moment; bankers want to move more slowly, think things over.

However, there are considerable benefits that banks can derive from working with small or medium-sized exporters. Involvement with an ETC can provide the bank with a broader client base. The bank is likely to be plugged into an extensive international information system; the ETC approach offers a way to make profitable use of this system. The ETC can provide the bank with a stepping-stone toward the internationalization of its own services.

True, there are sound reasons for bankers to think long and hard before getting involved with ETCs. Blending business entrepreneurship with banking regulations can be a challenge. The international debt situation makes many banks hesitant to increase the level of their international activities. Burned once, they are naturally cautious about going the world route again.

In the long run, though, U.S. banks will become more involved in international business. The increased pressures of a highly deregulated home market, coupled with the increasing opportunities available abroad, make the development inevitable.

Firms participating in trading companies need to be aware of the things that make the trading company successful. The participating firm must adjust its thinking. For example, companies (or some members of management) tend to use the trading company primarily as a way of disposing of merchandise. But the ETC—no matter what its members demand at the moment—must strike a balance between the demands of the market and the products offered by the companies.

The trading company itself should solicit continuous feedback on foreign market demands and changes in those demands so that its members will be able to maintain a winning international product mix. The ETC should also determine which activities to concentrate on, based on the types of suppliers represented and the types of products exported.

Participation in an ETC requires, to a certain extent, the relinquishing of corporate sovereignty. This is not easy for many executives. They look at the ETC in the same way they look at a domestic distributor. They reject the notion that the people running the ETC—which, after all, is the creature of the companies that form it—should have any input into strategy or tactics.

This mindset is a recipe for failure. If the ETC has been set up properly, with competent staff, it is far more than just a conduit for goods. It is the eyes and ears of its members in a potentially rich but unfamiliar area.

Getting Guidance into the World

For companies that are not ready to become all-out exporters, and whose products don't lend themselves to licensing or franchising, the answer may be to use an EMC or ETC as an intermediary. Today, many firms turn to export management or trading companies. Especially for a smaller firm, collaboration with an intermediary may be a good way to get started in international marketing.

Check Points

✔ Licensing and franchising are alternative possibilities for international market entry or expansion.

✔ Licensing requires less capital investment than most other forms of international involvement.

✔ The principal issues in negotiating licensing agreements are:

  • costs and compensation

  • scope of the rights conveyed

  • license compliance

  • dispute resolution

  • term and termination

✔ Franchising is a form of licensing that is expanding dramatically.

✔ Firms that cannot use licensing or franchising should consider using intermediaries: EMCs and trading companies.

CHAPTER 6

THE ART OF NEGOTIATION
Global Style

Good marketing people are good negotiators. In a way, they're always negotiating: within their own organizations, with finance people, production people, and research people; with suppliers and advertising agencies; and with dealers and distributors.

Negotiating styles vary. The best negotiators suit their styles to their personalities. They have enough flexibility to vary their approaches to the situation. But, whatever the style and approach, certain threads run through any successful negotiation. For one thing, expert negotiators are able to get inside the heads of their counterparts, to see things from the adversary's point of view. (And the person across the table *is* an adversary, no matter how friendly.) Good negotiators sit down before the bargaining session to assess not only their own priorities, but also the priorities of the other party.

The art of negotiating demands the ability to gauge the personal as well as the organizational priorities of the adversary. For example, the other party might be concerned about looking good to his or her own boss. A small concession that makes your opponent achieve this can bring a more valuable concession in return.

And people who negotiate long-term deals must be careful not to grind their adversaries down into the dust. Sometimes people negotiating from strength are tempted to use it to the maximum, extracting humiliating concessions amounting to unconditional surrender. Smart marketers know this is self-defeating. Your opponent's festering resentment will come back to haunt you.

International marketing negotiations involve the same general principles as bargaining in the domestic arena. However, the context is often so different that even the most experienced and capable negotiators need to rethink and reshape the tactics that have made them winners. When international marketers travel abroad they are often shocked to discover how the many variables of foreign behavior and customs complicate their efforts. The process of negotiation varies dramatically around the globe.

It's essential for the marketer to know as much about the foreign culture as possible. Talk to people who've lived and worked in the country. Are characteristic negotiations long or short? Marketers sometimes prepare for extended negotiation, only to find that in that particular place the bargaining stages are collapsed into one and the process rushes along. In other places, of course, the process is prolonged to the point of agony.

Long or short, telescoped or stretched out, the process of international business negotiations can be divided into four stages:

1. The offer

2. Informal meetings

3. Strategy formulation

4. Negotiations

The Offer

The offer stage allows the two parties to assess each other's needs and degree of commitment. The marketer should be open to new ideas and impressions. Progress is determined to a great extent by the backgrounds of the parties and the overall atmosphere (e.g., cooperative, suspicious, cautious). For example, many European buyers are skittish about dealing with a U.S. exporter, given the number of companies that have pulled out when an initial effort did not quite meet their expectations.

The other party in the negotiation might not always express such doubts, deeming it impolite to say, "I think you lack the guts to stay with us when things get tough." But the reservation will be there, influencing the negotiation. Good negotiators sense such unspoken objections and shape their approaches to meet them. During the offer stage be alert and look for such hidden snags.

Informal Meetings

After the offer has been made, the parties meet to get acquainted. In many parts of the world (Asia, the Middle East, Latin America), informal meetings often make or break the deal. Foreign buyers want to make sure they're doing business with someone who is sympathetic and whom they can trust. For example, U.S. exporters to Kuwait rate the relationship between the parties ahead of price as the critical factor driving buying decisions.

To some negotiators of the rough-and-tumble school, the handholding and "schmoozing" at this stage seem a waste of time. Marketers who are too impatient during the informal meetings will have a lot of trouble. In some cases, it is necessary to use facilitators to help establish these informal contacts. But there is no substitute for personal involvement and you must be ready to participate. The informal meeting is not a frill, but often essential.

Strategy Formulation

Strategy formulation should begin even before the offer is made. The informal meetings then help to sharpen the formulation of strategic approaches and objectives. Each side sets its priorities, goals, bottom-line requirements, and bargaining positions. The strategy should not be set in cement before the informal meetings. Based on the available facts and the "feel" obtained during the initial meetings, the firm formulates its strategy.

Here's where it's essential to factor in the other side's cultural approach to negotiation. Executives who consider themselves to be shrewd negotiators have found themselves at a loss in other countries when the ground rules they take for granted do not pertain. For example, studies show that negotiators outside North America have an advantage over U.S. and English-speaking Canadian bargainers because the Americans and Canadians are more trusting than other groups.

Negotiations

It is during negotiations that cultural and social differences come most heavily to bear. These are some key pointers. A combination of attitudes, expectations, and habitual behavior influences negotiation style. The course of negotiations in a specific country will, of course, vary with the culture. Here is a set of basic recommendations for negotiation in international marketing. Some will depart from what managers are familiar with at home, they are designed to allow the negotiator to adjust to the style of the host-country negotiators.

Team Assistance

Negotiations with bargainers from other countries is not a solo act, at least not until the negotiator has picked up substantial experience. The use of specialists strengthens the team and allows for all points of view to be given proper attention. Negotiators from some cultures don't like to have varying points of view expressed in domestic bargaining, because it causes ambiguity. But ambiguity is the norm when you are negotiating in certain countries around the world.

Using a negotiating team gives strength and diversity to the firm's position. Western bargaining teams average two to four people. A Chinese negotiating team usually consists of up to ten people. Membership on the team can be valuable training for less-experienced managers.

Traditions and Customs

Newcomers to international negotiations need to be thoroughly briefed by consultants or local representatives on status relations and business procedures. Rituals are important. For example, in Asian countries every first encounter is marked by an exchange of business cards. The business card should be offered with both hands. It should be received with both hands. The card must be read carefully, with great respect.

When Western executives first ran into this custom, many of them found this irksome, if not ludicrous. Some still do. They think the business card ritual, along with other rituals, is a meaningless gesture. It is not. It is fraught with meaning, an integral part of the negotiating process.

This is the kind of thing that negotiators must be informed about in detail and take very seriously. Furthermore, it's important to understand what is important to one's opponents. For example, Korean negotiators pay most attention to the oldest member of the opposing negotiating team, even if that person is not the senior in rank. In highly structured societies, like that of Korea, great respect is paid to age and tradition.

Finally, as one marketer puts it, "It's useful to remember, every now and then, that we look as weird to them as they look to us."

Language Capability

Ideally, the international marketer should be fluent in the customer's language, but that is not always possible. If the negotiator is just able to get by in the other language, it's better to work through a translator. Chapter 14 covers the topic of language in more detail. People who are serious about international marketing should start to learn other languages. But that doesn't mean negotiations should be conducted in the language of the foreign negotiators.

English is not exactly a lingua franca of world business, but it is used widely. Peter Drucker commented on the fact that languages embody the cultural characteristics of the countries where they are spoken:

There are . . . many companies in Germany today where the managers speak English with each other because they can use first names and no titles. . . . When German managers speak English, they can call each other Hans and Berthold and Karl; the moment they speak German they become formal.[1]

Therefore, the language of negotiation must be carefully selected. Negotiating through an interpreter is often the best bet. Sarah Pilgrim, president of OmniLingua, Inc., says it is wise to take an interpreter to important negotiations. "If you bring your own interpreter, you can be sure that person is on your side. The interpreter should be well briefed ahead of time so he or she is familiar with the product and can act as a company representative."[2]

The increase in emphasis on international marketing inevitably impels companies to hire people who can speak various languages, especially those of countries in which the company intends to operate in the future. Such individuals can be used as interpreters in addition to their main jobs.

There are drawbacks to using interpreters. They diminish the spontaneity of the presentation. Their use may offend a foreign business executive who thinks his or her English is adequate. (In this case, it's probably best to use English, even if it takes considerable patience.) There might be confidential information that the firm would rather not divulge to an outside interpreter. And, above all, interpreters slow down the exchange. But this can actually be useful by giving the parties time to formulate their responses and to consider what is being said. For example, we have seen Japanese trade negotiators who speak perfect English using an interpreter in their negotiations in Washington. It gives them much more time to think before responding.

Determining Authority Limits

Savvy negotiators set out early to discover how much authority the other party has. Must the final decision be referred to a higher level? "Limited agency" is a well-worn bargaining ploy. The negotiator shrugs and says, "If it were up to me, I'd waive these requirements, but my instructions. . . ." Then, at a critical moment, the negotiator does turn out to have full authority. A posture of limited authority is often perceived negatively by the other party. On the whole, however, it is probably a useful tactic for probing the other side's motives and strategies.

Patience

In many countries, such as the People's Republic of China, business negotiations take three times as long as in the United States and Western

Europe. Similar leisureliness is shown by negotiators in other countries, East and West. Showing impatience in countries like Brazil or Thailand will not speed up negotiations, it will prolong them.

And time elapsed is not the only thing that demands patience. It is also the perceived outlandishness of the bargaining positions. Most negotiators start with bargaining positions from which they are willing to retreat. U.S. negotiators tend to give these initial positions some degree of plausibility, so that the other party will not be insulted or tempted to laugh. In contrast, Chinese negotiators often start with "unreasonable" demands that must nevertheless be treated with a measure of dignity, not just brushed aside.

Negotiation Ethics

There are certain things the most hardboiled negotiator is unlikely to be willing to do. There are other things negotiators do as a matter of routine that would shock people from other cultures. Being tricky is valued in some parts of the world and frowned on in others. For example, Western negotiators assume that when agreement has been reached on a point, that's it. So British executives will be taken aback when Russian negotiators come back to request last-minute changes.

Silence

Knowing when to keep quiet is a crucial attribute of skillful international negotiators. Some people abhor dead air—when the conversation stops, they rush in to fill the vacuum. This is a social custom that carries over into business exchanges. If silence is interpreted as indicating disapproval in the negotiator's own culture, he or she tends to modify the position prematurely.

Typically, here's what happens. An American states a set of terms to a Japanese adversary, who simply sits there without changing expression. To the American, the moments seem to stretch into hours. Finally the American says, "Well, actually, we can do a little better than that" and proceeds to sweeten the deal. Japanese executives are comfortable with silence while they think things over. They have also learned that, simply by not reacting they can get Americans to offer lower prices or more favorable terms. Negotiators should learn to use silence tactically, not only in dealing with foreign executives, but also in bargaining domestically.

Persistence

Western executives conduct extended negotiations expecting that every meeting will result in perceptible progress. This is an understandable and laudable application of management by objectives. We establish a series of subgoals leading toward attainment of the main goal.

But foreign negotiators often see it differently. In some markets, negotiations are seen as a means of establishing long-term commercial relations, not as a precise series of steps toward a specific outcome. The negotiation, in this view, is not so much an event with winners and losers as a "getting-to-know-each-other" process.

Not that the foreign bargainers are uninterested in winning. They just define "winning" differently. So when Western executives insist on answers and push hard toward an outcome, the other party often sees this as a threat.

Patience and persistence are more important than adroitness in scoring negotiating points. Confrontations are to be avoided, because minds cannot be changed at the bargaining table; this has to be done informally.

Holistic View

A knack for the well-timed trade-off is a staple of successful negotiation. In international negotiation it's best to avoid concessions until all issues have been discussed. In the Far East and elsewhere, concessions traditionally come at the end of bargaining. So a trade-off proposed early in the process is often accepted by the other party, which gives back nothing in return.

The Meaning of Agreements

What constitutes an agreement will vary from one market to another. In many parts of the world, legal contracts are still not needed; in fact, reference to legal counsel indicates that the relationship is in trouble. This does not mean that a firm will not benefit from legal counsel in countries where that is the case. It means that "getting it on paper" is not the equivalent of breasting the tape successfully.

When oral agreements and handshakes are standard, there can be trouble ahead. This is not because the foreign party is planning to take advantage of the situation. In domestic or foreign negotiating, if you need an ironclad legal document to ensure honest dealing you are in difficulty right from the start.

The problem with oral agreements is that the two parties may have different perceptions of what they have agreed to. This is not necessarily a deliberate ploy, with one party trying to gain an edge by assuming elements in the agreement that are actually not there. It is, rather, a result of the universal human tendency to perceive events in the most favorable light.

Making a Bold Move to Get Negotiations Going[3]

John Stollenwerk wanted to show shoes made by his company, Allen Edmonds, at the Tokyo Trade Fair. He applied and was told, politely, that the fair was closed to foreigners.

"That really ticked us off," said Stollenwerk. He packed his bags, flew to Tokyo, called a press conference. The story was picked up by the international press.

And suddenly Stollenwerk found that Tokyo was welcoming him with open arms.

Going public with a high-profile gesture is a very risky negotiating move. But if you can't even get the negotiation started, sometimes it can be the best bet.

So, when the negotiation ends with a handshake, it's important to document the agreement by whatever means are feasible. Otherwise, certain elements of the agreement may be interpreted differently according to the hopes and expectations of the parties.

In the case of large-scale projects, details must be spelled out explicitly. One way to do this is to lay out at some length all the specific understandings in various pieces of correspondence. The details don't have to be loaded into one document; that might look too legalistic. But by touching all the bases in a series of written documents, the marketer builds a file containing a well-rounded picture of the understanding.

The idea is not to create legal bonds but to avoid misunderstanding. For example, in contracts that call for cooperative efforts, the responsibilities of each partner must be clearly specified. Otherwise, obligations that were thought to be the responsibility of one party can wind up costing the other. Rosenlew Oy, a major Finnish corporation, was the major contractor in the building of a plant for Hungary's Chemokomplex. Parts provided by Hungarian suppliers seldom arrived on time. Rosenlew Oy was not the cause of the resulting delays. Nevertheless, as principal contractor the Finnish firm was held responsible and had to pay a hefty fine.

Be Prepared to Be Patient

Negotiations in international marketing take longer than at home. Once you gear yourself to the extended time frame and the slower pace, you are better able to handle all the other differences. Many of the mistakes made by newcomers to international negotiation stem from impatience. They know people from other countries have a different approach to bargaining. They have been briefed on such customs as the ceremonial exchange of business cards. They have an intellectual grasp of the challenge. But when they are actually involved in the bargaining, their gut feelings take over. They try to contain their impatience and irritation, but their feelings get in the way of doing the best possible job of negotiating.

Check Points

✔ There are four stages in reaching an agreement:

1. Offer

2. Informal meetings

3. Strategy formulation

4. Negotiation

✔ Seizing a short-term advantage in the negotiation can endanger a long-term relationship.

✔ International negotiation is a team sport.

✔ It's vital to know the customs and traditions of the other parties.

✔ The ethics of negotiation vary widely around the world.

✔ International negotiations can take many times longer than the domestic variety. Persistence is essential.

✔ The agreement must be pinned down precisely, in writing, and mutually approved. Interpretations will differ.

CHAPTER

7

WHAT IF THE SHOE DOESN'T FIT?
Adapting Products for International Markets

Perception is all-important in marketing. No matter how good your product or service may be, people won't buy it unless they perceive its value.

The power of perception is so obvious that we take it for granted. However, realizing its importance is one thing; it's quite another to engineer the perception of buyers. And when you sell abroad, the difficulties are greatly magnified.

Companies entering the world marketplace must make some important decisions. The product or service itself may have to be changed. Or there may be no need for adaptation of the basic product, but customers must be impelled to perceive it favorably through packaging, positioning, promotion, or other means.

The end-user's perceptions—conditioned by cultural and economic factors—are not the only issues in product adaptation. Government regulations might also require changes. Climate and geography might dictate modifications. And the offerings of competitors will have a profound effect on how you shape your offerings for the world market.

The preliminary research process should produce information that helps management to make sound decisions about product adaptation. For example, a doughnut company that wants to sell in Brazil had better learn that Brazilians rarely eat breakfast. Doughnuts should be sold in Brazil as desserts and snacks. This is what Dunkin Donuts learned.

The company also learned that the product would sell better if it included local fruit fillings like guava and papaya. Another company, Campbell Soup, failed to sell its vegetable and beef soups in Brazil because Brazilians prefer the dehydrated products of competitors such as Knorr and Maggi; Brazilians like to use these dry products as soup starters, adding their own ingredients and culinary touches.

Because it costs time and money to adapt products, companies moving into international markets naturally prefer to sell the product as is or make the minimum necessary changes. This mindset creates tremendous opportunities for those who are bold enough and creative enough to outsell other offerings in the broad marketplace or to find a profitable niche. This chapter will discuss the most important issues bearing on your consideration of *how* and *how much* to adapt your product or service to sell abroad.

Government Regulations

Government regulations often present the most stringent requirements. Would-be international marketers are sometimes frustrated to the point of mania by the "senseless" restrictions certain governments place on imports.

That's not a useful way to look at it. No doubt many of these regulations are pointless when viewed with total objectivity. But the foreign government doesn't maintain these requirements because of their innate logic. Trade and domestic regulations are, very frequently, responses to political pressure.

The pressure that engenders them does not always come from domestic industries clamoring for protection. As a result, Sweden was the first country in the world to enact legislation against most aerosol sprays. Since 1979, when Sweden started to apply these regulations, environmental regulations have, of course, become widespread.

Environment is just one reason for government regulation. Another is specific countries' need to control standards and terms of reference. As an example, the metric standard applies to all commercial importation of distilled spirits to the United States. Bottle sizes must be 1.00 liters, 1.75 liters, and so on. Now, because the United States continues to resist the metric system internally, it is conceivable that an ambitious but untutored foreign distiller might run afoul of this regulation and have a shipment denied entry by customs.

It is vital that the research phase come up with all the relevant regulations and make sure they are current. Requirements change very rapidly. Check the country's track record. Are there frequent changes in trade laws? If so, that fact must be considered in planning. It would be

Going with the Green

The green movement is particularly strong in Europe. As the European Union (EU) struggles with its protracted birth pains, it becomes more and more apparent that environmental issues will loom large in the picture. Marketers in Germany, forced to develop less wasteful packaging, are espousing the environmentally correct Three R's: *reduce, reuse,* and *recycle.*

Germany's consumer goods marketers and retailers have joined with the German packaging industry to form Bonn-based Dual System Deutschland to collect, sort, and recycle empty packaging throughout Germany. Members, including Procter & Gamble (P&G) and Unilever, display Green Dot emblems on their recyclable packaging. Each German household would be issued a special yellow garbage can to dispose of packages from Green Dot products.

To pay for this costly system, all companies using the Green Dot agree to pay a volume-based levy amounting to, for example, less than 2¢ for a small 200–300 milliliter bottle.

Under the EU directive, within five years 60 percent of packaging waste by weight must be recoverable for recycling or other uses, with the proportion rising to 90 percent within ten years.

Thinking green in packaging is an imperative in Europe. For instance, P&G sells its Ariel liquid detergent in plastic containers containing 25 percent recyclable material. Although environmentally friendly packaging is expensive, it costs less than the alternative: even tougher measures that require all consumer-goods packages to be returned to the source.

The fact is that environmental considerations will soon be taken for granted in domestic as well as international marketing.

---

extremely embarrassing and expensive to modify a product to meet a certain requirement, only to discover that the regulation was undergoing modification at the same time as the product was being modified.

Remember also that government regulation comes wrapped in bureaucratic red tape. You have to be willing and able to cope with it if you are going to sell to the market. There's usually not much you can do about regulations, although firms with enough clout can influence the situation by lobbying directly or through industry associations. Sometimes one's own government is involved in the lobbying effort.

European economic integration reduces discriminatory regulation but does not necessarily eliminate it. For example, some national environmental restrictions will stay in place. For instance, a 1989 ruling by the European Court of Justice lets stand Danish laws requiring returnable containers for all beer and soft drinks. These laws severely restrict foreign brewers (and no doubt cut down the options for Danish beer drinkers), because the Danish market is not big enough to warrant setting up a system to handle returnables.

Obviously, marketers want to avoid restrictions when they can be avoided. However, there are occasions when it may be a good idea to seek government approval for a product even though it is not required. Testing by a governmental agency or an independent testing laboratory may add to the product's acceptability. And the process of gaining government approval may give the company some new insights into selling in the country.

Nontariff barriers are a troublesome aspect of government regulations. They involve such things as product specifications, approval procedures, subsidies for local products, and bureaucratic red tape. They are usually erected to keep foreign products out or to protect domestic producers.

Often nontariff barriers concern elements outside the core product. For example, France requires the use of the French language in any offer, presentation, or advertisement, whether written or spoken, in instructions for use, and in specifications or guarantee terms for goods and services, as well as for invoices and receipts.

This sort of regulation impels marketers to mutter about "Mickey Mouse" laws and claw their hair in frustration. It drives up the cost without affecting the product, and that's what it is intended to do. Even though the core product need not be modified, these mandatory changes may be the toughest single problem in international marketing.

Compliance with such regulations is a major cost factor. But even if the expense seems prohibitive at first glance, management should not succumb to sticker shock too quickly. For example, Mack International has to pay $10,000–25,000 for a typical European engine certification. On top of this, brake system changes to conform with other countries' regulations run from $1,500 to $2,500 per vehicle. Nor is this all; wheel equipment changes will cost up to $1,000 per vehicle. Confronted with these barriers, the company might be inclined to say, "Forget it!" Actually, though, Mack is able to compete successfully in the international marketplace in spite of these outlays and the resulting higher price. Infuriating as nontariff barriers can be, they must be evaluated like any other cost of doing business.

For many companies, especially smaller firms with limited resources, the seemingly arbitrary harassment is the ultimate barrier. Japan has found many ways to keep out foreign products. Product testing and certification requirements have made the entry of many foreign companies into Japanese markets quite difficult, if not impossible. Take, for instance, Japan's requirement that all pharmaceutical products be tested in Japanese laboratories. The ostensible reason was that Japanese might be physiologically different from other groups. Similarly, foreign ski products have been kept out because Japanese snow is considered unique.

Marketers trying to penetrate Japan found that it was futile to argue the validity of such claims or to offer proof to the contrary. It is not a matter of whether anybody, Japanese or otherwise, believes them. They are polite fictions.

Many exporters, rather than trying to move mountains of red tape, have found ways to accommodate Japanese regulations. Famous Amos, for example, creates separate product batches to meet Japanese requirements, thus avoiding problems with the Japanese Health and Welfare Agency.

Tariff barriers are diminishing or crumbling around the world. With the substantial decrease in these barriers, nontariff forms of protectionism have increased. On volume alone, agriculture dominates the list. Many barriers have been around for decades because of agriculture's exemption from the GATT framework, but new ones emerge as needed. In 1989, for example, the EC and the United States began a confrontation over beef produced with the aid of hormones. To hear certain European beef interests tell it, one might have thought that the hormones used by U.S. producers were the toxic equivalent of plutonium. The fact was that the hormones banned in beef imports to the EC were almost undetectable and had been declared safe by the United Nations health authorities in 1987.

The growth of regional trade combinations may make nontariff barriers more potent than those erected by individual countries. One example is the EC's postal and telecommunications administrators developing harmonized standards for equipment, causing U.S. manufacturers to worry that the new standards would reduce the U.S. share in this $12 billion-plus market. Similar policies had already excluded most imported equipment from the growing Korean market.

Pleasing the Customer

Customer characteristics and preferences are as important as government influences on the product adaptation decision. And they are more comprehensible to professional marketers.

Sometimes physical characteristics dictate product adaptation.

U.S.-based Erno Laszlo tried to market the same skin-care product to "fair-skinned Australians, swarthy Italians, and delicate Asian women."[1] The effort failed. The company found also that, in Asia, skin-care customs vary widely from region to region.

Physical size counts. GE Medical Systems redesigned its CAT scan equipment for the Japanese market. Internal anatomy does not vary from the United States to Japan, but Japanese people are smaller and so are Japanese hospitals.

Consumer products, of course, are especially affected by local behavior, tastes, attitudes, and traditions. This is a universal fact of marketing life. When British marketers, for example, sell in Britain, they can take certain baseline facts of consumer preference for granted and address the variables. When marketers venture abroad, they cannot make the same assumptions. What is important to a British customer might be a matter of indifference to a customer in Kenya, and vice versa.

Sometimes the product does not need to be changed, but only repositioned. For example, it's difficult to sell diet drinks in Japan, because in that country people (except for Sumo wrestlers) are not overweight by Western standards, and the word diet connotes a very unpleasant concept. Coke changed the name of the drink to Coke Light and shifted the promotional theme from "weight loss" to "figure maintenance." This positioning switch made the product acceptable to Japanese, mostly women, who do indeed watch their weight, but who would not like to admit that they are dieting.

Culture is the hardest variable for a company to accommodate. Culture abounds in symbolism. Symbolism is entwined with language and custom and perception. Had the woman in Unilever's Surf commercial in India not worn a *mangalsutra* necklace, many would have taken her white sari to indicate that she was a widow. In 1983, Coca-Cola introduced a product named Mello Yellow in Thailand. Before long, the name was shortened to simply Mello; "yellow" in Thai means "pus."

Religious customs shape culture in ways that can set traps for unwary marketers. When selling products in their own countries, of course, companies are careful to avoid offending religious feelings in any way. Without thorough grounding in the religions of other countries, it is easy to blunder. For example, a U.S. cologne manufacturer launched a product in North Africa with a label featuring a man and his dog in a rural setting. What could be more innocuous? Anyone familiar with Islam would know that dogs are said to have eaten one of the Prophet Mohammed's regiments, and Muslims consider them signs of bad luck and uncleanliness.

Even the number of units in a package can be significant. Our perception of certain numbers is a deeply ingrained cultural characteristic.

Don't Tell John Wayne[2]

Sales of Western footwear have risen dramatically in Europe since the mid-1980s because of growing interest in the American West and the Great Outdoors. At the beginning of the 1990s, Germans were buying half a million pairs of cowboy boots each year, with sales growing at a rate of eight percent annually. European young people wear boots that look as American as John Wayne's. However, John Wayne would have been dismayed to learn that most of these boots are made in Spain. Why? The toes of U.S. boots are not pointy enough.

"American brands are not very popular because they are of a different style," said the owner of Dynamo, one of the largest shops specializing in boots in Germany. American boots have toes that are too rounded and too wide. Now, real cowboy boots, as worn by the 19th-century riders of the purple sage, had rounded toes and ample foot room, because that made sense for working cowboys. But European customers don't plan to do much cowpunching. They are looking for boots that conform to their fashion ideas. The German retailer says of the American boots, "They are practical, but not very interesting."

American companies certainly did not lack the capacity to make narrow boots with pointy toes. They chose not to do so. They did not take the European market seriously, and they were unaware of, or indifferent to, European preferences.

It must be added that import duties, added to the already higher prices of American boots, place the U.S. products at a price disadvantage. However, European retail experts argue that price would not be a barrier if the style were right. European bootbuyers, especially in France, are willing to pay more for authentic boots made in the United States. They are turned off by the rounded toes.

In the West, 7 is lucky and 13 is unlucky. Those numbers have no similar connotation in Japan. However, the Japanese ideogram for the number 4 can also be read as "death." Therefore, consumer goods shipped in packages of four produce limited sales. The numbers 3 and 5 are considered luckier.

Economic Development

The stage of economic development may be a factor in the product adaptation decision. In some developing markets, the product or its packaging requires "backward innovation." This does not mean "dumbing down"; it means alteration to acknowledge the fact that people in the area don't have as much money to spend. In developing markets, products like razor blades are often sold by the piece. In Europe, soft drink cans are sold singly, even in big stores. Soft drink companies have found that six-packs sell poorly but four-packs do all right. In some markets, six-packs for drinks are not feasible because of the lack of refrigeration capacity in households.

On the other hand, products oriented to families, like food or soap, often appear in larger sizes in developing markets. Pillsbury packages its products in six- and eight-serving sizes for developing countries, whereas the most popular size in the North American market is for two.

Packaging

Packaging is the element that is likely to require adaptation even if all else remains the same. The most obvious packaging adaptation is in language. Certain countries require bilingual labeling: Canada (French and English), Belgium (French and Flemish), and Finland (Finnish and Swedish). Governments require more and less informative labeling. Inadequate identification, failure to use the required languages, or incorrect descriptions on labels can cause big problems. One simple way to avoid such problems is to study the labels of competitors in the market.

Color is of course a key element in package design. The assumptions that underlie choices of color for the domestic market do not always hold up abroad. African nations are considered to prefer bold colors. But in certain parts of Africa, the color red is associated with witchcraft or death. Would-be exporters have been dismayed to find that their bold package colors are banned in one country because the colors of its flag may not be used commercially. In a neighboring country, however, those colors might be preferred. Such considerations are part of the price of tapping into the world market.

Color is frequently a function of faddishness. In industrialized countries, as generic products grow in popularity, the color white is losing popularity with manufacturers, who don't want their products to be confused with the generics. Black, on the other hand, is increasingly popular, denoting quality, excellence, and "class."

Marketers are wise to monitor international packaging technology. One major innovation of the 1980s was in aseptic containers for fruit drinks and milk. Tetra Pak International, a $1.5 billion Swedish

New Life for Old Products[3]

Mature product lines can turn into spring chickens in international markets. Beral Inc., of Chatsworth, California, was no longer able to achieve desired growth in selling its medical laboratory products in the United States. So Beral entered the global market, starting its thrust by sending press releases to international bio-tech and laboratory journals, and placing advertisements in foreign professional publications. Another tactic was to advertise in the U.S. Department of Commerce's catalog magazine, *Commercial News USA*. As a next step, Beral's president, Ralph Garren, decided to participate in trade fairs in Mexico, Germany, Spain, and Italy.

Garren comments, "We are finding good, 'non-mature' markets overseas. Some countries are 20 years behind the United States in the use of disposable products of the type we make."

If the product is brand new to the new market, it may not take any adaptation at all.

---

company, converted 40 percent of milk sales in Western Europe to its aseptic packaging system, which keeps perishables fresh for five months without refrigeration.

Developing New Applications

New applications for existing products can substantially extend market potential. For example, Turbo Tek Inc., which makes a hose attachment for washing cars, has found that foreign customers are expanding the product's functions. In Japan, Turbo-Wash is used for cleaning bamboo. The Dutch use it to wash windows, plants, and the sidings of their houses.

Here is an area where the foreign marketing operation can provide useful feedback to the domestic operation. Watch what customers in other countries do with the product. Note the features that they value. Maybe there are profit opportunities in those new applications closer to home.

Method of Operation

Method of operation is, for some products (notably electrical appliances), a watershed issue in considering the need for adaptation.

Electric systems vary from country to country and even within some countries, such as Brazil. Exporters can learn about these differences through local government representatives or trade publications like *Electric Current Abroad,* issued by the U.S. Department of Commerce.

As the world moves closer to becoming one huge marketplace, many such complicating factors will be simplified or eliminated by standardization. Some companies have adjusted their products to operate on different systems. Japanese VCR equipment will record and play back on various color systems.

Failure to adjust to local systems can lead to disaster in international marketing. At the same time, though, the need to adapt to new systems can open up opportunities. When Canada adopted the metric system in 1977–78, many U.S. companies were affected, and quite a few resisted. Perfect Measuring Tape Company in Toledo, Ohio, for example, had to convert to metric if it wanted to continue selling disposable paper measuring tape to textile firms in Canada. Once the conversion was made, the company found an entire world of untapped markets. Soon Perfect Measuring Tape was shipping nearly 30 percent of its tape to markets as disparate as Australia and Zimbabwe.

Country of Origin

Country-of-origin connotations can affect efforts to sell abroad. In many places, there is a built-in positive or negative stereotype among customers based on where the product is made. A study found that machine tool buyers rated the United States and Germany higher than Japan, with Brazil ranked below all three.

In some places products made, say, in the United States are automatically rated higher than domestic products. In other places, Japanese products are just assumed to be better. In yet other countries, consumers tend to reject domestic goods and embrace any import.

County-of-origin effects lessen as consumers become more informed. Also, as more countries develop the necessary bases to manufacture products, the origin of the products becomes less important. Moreover, the issue is being blurred by the proliferation of so-called hybrid products, as when a Canadian multinational makes the product in Malaysia.

Keeping an Open Mind on Adaptation

Marketers who fight any modification until it is proven necessary are likely to be handicapped in entering the world market. Adaptation— whether of the product, the package, the merchandising, or the servicing—will probably be necessary.

The successful marketers of world brands are not producing identical products, but recognizable products. The prosperity of McDonald's in the world marketplace is based on adroit variation, not on offering the same product worldwide. Had it not been for the variations, McDonald's only customers overseas would have been American tourists.

Firms, especially smaller firms, are unquestionably confronted with risks and expenses in adapting for going global. The key to success in this phase lies in obtaining good research that pinpoints the need for adaptation; costing out the adaptations against realistic estimates of return; and, perhaps most important, looking toward the future to gauge the long-term consequences of not going international. Modifications made to sell abroad can be of considerable benefit in domestic selling, too.

Japan: A Special Case[4]

Japan presents some unique challenges in adaptation. When we consider marketing in most parts of the world, we talk about product rethinking.

The Japanese obsession with quality is so all-consuming that it leads businesspeople in other parts of the world to joke about it. The jokes betray frustration. The quality of Japanese goods is extremely high, and this is the primary reason for Japan's rise to the heights of the global economy.

Perfection has come to be expected in Japan. Leather goods with slight discolorations that are fully acceptable elsewhere are rejected by the Japanese. One U.S. maker of high-priced T-shirts had an entire shipment rejected because the seams had little stitching holes when the shirt was stretched. The Japanese customer explained, "We expect high-quality items to include hidden effort, even in areas that don't show. Whether that's really necessary is a different matter."

Similar standards are applied to industrial products, as the Bendix corporation found out when it supplied Toyota with disc brake pads. Matt Yoshida of Bendix Japan commented that "In the U.S., the quality of a part is judged to be satisfactory if it functions properly. But in Japan, perfection is expected over portions that have nothing to do with function, such as the finish of the paint job."

Entire shipments of merchandise into Japan will be inspected at all levels. If occasional defects are found, the entire shipment will be returned. To forestall such rejection, the Japanese will want to know about the quality control system at the point of manufacture. The exporter will have to provide assurances about quality control and live up to them.

Marketing executives who want to penetrate Japan must make sure that everyone in the firm—top management, manufacturing, customer

---

Reflections on Japan

A German marketing manager of OSRAM Ltd., a subsidiary of Siemens AG, which supplies the Japanese market with halogen lamps,
made the following remarks. "In not only Germany, but all countries
outside of Japan, the basic quality control stance is that among several
hundreds of thousands of products, the appearance of a few flawed
pieces is inevitable, so all that is necessary is replacement of such items.
But in Japan, a single flawed piece is considered highly problematic.
In the case of automobile makers, who are particularly strict about
quality, demands are made for detailed reports on clarification of the
cause and countermeasures to be taken for the appearance of even a
single flawed piece, and if such reports are not forthcoming, they will
discontinue further transactions. It was extremely difficult to convince
the German home office to provide such 'unprecedented' reports in
the early days. We finally persuaded them that such reports were
necessary to convince the users of our reliability. Once persuaded,
however, they quickly set out with a will to provide such reports and
improve product quality. As a result, quality that met with the demands of the users was achieved in an extremely short time." The
observations touch on several central issues. Most manufacturers, even
those who turn out extremely high-quality products, assume that they
will turn out some clinkers, that the customer will make the same
assumption, and that the defective item will be replaced or made good
under a standard procedure. Not only do the Japanese reject that
assumption, but they will also badger the manufacturer for all kinds
of paperwork explaining what happened. The headache and expense
of providing these explanations would, by themselves, either force the
manufacturer to change the system or drive the company out of the
Japanese market.

---

relations, finance—understands the peculiarities of the Japanese market. Is it outrageous? That depends on how you look at it. It is a fact
of life. If you're not prepared to deal with it, you had better forget about
Japan.

Product Holism

In Japan, consumers and channel members (distributors) tend to take
a holistic view of products, considering the total product, with all its

tangible and intangible components. For example, the packaging is considered an integral part of the purchase. Even slight faults or stains on the packaging make a product unsaleable.

But the holistic view extends far beyond packaging. The goal is to provide the utmost in value at every point, including price, promotion, packaging, and even those aspects of the product that the non-Japanese marketer would say have nothing to do with the way the product performs. The Japanese word *keihakutansho* means "lighter, slimmer, shorter, and smaller," which epitomizes the Japanese drive to create value by simultaneously lowering cost and increasing quality.

Emphasis on precision in product appropriateness is a hallmark of this approach. Products must be not just competitive, but truly superior, and they must offer a precise match with customer needs in order to succeed.

To achieve this match, Japanese firms are willing to go to great lengths in divining customer needs and doing the research necessary to meet those needs. Foreign firms are expected to do the same with respect to Japanese consumers. Manufacturers of electric shavers modified their products to fit the size of Japanese hands.

Spalding adapted its golf clubs to the Japanese physique and the company's sales in Japan tripled from 200,000 units to 600,000 units. Johnson & Johnson reformulated its baby lotion to be white and much less scented than the American product, and it became a hit in Japan. A German firm specializing in angora wool products developed an entirely new product, "Setany," made of silk and cotton rather than angora, to fit the tastes of the Japanese.

Salomon S.A., a French manufacturer of ski equipment, recognized early on that its products would have to be redesigned: "Japanese women, particularly from the knee down, can be a problem to fit. So we have to take this into account when designing our products."[5] If Salomon were selling in another country, perhaps the adaptation would be less necessary. The overall excellence and prestige of the equipment would, for most consumers, override the lack of perfect fit with the user's physical characteristics. After all, most skiers probably don't notice such matters. But in Japan, the whole system practically compels the manufacturer to make the adjustments before the products even get to the customers.

Values or Ploys?

Many marketers, confronted with these barriers to Japan, assume that they are all ploys to protect Japanese industry. When the Japanese insist that certain extraordinary standards be met, marketing executives from elsewhere might say, "Oh, sure; this is strictly an excuse." There is a measure of truth here. No doubt some Japanese interests use the *keihakutansho* approach to harass would-be competitors. But it is a mistake to assume that if—through diplomacy and pressure—the Japanese can be induced to reduce or eliminate the official and unofficial barriers, then Japanese customers will act just like customers everywhere else, and there will be no more need for extraordinary adaptive measures.

That's not the case. Ingrained in the Japanese system is a set of values and attitudes that will still reject goods that vary, even in "trivial" ways, from the Japanese standards of quality. And there will still be the invisible yet often unscalable wall the Japanese culture raises against *gaijin,* foreigners. Many middle-aged bureaucrats and company officials, for example, believe that buying foreign products is unpatriotic.

Younger Japanese consumers, of course, display great enthusiasm for things Western. In certain product categories, cultural differences can be a selling point. In Japan, Borden successfully sold Lady Borden ice cream and Borden cheese packaged and labeled in English, exactly as they are in the United States. Levi Strauss decided to promote its jeans with a television campaign featuring James Dean and Marilyn Monroe. It should be noted, however, that these Levi's jeans both measure up to Japanese quality standards and are designed and mostly made in Japan, where customers prefer a tighter fit.

Superficially there may seem to be contradictions here. The Japanese do indeed buy American products, but this does not mean their emphasis on perfection will change in any important degree, at least not any time soon.

Chances are that you can't crack the Japanese market by merely adapting. You have to be willing to adopt a fundamentally different approach to quality. This takes commitment and it takes money. So the Japanese market is for the long haul. The Japanese know this and structure it this way. Leases are for a substantial period, customers are only gradually developed, and market penetration and market share are emphasized over short-term returns.

So many companies, looking at the situation realistically, will conclude that Japan is not worth the effort, especially because the Four Tigers (Hong Kong, Singapore, South Korea, and Taiwan) are growing faster than Japan and increasing their shares of both inter- and intraregional business. Nevertheless, Japan is an immensely rich market and offers vast rewards to those who can enter it successfully. Here are some guidelines for considering the special circumstances relating to an effort to penetrate the Japanese market.

Be realistic. Base cost estimates on the need to meet Japanese expectations of perfection. Do not be sidetracked by the notion that the Japanese obsession with quality is strictly a protective ploy. It is *used* as a protective ploy, true, but it is a deeper, more pervasive element of the Japanese business and cultural psyche.

Be farsighted. There are few overnight successes in marketing in Japan. The commitment to go there must be part of a plan that stretches far into the future. It is a major commitment, one that may not show outstanding returns for quite a while. If the company can't afford the commitment, or is in no position to plan that far ahead, or will put too much pressure on the Japanese venture for quick profits, then it would be better to go somewhere else.

Be holistic. The Japanese take a holistic view, regarding every part of the product (including the package it comes in) as a component of value. Even when the product element has nothing to do with performance (like the paint trim on an appliance), it is still held up to the highest standards. This fact of life is irksome to many marketers. And yet, viewed positively, it can be a way of thinking that benefits the business in other countries and in the domestic sphere.

Adaptation—Is It Worth It?

The issue of product adaptation climaxes most often in the question "Is it worth it?" The answer depends on the firm's ability to control costs, estimate market potential, and, above all, sell profitably, especially in the long run. However, the question that should be asked at the same time is "Can we afford not to do it?" The question becomes particularly urgent when adaptation for one market may open others as well. For example, right-hand steering wheels are not just used in Japan, but also in England and other countries throughout the world.

The decision to adapt should grow out of thorough analysis of the market, including, if necessary, primary research. It's expensive to mount a specialized data collection and testing program, but it's a lot more expensive to fail because the product is wrong for the market.

The decision to adapt should be subject to rigorous standards. From the financial standpoint, some companies maintain specific return-on-investment levels that must be satisfied to justify adaptation. Other companies let the requirement vary as a function of the market and also with regard to other factors. For example, the firm decides to accept lower profitability at first in order to make a proper market entry, especially if it is a matter of beating competition to the punch.

It takes courage to commit the company to a product adaptation program. The people entrusted with the decision should know existing market conditions, the potential for the product in different markets, and be willing to take risks.

Check Points:

✓ Success abroad depends on perception as well as reality.

✓ Firms often prefer to sell abroad without adaptation, but firms that do adapt well have an advantage.

✓ Research should indicate possible needs for product adaptation.

✓ Government regulations often make adaptation necessary.

✓ Willingness to adapt to cultural variations can make the program successful.

✓ Adaptation decisions should be made by well-qualified people armed with adequate knowledge of the market.

WHAT PRICE THE WORLD?
Global Pricing Strategy

Price is a prime factor in buying decisions. In international marketing, it is also a weapon of penetration and a positioning tool. And, of course, it is a function of what competitors are charging and what customers are willing and able to pay. The price you put on your product or service reflects your marketing strategy. It also speaks volumes about how you want the market to perceive what you are selling.

Many companies operating in global markets have become adroit at creative pricing, setting different prices in different countries to suit the tactical thrust designed for that country. A product might carry a premium price in one market and a low price in another.

Now, as barriers between markets crumble around the world, marketing experts are finding that some pinpointed pricing strategies just won't work any more. For example, in the EU, goods sold for a lower price in one country can easily find their way into another country where the pricing structure for the same product is higher. In Germany, Badedas shower gel has been priced in the middle of the market by its marketer, Ligner & Fischer. In the United Kingdom, Beecham's approach has been to position the same Badedas gel as a high-price product. The result: U.K. retailers started importing the product from Germany.

The ground rules in international pricing are changing, but pricing remains a key element in the marketing mix. Price is the only element of the marketing mix that is revenue generating; all of the other elements are costs. Price should, therefore, be used as an active instrument of strategy in marketing decision making.

Pricing Basics for New International Players

When you decide to go global, pricing is a watershed issue. Do you intend to establish yourself in the market for the long haul? Is there a chance to make a quick killing by underselling competition? Conversely, does the absence of competition make it possible for you to charge at a premium level? Are you going head to head with your main competition or seeking a niche? How are you positioning your product? When Perrier was introduced into the United States, it could have been priced low. Instead, the sparkling water was positioned as a premium product and priced accordingly.

Of course, having folded all these strategic and tactical factors into your considerations, you must also make sure that your price is set to cover all your costs.

Duties and Currencies

Setting prices in international marketing is complicated. Duties have to be figured in, along with the margins claimed by intermediaries. Circumstances that are virtually unknown in domestic competition—dumping, gray markets, black markets—also affect pricing. Competition sometimes comes from government-owned entities whose pricing decisions seem to have little to do with logic or cost.

And then, of course, there are the vagaries of currency fluctuation. The latter half of the 1980s provides an example. Between February 1985 and the end of the decade, key foreign currencies climbed nearly 70 percent in value against the dollar.

Foreign companies selling in the United States were clobbered. They were faced with the choice of raising prices and losing market share or absorbing the shock of the currency swing and letting profit margins sink to protect their hard-won market share.

In a typical response, the British construction equipment maker J.C. Bamford Excavators Ltd., which had reached the point of selling 20 percent of its output to the United States, kept its price hikes to a minimum despite the pound's 40 percent rise since 1985. "Our competitors all produce locally," said the company's CEO, Gilbert Johnston. "We cannot increase our prices."

Taking Advantage of Currency Shifts

Some companies had planned for the possibility of wide currency fluctuations. These companies took advantage of the weak dollar in the 1980s, spending heavily to establish sales and distribution networks in the

United States. Having carved out a beachhead, they were able to take slimmer profits later. British Aerospace PLC set aside $350 million to cover anticipated foreign exchange losses. An official said, "We simply cannot go to the customer every time the dollar moves down and say we are going to put our prices up by 20 percent."[1]

Newton's third law of motion states that for every action there is an equal and opposite reaction. While foreign companies in the United States were squeezed between boosting prices and losing profit, U.S. companies in Europe were enjoying the luxury of being able to cut prices with ease because of the lower dollar. They had been able to build distribution and sales networks long neglected or abandoned during the years of the high dollar.

In computers, U.S. companies like Sun Microsystems, Hewlett Packard, and IBM were lowering prices in local currency, picking up market share, and putting pressure on their European rivals. Price differences were substantial enough to allow a Brussels-based computer dealer to buy U.S.-made computer hardware, add 20 percent profit, and still charge significantly less than the principal European competitor. Along with the big exporters like IBM, Boeing, and Caterpillar, hundreds of small and mid-sized U.S. companies took advantage of the situation, penetrating market niches where the price differential hampered European competition.

Many of the companies exploiting the exchange differential were not prepared to handle the situation that would develop when the dollar, inevitably, rose again. With the currency-driven price break their only rationale for a beefed-up export program, they were vulnerable to being forced to depart the field. Some companies (and this is a constant danger in international marketing) were lulled into the dangerous assumption that they were more competitive than was actually the case.

First-Time Pricing

The pricing strategy chosen by an exporter should accommodate such variables as currency fluctuation and should grow out of a well-conceived strategy. What is the exporting company trying to do in the short and long term? When that question is answered satisfactorily, the price can be set logically. In first-time pricing, the general alternatives are skimming, following the market price, and penetration pricing.

Skimming

The objective of skimming is to achieve the highest possible contribution in a short time. For an exporter to succeed with this approach, the

Governments is Your Big Brother in Pricing[2]

Governments around the globe are fighting what they see as the manipulation of intracompany pricing by multinationals to minimize tax bills. Japan has enacted special transfer pricing legislation that penalizes marketers for not providing information in time to meet government deadlines. German tax authorities carefully check intracompany charges. The U.S. Internal Revenue Service has filed suit against hundreds of firms on charges involving the rigging of transfer prices.

Multinationals must be ready to justify their transfer pricing policies on two or more fronts. Glen White, director of taxes at Dow Chemical, observes, "I don't think anybody can afford to have a transfer pricing system that cannot be revealed to all the relevant governments. If we were explaining to the Canadian tax auditor why we use our pricing system and our French tax inspector walked into the room, we would want to be able to invite him to sit down and then continue with the explanation.

product has to be unique, and a sufficiently large segment of the market must be willing to pay the high price. This segment should be identified and measured during the research phase. If the research findings are ambivalent or discouraging, then skimming is a highly risky policy.

As more segments are targeted and more of the product is made available, the price is gradually lowered. One vital element affecting the success of skimming is the speed and effectiveness of competitive reaction. If the research shows that competition is capable of fast and powerful counterattack, the tactic is not the best bet.

Market Pricing

If similar products already exist in the target market, the standard approach is market pricing. The final customer price is determined based on competitive prices, and then production and marketing must be adjusted to the price. This approach requires that the exporter have a thorough grip on product costs, as well as confidence that the product life cycle is long enough to warrant insertion.

Logically, the people planning the effort are marketers. The production know-how lies elsewhere, in another division or another company.

Controlling the Destiny of the Shipment[3]

For years Dixie-Narco let foreign buyers handle transportation. The Williston, South Carolina, company—a leading manufacturer of soda-vending machines—sells to dozens of countries, from Russia to Argentina.

A couple of years ago, Dixie-Narco scrapped its old transport system, which relied on up to 20 distributors to ship goods individually to each nation. Today the firm exports directly from the South Carolina plant to the customers' ports, where the foreign buyers take control. Dixie-Narco has won price reductions of about one-third from carriers.

These savings have been crucial in winning new business, says William J. Trier, the company's director of physical distribution. For example, in an Australian deal, Dixie-Narco was able to lower its delivered price by up to $1,800 on a $29,000 sale. This helped to win the deal against European and Japanese rivals.

That traditional disconnect can be dangerous at this stage. It's easy enough for the marketing team to determine the going price range. It's harder to figure back and bring production costs into line. Occasionally, wishful thinking takes over. The price is based on what the marketers would like it to be, ignoring the realities of actual cost.

Market pricing is a reactive approach. It can lead to problems if volume never rises to sufficient levels to provide a satisfactory return. Although firms typically use pricing as a differentiation tool, the international marketing manager often has no choice but to accept the world market price.

Penetration Pricing

Penetration pricing means low prices aimed at generating high volume and market share. It requires mass markets, price-sensitive customers, and the capacity to reduce production and marketing costs as volume increases.

Setting Export Price

Export pricing is affected by the same factors that affect domestic pricing. Internal factors include the company's goals, objectives, and philosophy;

the costs of developing, producing, and marketing; and the nature of the product and industry. In addition, there are factors relating to international markets in general or to a particular target market. These factors include customer, regulatory, competitive, and financial (mainly foreign exchange) characteristics.

The interaction of these elements causes restraints beyond those encountered at home. It may also offer distinct competitive opportunities. For example, a company decides to challenge its main foreign competitor in the competitor's home market. However, to seize that opportunity requires expensive product adaptation, the cost of which must be absorbed, at least for now.

As a company gets ready to establish its pricing strategy, it should work through four steps.

Analyze the target market. As in all marketing decisions, foreign or domestic, the intended target market establishes the basic premise for pricing. How much will price influence the buying decision? How strong is the perceived relationship between price and quality? How might various parties (including governments) react to what is seen as price manipulations?

Plan the marketing mix. The marketing mix must be attuned to the characteristics of the target market. Pricing will be a key factor in creating the desired brand image.

Select the appropriate pricing policies. Prices are not made in a vacuum. Besides profit maximization, those who set the prices have to consider the company's overall objectives as well as the goals for this particular product. This means thinking about such issues as return on investment and long-term survival.

Crank in the needs of the intermediaries. The reactions of distributors and other intermediaries are usually more influential in export pricing than in domestic pricing.

If the foreign intermediary is hurt competitively by too high a price or shorn of profit by too low a price, the intermediary might not go all out—might even pull out. The exporter in such circumstances can be hard-pressed to come up with a replacement.

Then, too, when an exporter is moving into a new foreign market, the brand image of the product will be heavily influenced by the price. The setting of price can be partly strategical, partly tactical. For example, an exporter entering a new market often allows wholesalers and retailers above-normal profit margins to maximize sales volume, shelf space, geographic distribution, and loyalty.

Pricing Strategy Determination

After taking preparatory steps, it's time to establish the pricing strategy. Three general pricing strategies in international marketing are a standard worldwide price; dual pricing, which differentiates between domestic and export prices; and market-differentiated pricing. The first two methods are cost-oriented approaches that are relatively simple to establish and easy to understand. The third strategy is based on demand orientation and is thus more consistent with the marketing concept. However, even the third approach is, in the long run, tethered to costs.

Standard worldwide price. The standard worldwide price might be the same price regardless of the buyer (if foreign product or marketing costs are negligible) or might be based on average unit costs.

Dual pricing. In dual pricing, domestic and export prices are differentiated. There are two basic approaches to dual pricing: the cost-plus method and the marginal cost method. The cost-plus strategy fully allocates domestic and foreign costs to the product and thus comes closest to reflecting true short-term cost. With this kind of pricing, the price is sometimes so high that customers don't buy.

This leads some exporters to use a flexible cost-plus strategy, allowing for variations in special circumstances. One familiar instrument of flexibility is the discount. Changes in prices can also be used to cope with exchange-rate fluctuations.

The marginal cost method establishes the direct costs of making and selling products for export as the floor beneath which prices cannot sink. Fixed costs for plants, R&D, and domestic overhead, as well as domestic marketing costs, are disregarded. The exporter can thus lower export prices to be competitive in markets that otherwise would have been unreachable.

Here an alarm bell rings and the word *dumping* lights up on the screen. Competitive pricing maneuvers that are part and parcel of the marginal cost method open a company to dumping charges. The determination that a company is dumping is based on average total costs, which include items omitted by this strategy, and which are therefore considerably higher.

The table on page 141 offers a comparison of cost-oriented methods. Notice how the rigid cost-plus strategy produces the highest selling price by full-cost allocation.

Three Paths to Pricing Success[4]

Typically there are three main approaches to export pricing:

- rigid cost-plus,
- flexible cost-plus,
- dynamic incremental.

Success may lie in picking the right approach—and switching to another approach when conditions change. Here are the pricing choices of three firms.

Autotrol—a Wisconsin manufacturer of water treatment and control equipment employing about 80 people. Exports account for around 60 percent of the company's $14 million annual sales. Principal markets include Western Europe, Japan, Australia, New Zealand, and Venezuela. Autotrol uses a rigid cost-plus approach, setting export prices three to four percent higher than domestic prices to cover costs including foreign advertising, foreign travel, and shipping. Autotrol, according to *Business Horizons*, has enjoyed 15 years of success using this strategy.

Badger Meter—a manufacturer and marketer of industrial liquid meters. The company employs 700, with annual sales of $60 million, and more than 50 years experience in international marketing. Its major markets are Europe, Canada, Taiwan, and the Philippines. Badger uses the flexible cost-plus approach, offering special discounts to gain market share or to offset exchange rate fluctuations.

Ray-O-Vac—a producer of batteries and other consumer goods, exporting successfully for more than 30 years. Its Micro Power Division employs 250 and has annual sales of $100 million. Exports account for 20 percent of total business; major markets include Europe, the Far East, and Japan. Ray-O-Vac relies on a dynamic incremental strategy. Branch managers may adjust prices day-to-day as dictated by the exchange rate. Ray-O-Vac adjusts export prices frequently according to current silver prices.

Export-Related Costs

In preparing a quotation, the exporter must be careful to take into account all the relevant factors, including (to the extent possible) unique export-

COMPARISON OF COST-ORIENTED METHODS

Production Costs	Standard	Cost Plus	Marginal Cost
Materials	2.00	2.00	2.00
Fixed costs	1.00	1.00	0.00
Additional foreign product costs	0.00	0.10	0.10
Production overhead	0.50	0.50	0.00
Total production costs	3.50	3.60	2.10
U.S. marketing costs	1.50	0.00	0.00
General & administrative	0.75	0.75	0.00
Foreign marketing	0.00	1.00	1.00
Other foreign costs	0.00	1.25	1.25
Subtotal	5.75	6.60	4.35
Profit margin (25%)	1.44	1.65	1.09
Selling price	7.19	8.25	5.44

related costs. This is not a chore to be taken lightly; a miscalculated cost can be expensive indeed in its effect on competitiveness and profitability. Costs to be considered include the following:

1. The cost of modifying the product for foreign markets.

2. Operational costs of the export process: personnel, market research, shipping, insurance, communications, overseas promotion.

3. Costs incurred in entering foreign markets: tariffs and taxes; risks associated with a buyer in a different market (mainly commercial credit risks and political risks); foreign-exchange risk.

The combined effect of both clear-cut and hidden costs results in export prices that far exceed domestic prices. This phenomenon of price escalation is shown in the table on the following page, which compares four export scenarios with a typical domestic situation.

The first case is relatively simple, adding only the CIF (cost, insurance, freight) and tariff charges. The second scenario adds a foreign importer and thus lengthens the foreign part of the distribution channel. In the third, a value-added tax (VAT) is included in the calculations. This is imposed on the full export selling price, which represents the "value added" to or introduced into the country from abroad. In Italy, for example, where most food items are taxed at two percent, processed meat is taxed at 18 percent because the government wants to use the VAT to reduce its trade deficit. The fourth case simulates a situation found in countries where distribution channels are longer. Lengthy channels can easily double the landed (CIF) price.

Shop Around for Shipping[5]

Shipping cost is an important element in pricing. Sometimes smaller firms find that carriers don't give them the same breaks that are given to larger firms.

One answer: join a shippers association.

Los Angeles-based Streamline Shippers Association (SSA), a full-service, not-for-profit entity, pools clients' cargo to achieve maximum flexibility and minimum rates. One importer says SSA saves him as much as 20 to 30 percent on an annual freight bill. SSA also helps clients set up in new markets. La Palaquita, a Texas-based general merchandise importer, says SSA was instrumental in identifying business contacts when La Palaquita opened in Bangkok.

Ray Camero, SSA's president, says that manufacturers of heavy, low-value products often run into trouble when they try to find consistent shipping service. Carriers, especially big ones, prefer to handle high revenue-generating cargo that inflicts less wear and tear on equipment. Smaller independent carriers often provide better service for high-volume, low value products. Camero advises the use of both: "The indies when I need the better price and the conference lines [larger carriers] when I need it faster."

Price escalation can be fought through creative strategies such as reorganizing the channel of distribution. The following diagram—based on one firm's import channels for spaghetti and macaroni in Japan—shows how the flow of merchandise through the various wholesaling levels has been reduced to include only an internal wholesaler–distribution center. The results are savings of 25 percent and an increase in the overall potential for imports.

There are other ways to reduce the bite of price escalation. One way is to modify the product to eliminate costly features or to enable the product to be included under a lower tariff classification.

The exporter must set up accounting procedures that truly assess export performance. Otherwise, hidden costs will bring unwelcome surprises. For example, negotiations in Russia or the Middle East often last three times longer than average domestic negotiations, drastically increasing the costs of doing business abroad. Without accurate information, a company is helpless in trying to combat such phenomena as price escalation.

EXPORT PRICE ESCALATION[6]

Export Market Cases

International Marketing Channel Elements and Cost Factors	Domestic Wholesale-Retail Channel	Case 1 Same as Domestic with Direct Wholesale Import CIF/Tariff	Case 2 Same as 1 with Foreign Importer Added to Channel	Case 3 Same as 2 with VAT Added	Case 4 Same as 3 with local Foreign Jobber Added to Channel
Manufacturer's Net Price	6.00	6.00	6.00	6.00	6.00
+ Insurance and Shipping Cost (CIF)	—	2.50	2.50	2.50	2.50
= Landed Cost (CIF value)	—	8.50	8.50	8.50	8.50
+ Tariff (20% on CIF value)	—	1.70	1.70	1.70	1.70
= Importer's Cost (CIF value + tariff)	—	10.20	10.20	10.20	10.20
+ Importer's Margin (25% on cost)	—	—	2.55	2.55	2.55
+ VAT (16% on full cost plus margin)	—	—	—	2.04	2.04
= Wholesaler's Cost (= Importer's Price)	6.00	10.20	12.75	14.79	14.79
+ Wholesaler's Margin (33⅓% on cost)	2.00	3.40	4.25	4.93	4.93
+ VAT (16% on margin)	—	—	—	.79	.79
= Local Foreign Jobber's Cost (= Wholesale Price)	—	—	—	—	20.51
+ Jobber's Margin (33⅓% on cost)	—	—	—	—	6.84
+ VAT (16% on margin)	—	—	—	—	1.09
= Retailer's Cost (= Wholesale or Jobber Price)	8.00	13.60	17.00	20.51	28.44
+ Retailer's Margin (50% on cost)	4.00	6.80	8.50	10.26	14.22
+ VAT (16% on margin)	—	—	—	1.64	2.28
= Retail Price (what consumer pays)	12.00	20.40	25.50	32.41	44.94
Percentage Price Escalation over Domestic		70%	113%	170%	275%
Percentage Price Escalation over Case 1			25%	59%	120%
Percentage Price Escalation over Case 2				27%	76%
Percentage Price Escalation over Case 3					39%

REORGANIZATION OF DISTRIBUTION CHANNELS

A. Conventional Route

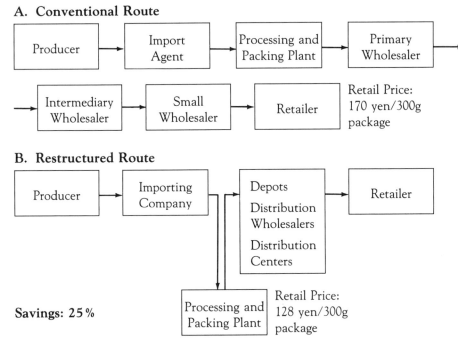

B. Restructured Route

Savings: 25 %

Check Points

✔ Price is a key factor in the international marketing mix.

✔ Price planning should consider currency fluctuations.

✔ The object of skimming is to achieve the highest return in the shortest time.

✔ Market pricing responds to competitive prices.

✔ Penetration pricing aims at generating high volume and market share quickly.

✔ Export price-setting begins with four steps:

1. Analyze the target market

2. Plan the marketing mix

3. Select appropriate pricing policies

4. Crank in the needs of intermediaries.

✓ Three general pricing strategies of international marketing are:

1. Standard worldwide price
2. Dual pricing
3. Market-differentiated pricing.

THE PAYOFF
Establishing Terms of Payment

Setting the right price is important. It's just as important to set up terms under which you can be sure to be paid the right amount, on time.

Companies involved in international marketing can enhance their profitability by signing the most favorable agreement possible and making that agreement work. The basic methods of payment vary in terms of their attractiveness to buyer and seller, from cash in advance (a bonanza for the seller) to consignment (a bonanza for the buyer).

Terms of Sale

Whatever the form of the agreement between exporter and intermediary, it's vital that the responsibilities of buyer and seller be spelled out. What is, and what is not, included in the price quotation? When does ownership of the goods pass from buyer to seller? Questions like these will come back to haunt the parties if they are not anticipated and settled in the initial agreement.

The first step in building a good agreement is to understand the terms used worldwide in buyer-seller agreements. This starts with a grasp of incoterms.

Incoterms are the internationally accepted standard definitions for terms of sale established by the International Chamber of Commerce.

Prices quoted ex-works (EXW) apply only at the point of origin, and the seller agrees to place the goods at the disposal of the buyer at the specified date or within the fixed period. All other charges are for the account of the buyer.

Free carrier (FCA) is a new incoterm that replaces a variety of FOB terms for all modes of transportation except vessel. FCA (named inland point) applies only at a designated inland shipping point. The seller is responsible for loading goods into the means of transportation; the buyer is responsible for all subsequent expenses. If a port of exportation is named, the costs of transporting the goods to the named port are included in the price.

Free alongside ship (FAS) at a named port of export means that the exporter quotes a price for the goods including charges for delivery of the goods alongside a vessel at the port. The seller handles the cost of unloading and wharfage; loading, ocean transportation, and insurance are left to the buyer.

Free on board (FOB) applies only to vessel shipments. The seller quotes a price covering all expenses up to and including delivery of goods on an overseas vessel provided by or for the buyer.

Under cost and freight (CFR) to a named overseas port of import, the seller quotes a price for the goods, including the cost of transportation to the named port of debarkation. The cost of insurance and the choice of insurer are left to the buyer.

With cost, insurance, and freight (CIF) to a named overseas port of import, the seller quotes a price including insurance, all transportation, and miscellaneous charges to the point of debarkation from the vessel or aircraft. Items that enter into the calculation of the CIF cost are (1) port charges: unloading, wharfage (terminal use) handling, storage, cartage, heavy lift, and demurrage (delaying the carrier or its failure to load or unload on time); (2) documentation charges: certification of invoice, certificate of origin, weight certificate, and consular forms; and (3) other charges, such as fees of the freight forwarder and freight (inland and ocean) insurance premiums (marine, war, credit).

With delivery duty paid (DDP), the seller delivers the goods, with import duties paid, including inland transportation from import point to the buyer's premises. With delivered duty unpaid (DDU), only the destination customs duty and taxes are paid by the consignee.

Ex-works places the maximum obligation on the buyer. Delivered duty paid places the maximum obligation on the seller. Between, there is a continuum of burdens to be allocated to either buyer or seller. The careful determination and clear understanding of terms used and their acceptance by the parties involved are vital if subsequent misunderstandings and disputes are to be avoided.

A discussion of the terms of sale in export might seem like trivia to some marketers, whose minds are occupied with the big, creative picture. However, when a company moves into the international arena, there may be no expertise in the firm on which the marketer can rely. Somebody has to know about these things, or else the most imaginative marketing plan can be badly hurt.

These terms are also powerful marketing tools. The exporter should learn what importers prefer in the particular market, and what the specific transaction requires. An exporter should quote CIF whenever possible, because it clearly shows the buyer the cost to get the product to a port or near a desired location.

An importer, especially an inexperienced one, might be deterred from going ahead by a quote like, for example, "ex-plant Jessup, Maryland," whereas "CIF Kotka" will enable a Finnish importer to handle the remaining costs because they are incurred at home. The responsibility for keeping track of the shipment until it reaches the destination remains with the exporter. Despite its customer orientation, CIF has its risks. The costs can change, sometimes dramatically, between the quote and the actual time of shipment. Freight forwarders are useful in determining costs, preparing quotations, and making sure that unexpected changes do not end up losing money for the exporter. Most exporters do not want to go beyond the CIF quotation because of unknown and uncontrollable factors in the destination country.

The exporter should find a good, reliable freight forwarder and rely on the forwarder not only as a link in the chain but also as a practical consultant who can suggest ways to keep down the export costs. When exporters take advantage of the know-how of freight forwarders and acknowledge that they value the service, they are forming ties to useful allies. True, exporters can set up their own freight forwarding functions on an in-house basis. However, that approach cuts the exporter off from a valuable source of experience and adds to cost. Rates for freight and insurance offered to freight forwarders are usually more economical than those offered to an individual exporter, because the forwarder is making large-volume purchases. So even with the forwarder's markup the exporter saves money. While export sales are still relatively infrequent, the best tactic by far is to use a facilitator.

Terms of Payment

In setting terms of payment, the exporter seeks an optimum arrangement that gives adequate profit and protection to the seller while it gives sufficient benefits to the buyer. The selection of the method of payment will be made within the competitive context. In international marketing especially, terms are a marketing tool.

The exporter considers the following factors in negotiating terms: (1) the amount of payment and the need for protection, (2) terms offered by competitors, (3) practices in the industry, (4) capacity for financing international transactions, and (5) the relative strength from which each of the parties is playing its hand. If the exporter is well established in the market with a unique product and accompanying service, price

BASIC PAYMENT OPTIONS[1]

BUYER'S PERSPECTIVE   SELLER'S PERSPECTIVE

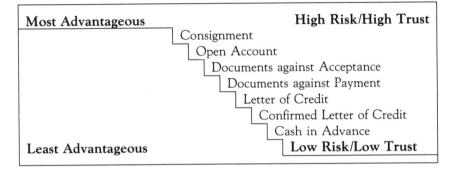

and terms can be made to suit the exporter's desires. (As we've mentioned elsewhere, however, if the exporter wants a smooth and profitable long-term relationship, it's best not to twist the buyer's arm.) If, on the other hand, the exporter is breaking into a new market, pricing and terms should be made attractive enough to be competitive.

The basic methods of payment are steps on a continuum running from maximum attractiveness to the seller to maximum attractiveness to the buyer. The above "stairway of terms" charts the principal options.

Cash in Advance

Cash in advance relieves the exporter of all risk. It is rarely used. If the ability of an importer to pay is highly dubious, the exporter might want cash in advance. A more likely scenario occurs when the order is for a custom-made product, where the exporter's risk is increased.

Letters of Credit

A letter of credit provides great security for the exporter. Letters of credit are among the most-used methods of payment in international transactions. A bank issues an instrument at the request of a buyer. The bank promises to pay a specified amount on presentation of documents stipulated in the letter of credit, usually the bill of lading, consular invoice, and a description of the goods. Letters of credit can be classified along three dimensions.

Irrevocable vs. revocable.   An irrevocable letter of credit cannot be canceled or modified without the consent of the beneficiary (exporter), thus guaranteeing payment.

Confirmed vs. unconfirmed.   Here, confirmation of payment is made by a domestic bank. In the case of a U.S. exporter, a U.S. bank might confirm the letter of credit and thus assume the risk. The single best method of payment for the exporter in most cases is a confirmed, irrevocable letter of credit. Banks sometimes also assume an advisory role without assuming the risk; the underlying assumption is that the bank and its correspondents are better able to assess the credibility of the bank issuing the letter of credit than is the exporter.

Revolving vs. nonrevolving.   Most letters of credit are nonrevolving, that is, valid for one transaction only. When parties have a long-standing relationship, a revolving letter of credit is issued.

The letter of credit has great benefits for the buyer as well as the seller, which accounts for its wide use. The approach substitutes the credit of the bank for the credit of the buyer. In custom-made orders, an irrevocable letter of credit facilitates the deal by enabling the exporter to get financing. The importer does not have to pay until the documents have arrived and have been accepted by the bank, thus providing an additional float.

The major caveat for the exporter is that the exporter has to comply with all the terms of the letter of credit. For example, if the documents specify crates measuring 4 × 4 × 4, and the goods are shipped in crates measuring 4 × 3 × 4, the bank may not honor the letter of credit. If there are changes, the letter of credit can and should be amended.

Letters of credit should be authenticated. Exporters can be victimized by fraudulent letters of credit, especially when they originate in less-developed countries.

We have spent some time on the nature and contents of the letter of credit. This is nitty-gritty detail of a type that decision-making marketing executives usually leave to others lower down in the organization. But it is the kind of detail that, if mishandled, can cause considerable damage to an international marketing venture. So it is important that care be taken about such nuts and bolts as the letter of credit. Responsible marketing managers should check them over, ask pertinent questions, and be assured that there are no booby traps.

The letter of credit is a promise to pay but not a means of payment. Actual payment is accomplished by means of a draft, which is like a personal check in that it is an order by one party to pay another. Most drafts are documentary, meaning that the buyer must get possession of various shipping documents before obtaining the goods involved in the transaction. Clean drafts—orders to pay without any other documents—are mainly used by multinational corporations in dealings with their own subsidiaries and in well-established business relationships.

LETTER OF CREDIT

This credit is subject to the Uniform Customs and Practices for Documentary Credits (1993 Revision) International Chamber of Commerce Publication No 400.

	INTERNATIONAL	CABLE: FSTAMERICA
	DEPARTMENT	TELEX: 80-2354 FSTAMERICA
1st American	740 15TH STREET, N.W.	240427 FSTAM UR
FIRST AMERICAN BANK, N.A.	WASHINGTON, D.C. 20006	197638 1STAM UT
	DATE February 10, 19__	

DOCUMENTARY CREDIT - IRREVOCABLE	──CREDIT NUMBER──	
	of issuing bank	advising bank
──ADVISING BANK──	ID-0000C	
	──APPLICANT──	

──ADVISING BANK──

Japanese Bank, Ltd.
P.O. Box 567
Tokyo, Japan

──APPLICANT──

XYZ Importers, Inc.
1234 Main Street
Anywhere, U.S.A. 54321

──BENEFICIARY──

ABC Exporters, Ltd.
9876 First Street
Anywhere, Japan

──AMOUNT──

Five Hundred Thousand and 00/100 United
States Dollars
(US$500,000.00)

── EXPIRY ──

November 10, 19

Dear Sir(s):
We hereby issue this letter of credit in your favor available by your draft drawn on us at sight

bearing the clause "Drawn under First American Bank, N.A. Letter of Credit, No. ID-0000C
accompanied by the following documents:

1. Commercial Invoice in Triplicate
2. Certificate of Origin
3. Insurance Policy or Certificate
4. Packing List in Duplicate
5. Full Set Clean On Board Ocean Bills of Lading Issued To Order of Fist American Bank, N.A. marked Notify XYZ Importers, Inc. Also to be marked Freight Prepaid.

covering Merchandise per P.O. Number 10203

Shipment from Any Japanese Port	Partial Shipments	Transhipments
to CIF USA Port	Permitted	Prohibited

Special conditions

We hereby engage with drawers and/or bonafide holders that drafts drawn and negotiated in conformity with the terms of this credit will be duly honored on presentation and that drafts accepted within the terms of this credit will be duly honored at maturity. The amount of each draft must be endorsed on the reverse of this credit by the negotiating bank.	[ ] This refers to our cable of today through the advising bank
	[×] This credit is forwarded to the advising bank by airmail
	Advising bank & notification
Yours very truly, First American Bank, N.A.	
_____ Issuing Bank (authorized signature)	Place, date, name and signature of advising bank

FORM NO.1045 REV 3 80

ORIGINAL

Documentary Collection

In documentary collection situations, the seller ships the goods, and the shipping documents and the draft demanding payment are presented to the importer through banks acting as the seller's agent. The draft, also known as the bill of exchange, is either a sight draft or a time draft.

A sight draft is payable on presentation. A time draft allows for a delay of 30, 60, or 90 days. When a time draft is drawn on and accepted by a bank, it can be sold in the short-term money market. With both sight and time drafts, the buyer can effectively extend the period of credit by avoiding receipt of the goods. Thus the buyer has the option of not having to pay until ready, while the seller has already absorbed the expenses of production and shipping. If this sort of situation becomes a problem, the seller might think about resorting to a date draft, which requires payment on a specific date, regardless of when the goods are accepted by the buyer. The date draft is the exception; sight drafts and time drafts are the rule.

Even if a time draft is not sold in the secondary market, the exporter can convert it into cash by discounting, selling the draft at a discount from face value.

Open Account

One frequent manner of doing business in the domestic market is open account (open terms). When an exporter sells on open account, things are made a lot easier for the importer. This is likely to make the deal more attractive to the importer. The downside is risk. No written evidence of the debt exists. The exporter has to put full faith in the assurances of the buyer and of the buyer's references (which ought to be checked out carefully).

Even worse, there is no guarantee of payment. If the debt turns bad, the problems of overseas litigation are considerable. Bad debts are far easier to avoid than to rectify.

The open account arrangement is common in trade between European countries; a European company that asked a company in another country for a letter of credit would be looked at askance. Trade practice does allow for letters of credit in certain industries or when goods are imported from countries more geographically removed, such as the United States, Japan, and Australia. In less-developed countries, importers will usually need proof of debt in applying to the central bank for hard currency. This precludes dealing on an open account basis. Again, open account is used by multinationals in their internal transactions and when there is implicit trust among the parties.

SIGHT DRAFT AND TIME DRAFT

U.S. $20,000.00   December 10,   _19xx_

180 Days Sight of this First of Exchange (Second unpaid)   _Pay to_

the order of _____

_____ Twenty Thousand and ---------------------- 00/100   _Dollars_

"Drawn under Any Bank, N.A. Letter of Credit ID-000C"

Value received and charge the same to account of XYZ Imports, Inc.

To _Any Bank, N.A._

123 15th Street, N.W.

No _Washington, D.C. 20005_   Howard J. Homeyer, President

ABC Textiles, Ltd.

U.S. $20,000.00   December 10,   _19xx_

At Sight of this First of Exchange (Second Unpaid)   _Pay to_

the order of _____

_____ Twenty Thousand and ---------------------- 00/100   _Dollars_

"Drawn under Letter of Credit ID-000C. Issued by Any Bank, N.A."

Value received and charge the same to account of XYZ Imports, Inc.

To _Any Bank, N.A._

123 15th Street, N.W.

No _Washington, D.C. 20005_   Howard J. Homeyer, President

ABC Textiles, Ltd.

Source: First American Bank, Washington, D.C.

Consignment Selling

Consignment selling is the most favorable deal for the importer, who does not have to pay until the goods are actually sold. All of the burden is on the exporter. If the exporter wants entry into a specific market through specific intermediaries, consignment is often the only way to do it. The arrangement requires absolutely clear understanding on the responsibilities of the respective parties (e.g., who is responsible for insurance until the goods have actually been sold).

Adjusting to Currency Fluctuations

What kind of money will the bill be paid in? Exchange-rate movements can louse up a vacation or ruin an international business transaction.

The currency of payment is a key matter to be resolved in the exporting process. Unless currencies are closely linked, as, for example, between Germany and Austria, swings in the rates can harm one or another of the parties.

Ideally, from the point of view of a U.S. exporter, the price will be quoted in U.S. dollars. This way the exporter is protected. The only trouble is, insisting on dollars might lose the sale.

Forward Exchange Market

Exporters who want the business often have to agree to payment in the importer's currency. When invoicing in foreign countries, exporters cannot insulate themselves from the problems of currency movements, but they can at least know how much money they will eventually receive by using the mechanism of the forward exchange market.

In essence, the exporter gets another party to agree to a rate at which it will buy the foreign currency when the importer makes payment. The rate is expressed as either a premium or a discount on the current spot rate. The bank accepts the risk. The exporter pays for accepting the risk. If the exchange rate does not move, or moves in a direction that would have been favorable to the exporter, then the exporter is worse off than it would have been if it had not bought forward. However, using the forward exchange market eliminates one uncertainty from a thicket of uncertainties.

Forward contracts provide a hedge against exchange risks. When the contract is signed, the forward quote (such as the 90-day quote for Germany) is the rate that applies, although no payment is generally made until the settlement date of the contract. The user pays the price of foregoing possible gains in order to be protected against possible losses.

Daily exchange rates are carried in newspapers like the *Wall Street Journal* and the *Financial Times*. However, the marketer has to contact a bank's foreign exchange trader for a firm quote. Forward markets exist for only a few major currencies (e.g., the pound, the franc, the mark).

Options and futures are a relatively new development in the foreign exchange markets. An option gives the holder the right to buy or sell foreign currency at a prespecified price on or up to a specified date. The difference between the currency options market and the forward market is that the transaction on the options market gives the participant the *right* to buy or sell, whereas a transaction on the forward market involves a contractual *obligation* to buy or sell.

Currency Futures Market

The currency futures market is conceptually similar to the forward market: that is, to buy futures on the pound implies an obligation to

Two Air Disasters, Two Cultures, Two Remedies[2]

When two jumbo jets crashed ten days apart in Dallas and in the mountains near Tokyo, Americans and Japanese shared a common bond of grief and shock.

But the two tragedies were followed by sharply differing legal events—and in that difference lies a significant point about varying standards of behavior and corporate responsibility. Lawyers hustled to the scene of the Texas crash. San Francisco attorney Melvin Belli boasted, "I'm not an ambulance chaser—I get there before the ambulance." The lawsuits promised to go on for years.

Several thousand miles away, Japan Airlines President Yasumoto Takagi humbly bowed to families of the victims, vowing to resign once the investigation was complete. Next of kin received "condolence payments" and negotiated settlements with the airline. Traditionally, in Japan, few, if any, lawsuits are filed after such an accident.

Japan's legal system encourages these traditions. Japan has far fewer lawyers per capita than does the United States.

Differences in culture generate differences in approach to compensation for damages—and, inevitably, to the requirements for insurance coverage.

---

buy in the future at a specified price. However, the minimum transaction sizes are considerably smaller on the futures market. Forward quotes apply to transactions of $1 million or more, whereas on the futures market transactions will typically be well below $100,000. This market, therefore, allows relatively small firms to lock in exchange rates and lower their risk.

Managing Financial Risks

After financial risks have been assessed, the marketer must decide whether it is worthwhile to do business in the particular environment. If the decision is to go ahead, the marketer can look for ways to minimize the risk.

Topping the list of risks may be the question of whether the buyer can pay. The marketer will want to do at least as much credit checking and financial analysis as with domestic buyers. However, assessing a foreign buyer is complicated by factors like the following:

1. Credit reports may not be reliable.

2. Audited reports may not be available.

3. Financial reports are often prepared according to a different format.

4. Many governments require that assets be revaluated upward every year, which can distort results.

5. Statements are in local currency.

6. The buyer might have the financial resources in local currency but be precluded from converting to dollars because of exchange controls and other government actions.

The marketer should obtain more than one credit report. It should be determined how each credit agency gets its reports. For example, if it turns out that two credit agencies get their information from the same correspondent agency, the marketer is just paying for the same information twice.

There are a number of useful sources for marketers seeking credit information on foreign buyers. One good source is the *World Traders Data Report* compiled by the U.S. Department of Commerce.

What Happens If the Customer Can't Pay?

No matter how thorough a job the marketer does of checking out the buyer, there is obviously still risk, perhaps considerable risk. If the customer doesn't pay, or doesn't pay the specified amount, rule one is not to panic. It might be a communications problem. When the marketer gets in touch with the customer, the difficulty might turn out to be a misunderstanding or error regarding the shipment. It doesn't hurt to assume that there has been a mistake. This avoids ruffling feathers unnecessarily. The seller can always cast off that assumption if it becomes untenable.

Maybe the customer has financial problems. The marketer has to be ready to reschedule the payment, if this seems like the best course. If the customer disputes the charges, it might be necessary to use a collection agency or to retain an attorney. That is definitely to be avoided if at all possible. One way to avoid it is to build a conflict-resolution mechanism into the agreement. Chapter 2 discusses the use of arbitration, which is a useful tactic, far superior to trying to fight it out in a foreign court.

MAJOR SOURCES OF CREDIT INFORMATION

Source	Response Time	Cost	Comments
1. Dun & Bradstreet	Same day to 50 days, depending on location	$122 to $495	Standard in the industry. Data are often sketchy, because subjects are reluctant to respond to a credit inquiry.
2. World Traders Data Report (U.S.D.O.C.)	Variable; if known name, quick; otherwise, lengthy delays	$100	If prominent name, comprehensive. Tendency to be out of date.
3. Local Credit Agency Report	Long, start from scratch	$100 to $200	Quality varies. International market perspective lacking.
4. Bank Reports	Slow	None	Limited in scope.
5. FCIB–NACM Corporation	Same day to 6 weeks	Part of membership fee ($730)	Network of 18 agencies abroad.

Forfaiting and Factoring

Forfaiting, developed in Europe, has only become widely known in the United States in recent years. In a typical forfait deal, the importer pays the exporter with bills of exchange or promissory notes guaranteed by a leading bank in the importer's country. The exporter can then sell them to a third party at a discount from their face value for immediate cash. The buyer of the notes assumes all of the risks. The discount rate takes into account the buyer's credit worthiness and country, the quality of the guaranteeing bank, and the interest cost over the term of the credit.

The most obvious benefit to the exporter is reduction of risk. A second benefit is simplicity of documentation (because the documents used are well known in the market). The exporter enjoys 100 percent coverage, which official sources such as import-export banks do not provide. In addition, forfaiting, unlike many official financing sources, does not involve content or country restrictions.

The major complaints about forfaiting center on cost and availability. Forfaiting is usually somewhat more expensive than using public sources of trade insurance. More to the point, it is not available where exporters need it most: the high-risk countries.

Factoring houses purchase an exporter's receivables for a discounted price (two to four percent less than face value.) Factors enable the exporter to receive payment for goods while getting out from under the administrative burden of collection. Unlike forfaiting, in which the buyer of the notes takes on all of the risk, the exporter is ultimately liable for repaying the factor in case of a default. Some factors are willing to accept export receivables "without recourse" (meaning they assume the whole risk), but for this they require a large discount.

Check Points

✓ Terms range along a continuum from maximum benefit to buyer to maximum benefit to seller.

✓ Letters of credit may be:

1. Irrevocable or revocable

2. Confirmed or unconfirmed

3. Revolving or nonrevolving

✓ Exporters use the forward exchange market as insurance against currency fluctuations.

✓ It is difficult to get reliable credit information on some foreign businesses.

✓ Government agencies can help by suggesting ways of checking credit.

✓ Forfaiting and factoring are increasing in popularity.

CHAPTER
10

TAPPING INTO PUBLIC FINANCING
Commercial Loans and Lines of Credit

Sales in the international marketplace are often won or lost on the availability of favorable credit terms. Winning companies are able to offer favorable terms because they are backed by favorable financing deals.

An example may be the international consortium that won a major contract from the Turkish government to build a bridge over the Bosporus with a package including a $205 million Japanese loan at 5 percent, at least $130 million in Italian export credits at 2.5 to 7.75 percent, and commercial loans totaling $230 million.

International trade is an extension of national foreign policy. For years, industrialized nations such as France, Italy, and Japan have been assisting private companies with development aid and with export credits at below-market interest rates.

Many companies, especially U.S. companies, lose out in the international marketplace because they cannot match the terms offered by competitors. All too often, these failures could have been avoided if the companies had known about, and taken advantage of, financing available from U.S. and international sources.

In this chapter you'll find out more about how favorable financing can spell international success—and how obtaining it may be easier than you think.

Sources of Financing

International marketers should be ready to assist their foreign customers in obtaining appropriate financing. Export financing terms can significantly affect the final price that buyers pay. Consider, for example, two competitors for a $1 million sale. Exporter A offers a four percent rate over a ten-year payment period, and B offers nine percent for the same term. Over the 10 years, the difference in interest is $220,000. In some cases, buyers will overlook differences in price and quality and award a contract to the supplier that can offer cheaper credit.

Financing assistance is available from the private and the public sectors. The international marketer should assess not only the financing arrangements available in the marketer's home country, but also the resources in other countries. For example, Japan, Taiwan, and South Korea have import financing programs that offer exporters added potential in penetrating these significant markets.

Commercial Banks

Commercial banks worldwide provide trade financing, depending on their relationship with the exporter, the nature of the transaction, the country of the borrower, and the availability of export insurance. This usually means that financing assistance is provided only to first-rate credit risks. Many U.S. exporters encounter major problems in enlisting assistance from U.S. commercial banks. The problem is most serious when the buyer is in a developing country. Many banks see profits from international trade transactions as too small, too risky, and too time-consuming.

Official Trade Finance[1]

Official financing can take the form of either a loan or a guarantee, including credit insurance. In a loan, the government provides funds to finance the sale and charges interest on those funds. The government lender accepts the risk of a possible default. In a guarantee, a private-sector lender provides the funds and sets the interest rate, with the government assuring that it will reimburse the lender if the loan is unpaid.

Working Capital Guarantee Program. The Export-Import Bank of the United States (Eximbank) was created to aid in financing and facilitating exports.

One major impediment to export success for small businesses is lack of capital to build the necessary inventory to fulfill the order. In response

Penetrating the European Market

In 1989, Anadigics, Inc., based in Warren, New Jersey, began to penetrate key foreign markets with its RF, microwave, and high-speed digital integrated circuits for wideband communications applications.

It was imperative that Anadigics acquire more working capital if it was going to participate effectively in this growing market. Specifically, the company needed working capital to support a $5.3 million contract from a European communications firm.

Anadigics applied for a $1.5 million working capital guarantee from Eximbank. Within two months, the company received preliminary approval for the loan guarantee. Anadigics then used the Eximbank preliminary commitment to obtain the working capital necessary to maintain and finance its European contract, as well as to begin a concentrated international expansion effort.

---

to this need, Eximbank created a Working Capital Guarantee Program (WCG). It is the only *pre*-export program offered by Eximbank. All other programs finance exports after shipment.

Under WCG, Eximbank guarantees the lender against default by the exporter. As of this writing, the guarantee is for 90 percent of the loan, with interest up to one percent over the Treasury borrowing rate. The lender must retain ten percent of the risk. Should the exporter default, only the commercial bank exposure is covered. If the foreign buyer defaults, only the exporter's outstanding loan from the commercial bank is covered under the WCG.

For this reason, many exporters secure Eximbank insurance to protect themselves against failure of the foreign buyer to pay the obligation, for either commercial or political reasons.

The WCG may be used for single sales or as a revolving facility. It may also be used for marketing and promotion purposes. However, most of the WCGs approved by Eximbank are for single-sale transactions. The exporter must put up collateral equal to 110 percent of the value of the loan. Eximbank takes a broad interpretation of what constitutes acceptable collateral. It will accept raw materials, fixed assets in certain cases, foreign receivables, etc. Frequently, the personal guarantee of the exporting company's officers is also required.

Eximbank and Working Capital

Semiconductor Test Solutions Inc. (STS) of Santa Clara, California, wanted to sell into the expanding worldwide semiconductor industry. The company had surpassed the legal lending limit of its current financial institution. STS needed to find alternative sources of financing for its export receivables, inventory, and marketing expenses.

STS's financial needs were met with a $2 million loan from Eximbank's Working Capital Loan Guarantee Program, which provides U.S. exporters access to export-related working capital loans from private-sector financial institutions. STS put up export receivables and inventory as collateral for the loan guarantee. The additional $2 million that STS was empowered to borrow enabled the company to finance export receivables and to meet the growing inventory and marketing expenses needed to support its export program.

Medium-term guarantees. Eximbank provides medium-term guarantees for export transactions up to $10 million, with a maximum repayment term not to exceed seven years. Most typically, medium-term guarantees are used by commercial banks that do not want exposure in a certain country or that have reached their internal "exposure limit" in a given country. The Eximbank guarantee overcomes these limitations. The medium-term guarantee provides the lender 100 percent commercial and political risk protection. However, the exporter must provide a two percent counterguarantee for the commercial risk. Under this guarantee, the foreign buyer is required to make a 15 percent cash down payment, so the guarantee covers the financed portion of 85 percent.

Eximbank's fee schedule is determined by country risk and by the repayment terms of the transaction. Rates vary from the highest-rated "A" country to the lowest-rated "E" country. By having a rate schedule based on perceived risk assumption, Eximbank is able to remain open for business longer in more countries, because it is compensated for the risk it is being asked to bear.

Long-term guarantees. For transactions of more than $10 million and repayment periods of eight or more years, Eximbank offers long-term guarantees. The commercial and political risk coverage is 100 percent, and there is no requirement for an exporter to post a two percent commercial risk counterguarantee. The fee structure is the same as under medium-term guarantees.

One major difference in the long-term guarantee is that loans made under the long-term guarantee may be made in foreign currencies acceptable to Eximbank. This enables foreign buyers with access to foreign currency earnings to use this currency to repay loans. A good example of this would be a foreign airline with earnings in Japanese yen. The airline wishes to buy U.S.-made planes but wants to borrow in yen and use its yen earnings to service the debt. An Eximbank long-term guarantee could be used for such a transaction.

Eximbank, by statute, does not compete with commercial banks. It complements and supplements commercial bank support for exports by assuming risks unacceptable to the banks. It is well known that commercial banks rarely provide fixed interest rate loans for any type of commercial transaction. Yet today, in the highly competitive international marketplace, many foreign buyers can demand financial support as a precondition of their purchase of goods from abroad. These foreign buyers often require fixed-rate financing as a condition of the deal.

Medium-term loans. Eximbank offers medium-term loans to commercial banks at a discount from the official OECD rates for the country of the purchaser. The commercial bank then lends to the foreign buyer at the full OECD rate. The maximum amount a bank can borrow from Eximbank under this program and still receive the discount is $10 million.

Long-term loans. For fixed-rate loans above $10 million and repayment periods of eight years or longer, Eximbank lends directly to the foreign buyer. This is because most banks simply do not make this kind of loan for longer than a seven-year period. Often, too, these transactions involve large amounts, in excess of $100 million; commercial banks don't want that much exposure for long periods in one country. So without Eximbank participation, U.S. exporters would be unable to compete successfully.

The table on the next page matches products and services with the customary financing term and the appropriate Eximbank programs. Obviously, the applicability of a particular program depends on the details of the transaction. For more information on selecting an appropriate Eximbank program, call Eximbank's Export Finance Hotline at (800) 424-5201 and request a copy of its "Program Selection Guide."

Any entity—including a U.S. exporter, a U.S. or foreign bank, or a foreign buyer—may apply to the Eximbank for a premium quote,

EXIMBANK PROGRAMS

Exports	Appropriate Programs
Pre-export	
Any product or service when working capital is needed to fill an export order	Working capital loan guarantee
Short term (up to 180 days)	
Consumables	Export credit insurance
Small manufactured items	
Spare parts	
Raw materials	
Services less than 1 year	
Short Term (up to 360 days)	
Consumer durables	Export credit insurance
Bulk agricultural commodities	
Medium term (181 days to 5 years)	
Capital equipment	Export credit insurance
Mining and refining equipment	Intermediary credit
Construction equipment	Financial guarantees
Agricultural equipment	
General aviation aircraft	
Planning/feasibility studies	
Breeding livestock	
Long term (5 years and longer)	
Power plants	Direct loans
LNG and gas processing plants	Financial guarantees
Other major projects	PEFCO

at no cost. Eximbank offers ten standard policies, which fall into two basic categories: multibuyer and single-buyer. Premiums are based on the buyer, the length of the repayment term, the country of importation, the experience of the insured, and the volume of business. The coverage offered may be political only or comprehensive, covering both commercial and political risks. Because of the difficulty in predicting events, you should consider a comprehensive policy. For one thing, devaluation is not covered as a political risk, but, if it causes default, it might be covered as a commercial risk. Eximbank does not offer commercial risk coverage alone.

The policies have U.S. content requirements. Products sold with short-term repayment periods must have at least 50 percent U.S. content, exclusive of markup. Products sold with medium-term repayment periods must be 100 percent U.S. content. No value may be added after shipment from the United States.

Multibuyer policies. These policies cover short- or medium-term sales or a combination of the two. They require that the insured pay premiums on all, or a reasonable spread, of export credit sales. This requirement is put in to prevent the insured from choosing only the riskiest sales to be covered, thus increasing Eximbank's risk.

Typically this kind of policy is used by an exporter for comprehensive coverage on worldwide short-term sales. Eximbank assigns an aggregate policy limit, which is the maximum dollar amount in claims that will be paid in a policy year.

The insured must submit credit information to Eximbank and receive approval for each buyer whose receivables are to be covered. Experienced companies are sometimes granted a discretionary credit limit to relieve them from obtaining pre-approval every time they make new sales. There is a ceiling on the dollar amount of each sale covered under this provision. The firm is required to maintain a credit file on the buyer. A first-loss deductible for commercial bank risks is typical. The minimum premium is usually $500 per year paid up front. The insured pays premiums monthly, based on shipments.

Single-buyer policies. These policies, like multibuyer policies, cover short- or medium-term sales or a combination of both. However, one notable difference is that this type of policy allows exporters to select the sales they want to insure. There is no first-loss deductible. It may cover single or repeated sales to one buyer. Here is an example of an Eximbank medium-term single-buyer policy.

(1) Contract value	$100,000
(2) Cash payment (15%)	15,000
(3) Financed portion (85%)	85,000
(4) Exporter commercial retention (10% of line 3)	8,500
(5) Eximbank commercial risks coverage (90% of line 3)	76,500
(6) Eximbank political risks (100% of line 3)	85,000

A combination of short- and medium-term insurance is available, used mainly to protect U.S. exporters that offer floor plans to overseas dealers and distributors. This option offers protection on parts and accessories sales on terms up to 180 days and capital equipment inventory financing up to 270 days that can be converted to a medium-term receivable of up to three years.

To insure against risks from the date of signing the sales contract instead of from the date of shipment, Eximbank offers comprehensive preshipment coverage. This coverage is necessary when goods are specially manufactured or require a long factory lead time. The exporter is insured against the arbitrary refusal of the buyer to accept products that conform to the contract of sale. There is no extra cost in addition to the normal preshipment coverage, except when greater-than-normal risk exists, as with perishable items.

In addition, Eximbank will insure political risks for goods on consignment, where payment is made only after the goods have been sold. Should an exporter consummate a sale requiring payment in foreign currency rather than U.S. dollars, Eximbank will cover such transactions under all policies. However, coverage is limited to "freely transferrable" currencies.

Eximbank provides several policies for financial institutions, such as banks. These policies cover risks on, for example, letters of credit.

We have been talking about Eximbank policies covering the exporting of products. Today there is a strong and growing demand overseas for services. Eximbank has developed policies to benefit management consultants, engineering service firms, transportation companies, and other firms offering the services of U.S.-based personnel to foreign buyers with payment in U.S. dollars in the United States.

The new-to-export policy is for companies without exporting experience or those with limited export experience. The policy gives added commercial risk protection of 95 percent to further cushion potential losses. To qualify, a company must meet the following criteria: average annual export credit sales of less than $2 million per year during the preceding two years and *no* prior direct coverage under any Eximbank program.

Eximbank is insuring export sales, not financing them, but an Eximbank policy can give a powerful boost to financing because the exporter is able to obtain financing from banks more easily. As a result, the exporter can extend credit on more favorable terms to overseas customers.

Claims under Eximbank policies are often submitted immediately upon default, or there might be a waiting period of up to eight months, depending on the provisions of the policy and the cause of the default. In making the claim, the exporter must submit such corroborating documents as copies of bills of lading, the debt instrument, evidence of attempts to correct, and evidence of compliance with any special conditions imposed by Eximbank. This is just one more reason why exporters must keep all documents in good order until the deal has been completed with total satisfaction or the insurance claim has been paid.

Government Plays Hardball with Soft Loans[2]

In the developing world, where demand for electric power far outstrips supply, the Japanese trading giant Mitsui has become largely unbeatable, owing to Japanese government aid in the form of "soft" loans from its Overseas Economic Cooperation Fund (OECF). One of Mitsui's biggest recent projects, the construction of two 550-megawatt electric generating facilities at Anpara, India, was clinched by a $600 million OECF loan carrying a 2.5 percent annual rate of interest, a 10-year grace period, and a repayment period stretched over 30 years. Virtually all OECF loans to developing countries bar European and U.S. companies from competition, but companies from developing countries are allowed to compete. In the rare instances when they beat out a Japanese competitor, subsequent negotiations often lead to a tieup with a Japanese company.

While economic conditions will affect—in Japan and elsewhere—this kind of government involvement, there is no .question that government-assisted financing is a reality of modern foreign policy.

How To Get Help from Eximbank

The bad news is that the process of applying for help from an Eximbank program is complicated. There are, as you might imagine, a lot of forms, and some of them are quite detailed and complex.

The good news is that businesses don't have to cope with the process on their own. In the 1980s, the U.S. federal government—recognizing that the application process could be formidable—enlisted regional and local banks around the United States as affiliates of Eximbank. Eximbank works with these affiliates and trains their personnel in how to fill out the forms, expedite the process, and get help. At around the same time, Eximbank undertook a major revision of its programs to streamline them and make them more responsive to the needs of business. So, while it is still not exceptionally easy to apply—the company must document its situation and present its case thoroughly—businesses that apply are able to get guidance from nearby banks.

Interested marketers who don't know where to obtain help should get in touch with Eximbank and ask for the names of the affiliates nearest to their own locations. The Department of Commerce should be able to furnish this information as well.

Other Public Sector Sources

Other countries have import-export banks, including the Export-Import Bank of Japan and the Export Development Corporation of Canada. Interested exporters can check out their structures, terms, and rates relating to programs to finance import and exports of goods and services.

Overseas Private Investment Corporation

The Overseas Private Investment Corporation (OPIC) is a federal agency offering guarantees and insurance coverage comparable to those offered by Eximbank. These services are offered to U.S. manufacturers that wish to establish plants in less-developed countries, either by themselves or as a joint venture with local capital. OPIC finances or insures only foreign direct investment through (1) direct loans from $100,000 to $6 million per project with terms of 7–12 years, (2) loan guarantees to U.S. institutional lenders of up to $50 million per project, and (3) political risk insurance against currency inconvertibility, expropriation, takeover, and physical damage resulting from political strife. The importance of this activity is increasing rapidly because foreign direct investment enables firms to remain competitive in the world marketplace. It is difficult to maintain market share without presence as a producer, so trade is more dependent on investment.

Agency for International Development

The Agency for International Development (AID) administers most of the foreign economic assistance programs for the U.S. government. Because many AID agreements require that commodities be purchased from the United States, exporters can use this support mechanism. AID estimates that 70 percent of all U.S. aid comes back in purchases of goods and services from U.S. companies. In the long term, one of the agency's objectives is to increase potential for exports by encouraging follow-up sales.

U.S. Trade Development Program

As a sister agency to AID, the U.S. Trade Development Program (TDP) uses foreign assistance funds to increase U.S. exports by financing the planning of projects and making grants for feasibility studies of development projects.

People in business often chafe with frustration at what seems to be the anti-business mindset of the U.S. federal apparatus. Among the benefits of going global is the fact that the interest of the exporter and the interest of the government coincide. The government wants more U.S. companies to be successful international marketers and is ready to assist those companies with considerable resources.

A phone call to the Department of Commerce can bring detailed information about these programs and how they might be used. Eximbank affiliates are likely to have information about the other public-sector sources. It is amazing and sad that some marketers try to go forth into the international arena without even finding out how the U.S. government can help them.

Other Financing Assistance Sources

In addition to the U.S. entities mentioned above, the international marketer will find it worthwhile to learn about the activities and programs of development banks such as the World Bank, regional development banks (such as the Inter-American Development Bank), and many national development banks. These institutions specialize in financing investment activities. They can help in financing initiatives already decided on as well as providing valuable leads for future business activity.

The World Bank Group provides financing for projects extending over a broad spectrum, including agriculture, industry, transportation, telecommunications, and population planning. Loans are at variable rates, for 15- to 20-year terms. All loans must be guaranteed by the government of the borrowing country. To get business from World Bank projects, international marketers must closely monitor the entire process, from the identification of the project to the approval of the loan.

The Multilateral Investment Guarantee Agency (MIGA) is an affiliate of the World Bank that was set up to encourage the flow of financial resources to its developing member countries. To accomplish this goal, MIGA is authorized to issue guarantees against noncommercial risks in host countries, so that investors can assess the benefits of projects on economic and financial grounds, without being bogged down in the question of political risk.

So, like similar programs, the general thrust of the MIGA approach is to allow businesses to use their strengths and not worry about areas in which they have no expertise. Marketers can and should be able to size up the chances of success or failure of a particular marketing venture, along with the financial risks involved. They are not likely to be able to calculate the odds on a sudden change in government and what that might mean. (Indeed, few career diplomats can do that.) When marketers are protected against political risk, they can focus on the other risks, which, though large, are more understandable.

Private-Sector Export-Credit Insurance

The Private Export Funding Corporation (PEFCO) is a private corporation that makes fixed-rate U.S. dollar loans to foreign importers to finance purchases of goods and services of U.S. manufacture or origin. PEFCO's stockholders consist of more than 50 banks, including most of the major U.S. banks involved in export financing. The stockholder group also includes an investment bank and manufacturers like Boeing, General Electric, and United Technologies.

Eximbank and PEFCO maintain an agreement under which Eximbank guarantees the principal and interest on debt obligations issued by foreign purchasers of U.S. products and services under the PEFCO aegis. PEFCO thereby acquires a portfolio of Eximbank guaranteed paper that can be used as the basis for raising funds in the private market. Because all of its loans are guaranteed, PEFCO does not evaluate credit risks, appraise economic conditions in foreign countries, or review other factors that might affect the collectibility of its loans.

The role of private export credit insurers has increased in the past few years. For example, American International Underwriters, a division of American International Group, offers coverage of commercial credit and political risks similar to that offered by FCIA. Other firms offering limited forms of commercial and political risk coverage include Citicorp International Trade and American Credit Indemnity. Private underwriters offer political risk coverage for confiscation, expropriation, and nationalization risks, coverage similar to that provided by OPIC.

Proponents of the private insurers cite certain benefits. The private firms process applications faster. They can charge lower rates because they can select preferred risks. They have no U.S. content or origin requirements. And they can do business in countries embargoed by the U.S. government.

There are drawbacks. The private insurers require a substantial amount of business as a minimum to be covered. They cater mainly to the large multinationals and are not especially interested in smaller firms. The most important caveat is that the insurance provided by these firms may not be as acceptable as public coverage to the commercial banks that provide the financing.

Check Points

✓ Credit and terms are important marketing tools.

✓ The international marketer's credit policy involves getting paid and avoiding unnecessary risk in the process.

✓ The U.S. government wants international marketing to flourish.

✓ There are various government and private programs to help marketers cope with financial risk.

✓ Support systems exist to give marketers vital information on credit risks and country conditions.

✓ Foreign exchange risk crops up whenever payment is to be in a different currency.

✓ There are resources to support marketers in penetrating higher-risk foreign markets.

✓ Use of the resources described in this chapter will help exporters to offer competitive terms, achieve flexibility and liquidity in administering the foreign receivables, and get protection for the magnified risks of operating abroad.

CHAPTER
11

COUNTERTRADE
The Old Barter System Takes on New Life

Brazil and Mexico have a deal. Brazil sends soybeans, sunflower seeds, and other foodstuffs, along with chemicals and oil-drilling equipment, to Mexico. The payment flowing back to Brazil is not measured in money. It is Mexican oil, 80,000 barrels a day.

This is the modern equivalent of the age-old barter system, which is still carried on in such locations as the Russian town of Blagoveshchensk and the northeast China town of Aihui, which face each other across the border between their two countries. Hundreds of merchants, carrying huge bundles of goods, plod between the two towns every day, bartering in a centuries-old tradition.

Today bartering has taken on a new life and a new name: countertrade. It's not just merchants trudging across borders loaded with bundled goods. It's giant multinationals and much smaller companies from countries around the world.

Among the latecomers to this form of trade are U.S. companies, which have had to learn the ancient and exotic art of barter. Control Data swaps computers for Polish furniture, Hungarian carpet backing, and Russian greeting cards. General Motors trades automobiles for a trainload of strawberries. In exchange for soft-drink concentrate, Pepsi accepts products ranging from sesame seeds to sisal for making rope. Ford swaps cars for sheepskins from Uruguay, potatoes from Spain, toilet seats from Finland, cranes from Norway, and coffee from Colombia.

Countertrade is thriving today because it gives companies and governments everywhere a way of doing business with each other when many of the conventional avenues to trade are blocked.

Many countries are deciding that countertrade transactions are more beneficial to them than transactions based on financial exchange alone. One major reason is that the world debt crisis has made ordinary trade financing risky. Many countries, particularly in the developing world, simply can't get the trade credit or financial assistance necessary to afford desired imports. Heavily indebted countries, faced with the possibility of not being able to afford imports at all, resort to countertrade to maintain at least some trickle of product inflow.

A second reason is encapsulated in the old saw, "You scratch my back and I'll scratch yours." Many countries are newly enamored of the notion of bilateralism. For various reasons, some of them economic, some of them political, they prefer to exchange goods with their major business partners.

Countertrade can be an excellent mechanism for gaining entry into new markets. Say, for example, that a producer believes marketing is not its strong suit in a highly competitive area. A countertrade arrangement gets the firm's goods into the country. The producer hopes the party receiving the goods will serve as a new distributor, opening up new international marketing channels and ultimately expanding the original market.

Why Countertrade Is Spreading

In the 1950s, countertrade and barter were mainly carried out between countries in the Eastern bloc. Their currencies were not acceptable outside these countries because they were not freely convertible. At the same time, the countries lacked sufficient hard currency to buy the Western goods that were crucial for further economic development.

In 1972, countertrade was used by only 15 countries. By 1979 the countertraders numbered 27, and by 1993 there were 108 countries conducting countertrade transactions. A U.S. Department of Commerce list of countries requesting countertrade includes Canada, Germany, Sweden, Italy, Brazil, Australia, and France.

Traditionally, the U.S. government has taken a dim view of countertrading. However, in acknowledgement of the great gap between theory and practice, some U.S. government departments, notably the Department of Commerce, maintain a more supportive view of the practice. Commerce now has its own office of Barter and Countertrade, which provides advice to firms interested in such transactions.

Whatever any particular segment of the government thinks about it, countertrade is a major medium of commerce in the world today, for U.S. firms as well as those of other countries. The world, with a surging flux of new and developing countries and a massive debt crisis, is reverting in many ways to an older way of doing business. Because of a shortage of hard cash, lack of credit, unwillingness to part with precious hard currencies, the riskiness of cash transactions, and balance of payments problems, more and more countries and organizations are using countertrade.

Types of Countertrade

Under the traditional types of barter arrangement, goods and services are swapped directly for goods and services of equal value. Here are some examples:

- **United States/Jamaica.** Chrysler trades 200 pickup trucks for equivalent value in iron ore.

- **United States/Rumania.** General Electric swaps two nuclear steam-generating turbines worth $121 million for equal value in miscellaneous Rumanian goods.

- **China/United States.** China trades 100 Chinese-made tailfins for 737 jetliners for assistance in qualifying personnel and machinery to meet FAA standards. Contracts valued at U.S. $39 million.

- **China/United States.** China supplies silks and cashmeres to Pierre Cardin in return for technical advice.

- **Russia/Ecuador.** Russia sends LADA and NIVA cars and SKM pickup trucks in exchange for bananas.

- **United Kingdom/CIS (Former Soviet states).** Raleigh Bicycle trains CIS scientists in mountain-bike production in return for enough titanium to make 30,000 bike frames per year.

Companies that swap expertise for goods must recognize that they are training future competitors. It could also be that such barter arrangements will serve as the forerunners of continuing associations between firms in different countries. Straightforward barter transactions, quite frequent in the 1950s, are used less often today, because it is too difficult to work out simultaneous swaps of equivalent value.

Counterpurchase or Parallel Barter

Increasingly, participants in countertrade resort to more sophisticated transactions that often include some use of money. One refinement of simple barter is the counterpurchase, or parallel barter, agreement. The parties sign two separate contracts specifying the goods and services to be exchanged. Frequently the exchange is not of equal value; therefore, some cash is involved. Nor need the swap be simultaneous. One sale depends on a reciprocal sale of goods. The two sales are back-to-back.

Buyback

Another common form of countertrade is the buyback. In this form of trade, also called a compensation agreement, one party agrees to provide technology or equipment enabling the other party to produce goods, with which the supplier of the technology or equipment is repaid. Such deals often involve more money, time, and goods than straight barter arrangements. One example is an agreement between Levi Strauss and Hungary. The company transferred the know-how and the Levi's trademark to Hungary. A Hungarian firm began producing Levi's products. Some of the output is sold in Hungary. The rest is marketed throughout Europe by Levi Strauss. Such buyback arrangements are being used with many developing and newly industrialized countries.

Clearing Agreement

One difficulty of the traditional barter deal is immediacy. It's tricky for two parties to be ready to make a complicated trade simultaneously. The clearing agreement reduces the problem by establishing clearing accounts to hold deposits and effect withdrawals for trades. The currencies in the account represent purchasing power. They are not directly withdrawable as cash. As a result, the parties can agree in a single contract to purchase goods or services of a specified value. The account may be out of balance to one side or the other on a transaction-by-transaction basis; however, the agreement provides that over the long term a balance in the account will be restored. Frequently, the goods available for purchase with clearing account funds are tightly stipulated. Funds have been labeled "apple clearing dollars" or "horseradish clearing funds."

Switch-Trading

Sometimes the clearing account is given additional flexibility by permitting switch-trading, in which credits to the account can be sold or transferred to a third party. This provides creative intermediaries with opportunities for dealmaking by identifying clearing account relationships with major imbalances and structuring transactions to reduce those imbalances.

Offset

Offset is another major form of barter arrangement. Offset is found most frequently in the defense-related sector and in sales of large-scale, high-priced items such as aircraft. Here a purchase depends on certain conditions or arrangements, rather than on a counterpurchase of a product or service. Examples of such conditions or arrangements include on-site assembly of the product, coproduction, licensing, subcontracting, and joint ventures. For example, when Saudi Arabia buys military aircraft from a U.S. company, the contracts call for offsetting the cost through related investments. This arrangement, called the "Peace Shield" program, sparked investment in manufacturing plants and other defense-related industries on Saudi soil. Such requirements are often a condition for the award of the contract and are frequently used as the determining factor in contract decisions.

Debt Swaps

Debt swaps are a newly emerging form of countertrade. These swaps are particularly prevalent in deals involving less-developed countries in which both government and the private sector carry large debt burdens. Because the debtors are unable to pay up any time soon, debt holders have increasingly grown amenable to exchange the debt for something else.

Debt for debt. Four types of debt swap are most prevalent. One is the debt-for-debt swap, in which the loan held by one creditor is simply exchanged for a loan held by another one. For example, a U.S. bank may swap Argentine debt with a European bank for Chilean debt. Through this mechanism, debt holders are able to consolidate their outstanding loans and concentrate on particular countries or regions.

Debt for equity. A second form of debt swap is debt for equity. Debt is converted into foreign equity in a domestic firm. The swap therefore serves as the vehicle for direct foreign investment.

Debt for product. And then there are debt-for-product swaps. Usually these transactions require that additional cash payment be made for the product. For example, First Interstate Bank of California concluded an arrangement with Peruvian authorities through which a commitment was made to purchase $3 worth of Peruvian products for every $1 paid by Peru against debt.

Debt for social purposes. The newest emerging form of debt swap is debt for social purposes. For example, the green movement has inspired swaps in which debt is applied to the preservation of nature. These sophisticated variations of countertrade stray from the original form

Debt for Education

Debt-for-education swaps can be used to permit more students to study abroad. Harvard University agreed to sponsor a program that converts Ecuadorian debt into a fund providing scholarships for Ecuadorian students and U.S. students and professors. This is how it works:

1. Harvard purchases $5 million of nonperforming Ecuadorian loans from banks at 15 percent of face value, or $750,000. The banks, faced with the possibility of having to eat the loans altogether, are happy to sell at the heavily discounted rate.

2. Harvard then presents the debt to Fundacion Capacitar, an educational foundation in Ecuador. The foundation sells the debt to the Ecuadorian government in exchange for bonds worth $2.5 million, or 50 percent of the original face value of the debt. The transaction reduces the government's outstanding debt by 50 percent.

3. Fundacion Capacitar then sells the bonds, which are valued in Ecuadorian currency, to local investors.

4. Income from the sale of the bonds is converted back into U.S. dollars, invested in the United States, and used to set up a scholarship fund primarily for Ecuadorian students. Secondarily, the fund finances research grants to American students and professors.

Other U.S. universities are involved in similar agreements with Ecuador.

---

of straight barter. They underscore certain realities about international marketing today.

For one thing, the examples of countertrade drive home the dominant role of government in business deals in so many parts of the world. Within the friendly confines of the U.S. version of free enterprise, the norm is a deal in which goods or services are exchanged for money. Marketers venturing out into the world should rid themselves of the idea that this is the only way to do business. Vast numbers of countries carry such a huge debt load that they will never repay their debts fully in the traditional sense. Nevertheless, these countries and enterprises within them teem with activity and potential. They produce things of value, even if those things are hard to translate into dollars. They are well worth doing business with if the right structure for that business can be built.

Changing Attitudes toward Countertrade

A few years ago, most Western executives shunned countertrade, viewing it as a hindrance to international marketing. Things have changed. Some companies still do not like countertrade transactions, but they must face the fact that continuing refusal to engage in them will lead to the loss of profitable business and important markets to rivals who are willing to engage in countertrade.

To grasp leadership in international business, firms must be proactive, not reactive, using vision and creativity to spot opportunities and come up with innovative ways to seize those opportunities. In the past, corporations would resort to countertrade only if they were compelled to do so by local circumstance (usually the mandate of the foreign government). Now forward-looking companies are using countertrade as a tool to improve market position. Rockwell International Corporation, for example, has set up a trading subsidiary through which the company makes barter deals. As a result, Rockwell's products have a special appeal abroad because of the firm's willingness to engage in countertrade.

Companies that accept countertrade grudgingly—on the basis that, bad as it is, it's better than no sale at all—will find that attitude a drawback. Increasingly, firms are seeking out countertrade opportunities that could lead to an expansion of their markets. These companies go beyond the view that countertrade is a necessary evil, to be adopted only when all else fails, and that one fine day we will all return to a state of cash-for-goods equilibrium. These companies accept countertrade as a legitimate alternative form of transaction. They are using countertrade systematically as a marketing tool that has considerable advantages, including favorable government consideration and a larger measure of pricing flexibility. Willingness to countertrade can enhance the overall attractiveness of a firm to its customers and can lead to some remarkable business-building synergy.

Companies and countries imposing countertrade believe there are more merits to these transactions than purely conserving foreign currency. For example, the countertrade partner can be used as a means of exploring new markets. Long-term countertrade deals can assure markets for future output. This is especially important to producers

Countertrade As the Only Alternative[1]

Competing in the tough worldwide automotive arena, Daimler-Benz has determined to use barter, offset, and countertrade. Company executives acknowledge that, to do business in many countries, they have no choice.

Writing in the *German Tribune* Klaus Dieter Oehler pointed out that for "many developing or threshold countries, commodities are the only means of payment that they can call their own. Daimler-Benz management, lacking any idea of how to sell freighter loads of ore, has joined forces with Metallgesellschaft, which has the know-how. In February 1988, a joint countertrade subsidiary was formed between the two firms. Metallgesellschaft is rated number two world-wide in countertrade and deals mainly in raw materials."

A Daimler-Benz executive commented, "We are now in a position to talk countertrade terms with the government of countries without money. Now we are going on to the offensive."

in industries that are vulnerable if they don't use their full capacity. Security and stability of purchasing and sales arrangements are also desirable features of certain countertrade relationships.

Some countries and companies like counterpurchases because they help guarantee the availability of quality products. There are, for instance, numerous deals in which A transfers technology to B in another country. B uses the technology to make components that are shipped back to A. In this case, A is making sure the technology transfer is carried out as promised, because the transferor will have to take back the product. If the technology is misused, the products will be no good.

As some of our examples point out, countertrade agreements can be set up for the long term. Some companies are unwilling to incur the risks involved. Many economic, political, and technological factors can change over, say, ten years. So for long-term risks, a substantial number of firms still insist on cash (preferably dollar) deals. However, the number of stalwart defenders of strictly non-countertrade deals is decreasing.

One drawback to countertrade is that one partner might not need the goods offered in exchange or might have considerable trouble deriving a profit from them. A firm can waste valuable time trying to find buyers for goods received. Meanwhile, the goods languish in expensive ware-house space.

Bartering Tourism for Technology

The Arab Company for Transistor Radios and Electronic Equipment (Actree) produces NEC television sets in Egypt using Japanese-made components. But there was a problem: Egypt's lack of hard currency to buy the components meant that shipments were often delayed.

As Abla Adel-Latif describes it in the *Journal of World Trade*, "In 1986, NEC proposed a plan to set up a company in Egypt whose profits would provide Actree with badly needed foreign money. Reacting to a desire of the Egyptian government to stimulate the travel industry, NEC chose to set up a business promoting Japanese tourism in Egypt. All profits from the business would be given exclusively to Actree for purchasing the NEC television components."[2]

For NEC, one major benefit of this arrangement is guaranteed sales. Because the NEC tourist business is supplying the currency, the Japanese firm avoids the hangups that took place when Actree ran short of acceptable funds.

There is a second large benefit for NEC; though intangible, it is nevertheless important. By showing an understanding of Egypt's economic problems and contriving a solution that not only gives Egypt a dignified role but also promotes tourism to the country, NEC builds rapport with the Egyptian government that will be of considerable help in generating future business. (Of course, NEC's goodwill could evaporate swiftly in the case of a radical change in the Egyptian government, say, in the direction of Muslim fundamentalism. But in the meantime, NEC is getting paid in hard currency for its products.)

This example underscores the fact that countertrade is flexible in connecting seemingly unrelated industries and national interests. Adept countertraders do what any good marketer does. They identify needs and arrange to meet them for a profit. In countertrading, you deal with a bigger game board and more varied pieces.

Another disadvantage is the complexity of many countertrade deals. There is government involvement and a heavier infusion of the vicissitudes of politics than in cash sales. The restrictions imposed by one party sometimes cause the other party's costs to rise in ways that were not anticipated, thereby eroding the profit. Also, because a transaction is dependent on other transactions, it can be difficult to determine the actual value for accounting and tax purposes.

Preparing for Countertrade

Any organization that wants to participate in international marketing should be prepared to engage in countertrade, or at least to be able to evaluate a countertrade proposition when it is offered.

One way to get into the action is to engage one of the new breed of countertrade intermediaries. International banks have begun to increase their countertrading capabilities. Banks can apply their experience in international trade finance to the financial aspects of countertrade. Banks also have an advantage over trading firms because of their knowledge and expertise in financial risk management. Then, too, a bank will have more information about, and contacts with, the global market.

Independent trading houses specializing in countertrade are springing up all over the world. By being willing to buy unwanted inventories, some intermediaries solve the problem of what to do with the goods received in countertrade transactions. Of course, there is a price; the intermediary buys the goods at a steep discount to assure itself a high profit margin for its services and the risk it incurs.

Some trading houses act as facilitators, guiding the parties through the transaction. Firms that deal with trading houses to receive help in countertrading should be aware that the fees are often quite steep and often increase cumulatively. There may be an initial consulting fee just for talking it over and deciding whether to proceed, a big fee for the consummation of the acquisition, and a subsequent deep discount for the disposal of the acquired products. Also, these trading houses frequently refuse to take countertraded goods on a nonrecourse basis. They insist that the client share some of the risks.

Countertrade intermediaries need not be big. Some of the best are confined to a few principals, maybe even just one or two savvy, experienced people. Smaller firms can compete successfully by finding niches. An entrepreneur who exploits specialized product or geographic knowledge or contacts and develops countertrade transactions that are too small for a multinational firm can conduct trades with little capital while garnering ample profits.

Another new type of intermediary is the countertrade information provider. These firms are exemplified by Batis Ltd. in London and ACECO in France. They provide databases on countertrade products and regulations in various countries. Subscribers can tap into these databases. These intermediaries are also beginning to provide computerized matchmaking services, matching companies in debt to some country's counterpurchase system with companies in credit, or willing to buy counterpurchase items.

Building an In-House Countertrade Capability

Because dealing through intermediaries is so expensive, companies should consider carrying out countertrade transactions in-house. This step should be taken only if the company is in international marketing for the long haul and is willing and able to look at countertrade, not as a last-ditch necessity but rather as a useful way of conducting business abroad.

First, from a strategic corporate perspective, the company should find out how important its products are to the target country. If the goods are highly desirable or necessary, the country is less likely to insist on countertrade or to impose especially stringent requirements. If the goods are deemed luxuries or are not essential to the country's development, then the company may have no choice but to countertrade.

Next comes a study of the countertrade arrangements and regulations in the country. What countertrade percentages are demanded? What alternatives are available? It's important to gather all the facts to strengthen the company's bargaining position and to help to cost out the venture. Sometimes the cost and complexity of countertrade will rule out a transaction. The assessment can't be made without all the facts.

Also, it is vital to incorporate the entire projected cost of countertrade into the pricing scheme (see Chapter 10 on pricing). It's quite difficult to increase the price of goods once a cash-deal price has been quoted and a subsequent countertrade demand is presented.

The company should, at this stage, identify the best countertrade arrangement. Why is this particular arrangement the best? What other forms of transaction might meet the objectives of the other party? To answer these questions, the company needs to determine the goals and objectives of the countertrading parties: import substitution, preservation of hard currency, export promotion, and so on.

The next step is to match the strengths of the firm with current and potential countertrade situations. This requires an assessment of corporate capabilities and resources. What internal resources can be used to fulfill a countertrade contract? What raw materials or components, currently being sourced from suppliers, can be obtained on better terms from the countertrading partner?

The assessment of company capability should not be restricted to existing products. Can the company's distribution capabilities or contacts with other customers and suppliers be of help in carrying out the countertrade transaction?

Sometimes main contractors will demand that their major suppliers participate in disposing of the countertraded goods. Would it be necessary or desirable to involve suppliers or other organizations in the transaction? Is it feasible? What would such a step do to existing and future relationships?

Having thoroughly considered the implications, the company can decide whether to engage in countertrade. The accounting and taxation aspects are key issues. They are quite different from conventional procedures. They can be difficult, and they cost money. The company will have to use the services of accounting or tax professionals who can blaze a path through the tortuous and obscure IRS regulations in this area.

Next, all of the risks of countertrade must be assessed. The goods to be obtained must be specified. The delivery time must be determined. The reliability of the supplier and the quality and consistency of the goods have to be gauged.

What will be the effect of countertrade on future prices? There will be some, and perhaps considerable, impact on the price of the specific goods obtained and on the world market price for that category of goods. For example, a countertrade deal that looks profitable at the time of the agreement might be worth much less months, even years, later when the transaction is actually consummated. A change in world prices can severely affect the profitability.

The length of time involved in countertrade also makes it difficult to determine the value of the transaction, not only for accounting and taxation purposes, but also for measuring the success or failure of the deal with an eye toward shaping future policy. It is difficult to establish just when the transaction took place, when the income was received, whether a profit or loss was incurred, and in what country.

The product to be received in countertrade must be specified in as much as detail as possible. (The other party will probably resist specificity, preferring to leave the matter open.) There will be plenty of give and take in the negotiation, but the company is asking for trouble if it does not specify the goods. For one thing, the company must explore the market for these products. The deal can turn disastrous if the receiving party has to hold a fire sale.

Forecasting the market for the incoming products (if they are to be resold) will take expert analysis. The company no doubt is fully extended in forecasting sales of its own familiar products. Now it must peer into the future possibilities for less familiar goods. Also, it's important to consider the impact of the countertraded products on the sales and products of lines currently marketed by the firm.

Countertrade Terminology

Balance of Payments. The total of receipts (credits) and payments (debits) in transactions between residents of two countries during a given period, usually considered in terms of how much debits exceed credits and vice versa.

Barter. One-time transaction bound under a single contract that specifies the direct exchange of selected goods or services for another of equivalent value.

Blocked Currency. Currency that cannot be freely transferred into convertible currencies and expatriated. Usually synonymous with foreign-owned funds or earnings in countries where government exchange regulations prohibit their expatriation.

Buyback. Agreement whereby the primary supplier accepts as full or partial repayment products derived from the original exported product.

Clearing Agreement. Reciprocal trade arrangement whereby two parties agree to a trade turnover of specified value over one or more years. The value of the products traded under the agreement is denominated in accounting units expressed in major currencies—such as clearing U.S. dollars, clearing Swiss francs, etc. Exporters in each country are paid by designated local banks in domestic currencies.

Counterpurchase (or Parallel Barter). Agreement whereby the primary supplier accepts as full or partial repayment products unrelated to the original exported product.

Countertrade. A generic name for a reciprocal exchange of goods and services, inclusive of licenses, technical documentation, and equipment.

Debt Swap. Transaction by which external debt, usually owed a commercial bank in a developed country, is swapped for other assets. Devalued debt paper of developing countries has been swapped among creditor banks wishing to consolidate their debt portfolios. Developing country debt has also been swapped for products exported from the debtor country, for equity investment in the debtor country, or for the promotion of socially useful goals in the debtor country—i.e., education, charity, nature conservation, and environmental protection.

Hard Currency. Currency that has sound value, is generally acceptable at face value internationally, and is convertible in the open market. Also known as *convertible currency.*

Offsets. Umbrella term for a broad range of industrial and commercial compensation practices required as a condition of purchase in commercial or government-to-government sales of either military or high-cost civilian hardware. Both defense and nonmilitary offsets may result in the creation or expansion of industrial capacity in the importer's country. The offset arrangements may include overseas coproduction, licensed production, subcontractor production, investment, technology transfer, and countertrade initiatives.

Parallel Barter. *See* **Counterpurchase.**

Switch Trading. Trade activities connected with converting bilateral clearing imbalances into convertible currencies through the sale of the clearing imbalance to switch traders at discounted prices. The switch traders then reduce or eliminate the imbalance through import/export transactions that they arrange. The term is also used to denote nonclearing transactions involving triangular or multiple sales of different goods by various brokers. By a series of trades at discounted prices, a primary exporter can convert a soft currency payment or a countertraded product in low demand into hard currency.

Another question: what, if any, repercussions will come from outside sources? Such reactions consist of antidumping actions brought by competitors or reactions from totally unsuspected quarters. For example, McDonnell Douglas probably did not consider it risky to use bartered Yugoslavian ham in the employee cafeteria and as Christmas gifts. The local meatpackers union complained strenuously that McDonnell Douglas was threatening the jobs of its members.

Using all the information it can get, the company can finally estimate the length of the intended relationship and the importance of this relationship for future plans and goals.

Countertrade will continue to increase because of the large number of debtor countries and their lack of hard currency, not to mention their cash flow and balance of payments problems. However, there are factors that will tend to slow the growth of the practice. Third-party firms and countries will protest the concessions given to other firms and countries as unfair. International organizations will not give countertrade much support. Other factors adversely affecting countertrade are the prolifer-ation of government regulations and the inefficiency involved in finding third-party buyers.

Nevertheless, countertrade is a major factor in international com-merce. Marketers should be familiar with how it works; should be willing to consider it, especially as a door-opener; and, if engaged in countertrading, should be equipped to carry it out with patience and skill.

Check Points

✔ Countertrades are transactions in which the sale of goods is linked to other goods rather than money only.

✔ Because of hard-currency shortages, countertrade is on the rise.

✔ Although governments are concerned about countertrade, they tend to give it free rein or even encourage the practice.

✔ International marketers are increasingly using countertrade as a competitive tool.

✔ These transactions require careful planning. For example, how will the acquired goods be disposed of?

✔ New intermediaries are available to facilitate countertrade. They are expensive, but they are often the best bet for companies without experience.

BETTING ON THE WINNERS

Foreign Direct Investment, Joint Ventures, and Management Contracts

Swiss-based Nestlé has more than 400 plants in 60 countries, with nearly 200,000 employees. Only two percent of the company's sales come from Switzerland. About half Nestlé's sales are generated in Europe, around 25 percent in North America, 11 percent each in Asia and Latin America, and the rest comes from Africa and the Pacific Islands.

Nestlé is marketing products for people of many ethnic and cultural backgrounds. Central to the company's strategy is understanding local tastes and customs and nurturing relationships around the world. The firm has developed a strong capability to adapt to local markets.

For example, for years the world's major food products companies have been trying to break into the Japanese breakfast market. Kellogg Co. sold the Japanese the same kind of Corn Flakes and Sugar Pops sold in U.S. supermarkets, but kids ate them mostly as snacks, not as breakfast food. Nestlé took a different tack, developing one cereal that tastes like seaweed, carrots, and zucchini and another that tastes like coconuts and papaya—flavors that appeal to Japanese used to eating fish and rice for breakfast. Nestlé succeeded, gaining substantial penetration into the Japanese market.

Nestlé couldn't carry on this kind of international business by exporting. The company establishes a presence in countries around the world through direct investment. The capacity to innovate products like seaweed breakfast food is one reason for working from *inside* the target

Contesting the European Computer Market

At the outset of the 1990s, the European computer market seemed to many to be up for grabs. Japanese firms rushed into the market. Fujitsu took over International Computers, Britain's flagship mainframe company; Mitsubishi Electric bought PC maker Apricot; NEC Corp. purchased a stake in French computer maker Groupe Bull.

IBM, for one, was not willing to sit back and let this market go to the Japanese by default. IBM teamed up with Siemens to develop high-capacity 64-megabit memory chips. It formed an industrial alliance with Groupe Bull in which IBM supplies Bull with its reduced instruction set computing (RISC) technology, useful in high-powered computer workstations, while Bull provides IBM with opportunities to expand in European markets, as well as multiprocessor computers and a full range of portable and notebook computers made by Bull's U.S. unit, Zenith Data Systems.

In an effort to forge new links, IBM has also become a major source of venture capital for independent suppliers of software and services. In two years, IBM plowed more than $100 million into nearly 200 joint ventures and partnerships, from a German software maker to a Danish supplier of network services.

market, rather than from outside. Another reason is highlighted by the battle for the European computer market.

The Wave of the Future

The wave of the future in international marketing is full participation in the global arena through direct foreign investment or management contracts. Typically, these activities grow out of previous international experience and exposure, usually exporting. The multinationals are, of course, the most visible players. However, any firm that is serious about international business should know the pros and cons of making strategic alliances abroad.

Foreign Direct Investment

Direct investment in firms in foreign countries has been used by companies in some countries for many years. Other areas are relative newcomers to the concept. Two decades ago, for example, there was no comprehensive listing of foreign firms investing in the United States. No one knew which U.S. companies were foreign owned. Data about foreign direct investment in other countries was even sketchier. It did not seem to be a matter of great importance.

The Global Boom in Foreign Investment

Then came the 20-year boom in this activity. In 1967 the total global value of such investment was estimated at $105 billion. By the end of 1992, it had soared to an estimated $1.8 trillion.

The United States had become a major player. In 1992, foreign direct investment by U.S. firms amounted to $421 billion. In the same year, direct investments by foreign firms in the United States totaled approximately $408 billion, up from $6.9 billion in 1960. Obviously, foreign direct investment is a major avenue for foreign market entry and expansion.

Why Is It Happening?

There are several reasons why foreign direct investment is being adopted by more companies—and not just the giants—as an integral part of their global strategies.

Speed.   Business moves with lightening speed these days. Companies must strike fast to seize opportunities. Buying into a foreign firm achieves wider market access much faster than exporting.

Leaping barriers.   Foreign direct investment permits corporations to circumvent barriers to trade. The efficacy of the tool is changing the face of the world. For example, many Canadians are distressed by the enormous amount of U.S. investment in Canada. The U.S. investment moved into Canada, to a great extent, because of the barriers to trade created by the Canadian government to protect domestic industry. The U.S.-Canada Free Trade Arrangement—a prelude to NAFTA—reduced these barriers and led to much more balanced investment growth.

Pleasing consumers.   Not all barriers are government built. Restrictions are imposed by customers through their insistence on domestic goods and services, as a result of nationalistic tendencies or cultural differences. Moreover, local buyers often prefer to buy from local producers because they view them as more reliable. By becoming, in effect, a domestic company, the foreign firm begins to ease these antipathies.

Maintaining profitable relationships.   Let's say a firm has built up a good relationship as a supplier to a manufacturer. The manufacturer opens up an operation abroad and encourages the supplier to follow suit. For example, many Japanese automakers have urged their suppliers in Japan to begin production in the United States to give the new Japanese plants in the United States a flow of familiar products.

The same phenomenon holds true for service firms. For example, advertising agencies often move abroad to service foreign affiliates of their domestic clients. Similarly, engineering firms, insurance companies, and law firms are often invited to provide their services abroad.

Forestalling competition.   Not all moves abroad by a dependent firm are made because the customer or client suggests it. Often suppliers invest abroad out of fear that their customers will find good sources abroad and not only use those suppliers abroad but also begin to import their products or services.

Government incentives.   Governments are under great pressure to provide jobs for their citizens. This mounting pressure will be a dominant world force in years to come. More and more governments are recognizing that foreign direct investment can serve as a major means of increasing employment and income. Some countries—Ireland, for instance—have been promoting government-incentive schemes for foreign direct investment for decades. Increasingly, in the United States, state and local governments are starting investment promotion activities. Cities and provinces of other countries are moving onto this path as well.

So the firm that moves from export to foreign direct investment enjoys the rare and exhilarating experience of being welcomed with open arms and even subsidized, rather than having to fight its way through a thicket of legal obstacles and red tape. The incentives might be tax breaks, the furnishing of land or buildings, loans and loan guarantees, wage subsidies, guaranteed government purchases, special protection from competition, dispensation from local content requirements, and so forth.

Monopolies

Western companies planning to move into Eastern Europe should be aware of some significant differences between the situation there and the ground rules the Western marketers are used to.

One fundamental fact about the countries of the old Soviet bloc was not picked up at first by many Western companies. The *Wall Street*

Journal observed that advisers were now warning Western businesses that because of the legacy of Communist central planning, "many companies for sale in the East are near monopolies. Buying one can give an unprecedented foothold that competitors can't replicate for decades, even if the government eventually lets in rivals."[1]

When Philip Morris bought the Czech state tobacco company Tabak SA, the U.S. company acquired a state-enforced monopoly. More than a year after the sale, the Czech parliament had yet to allow anybody else to make cigarettes in the country. Obviously, Philip Morris was handed a tremendous advantage.

Astute Western corporations have been able to pick up a monopoly along with the rest of the acquisition. In some cases, the monopoly is a specified part of the deal. In 1991, Volkswagen AG bought 31 percent of the Czech auto maker Skoda. The government gave VW tariff protection for four years. The *Wall Street Journal* reported that Skoda "made full use of its protected market, nearly doubling prices in the past three years and spurring anger among the populace."

Ford Motor Company, in establishing a parts factory in Hungary, got at the same time an exemption from Hungary's 18 percent tariff on imported pickup trucks. Competitors and legislators raised an uproar and the exemption was extended to other trucks.

Similar situations are reported in other Eastern European countries. Eventually, such relics of Communism will die out, as competitors and customers revolt against this assault on free market principles. Moreover, the boon of turnkey monopoly is not always as great as it appears at first. Says the *Wall Street Journal:*

> Italy's Ansaldo SpA . . . bought its 51 percent stake in Budapest's Ganz Electric Works, in part, because at the time Ganz had a monopoly. But Ansaldo then was forced to hasten the money-losing Hungarian company's restructuring when the government abruptly ended Ganz's monopoly.[2]

Marketers headed for Eastern Europe should make sure an earlier competitor does not enjoy a monopoly.

Types of Ownership

In making a direct foreign investment, a corporation has a spectrum of choices, ranging from 100 percent ownership to a minority interest. The different levels of ownership lead to varying degrees of flexibility and control for the corporation. A lower level of participation means less control. The trade-off is that the risk is also lessened. The decision on degree of ownership should be a strategic response to corporate objectives. In

Maintaining International Advertising Control[3]

The Crane Company manufactures plumbing fixtures, pumps and valves, and similar equipment used in oil refineries, paper mills, and many other types of installations. The firm sells through design engineers throughout the world: these engineers might not be actual buyers, but they design equipment into the plants they build and so they specify, or at least strongly recommend, the equipment to be used.

In advertising to this important segment of the market, Crane recognizes that the design engineer in São Paolo reads engineering journals published in the United States, Great Britain, Germany, and France as well as Latin America. So Crane wants its advertising in these journals to be consistent. Therefore, the company does not let its foreign subsidiaries conduct their own advertising without clearance from New York headquarters. If Crane were to use joint ventures abroad, the partner would have to yield advertising authority to New York. This could lead to destructive friction. To avoid arguments on advertising policies, Crane insists on full ownership.

practice it will be modified by such realities as government regulation and financial limitations.

Full Ownership

For many firms, the direct foreign investment question is approached in "all or nothing" terms. Sometimes this is a matter of gut feeling that no outside entity should have an influence on corporate decision making. The issue can transcend strategy and policy and reach the rarefied levels of principle. For example, IBM used to maintain a traditional position that relinquishing portions of its ownership abroad would be setting a precedent for shared control with local partners and would cost more than could possibly be gained. (This does not affect IBM's strategic alliances with companies like Siemens and Groupe Bull, which don't involve ownership.)

To make a rational decision, management must evaluate—dispassionately and carefully—the extent to which total control of the foreign entity is important to the international marketing effort. Often, full ownership is desirable but not essential.

When companies insist on full ownership for strategic reasons, it's important to subject these policies to fresh scrutiny. Are they as important now as they have been in the past? Are they sacrosanct or can they be modified? Are there new considerations in a changing world that might outweigh the policy?

In many parts of the world, full ownership is simply not an option, no matter how well it fits company strategy. Governments often limit ownership options through legal restrictions or measures designed to make foreign ownership less attractive—such as profit repatriation limitations. So the international marketer faces the choice of accepting reduced control or losing the chance to operate in the country.

Joint Ventures

Joint ventures are a collaboration of two or more organizations for more than a transitory period. The partners share assets, risks, and profits. The partnership might be equal, or one partner holds the majority ownership.

Advantages of joint ventures.   The two major reasons for entering a joint venture are environmental and commercial. Environmental reasons consist mainly of government pressures. Obviously, circumventing government ownership restrictions is an essentially negative consideration and not by any means a sufficient reason for a joint venture.

The positive area of consideration involves commercial reasons. If a corporation can find a partner with a common goal, and if the international activities are sufficiently independent from each other not to infringe on the autonomy of the individual partner in undesirable ways, joint ventures represent the most viable vehicle for international expansion. Joint ventures work well when pooling resources creates a better outcome for each partner than if they went their separate ways.

Joint ventures also permit better relationships with government, local authorities, and labor unions, particularly if the local partner has clout. The local partner's familiarity with the culture and environment of the country can be a valuable resource for the other partner, providing profitable insights into market conditions and needs and providing early warning of changes. (Many companies overlook this benefit.)

Another advantage of joint ventures is that they can make it possible to minimize the risk of exposing long-term investment capital while at the same time maximizing the leverage on the capital that is invested. This is an important benefit, as economic and political conditions in many countries will continue to be volatile, leading corporations to shorten their investment planning time span.

A Joint Venture Made in Heaven[4]

The Trailmobile Company of Cincinnati, Ohio, produces truck trailers. Trailmobile has formed more than 25 joint ventures abroad. Truck trailers do not move in international markets in significant numbers because transportation costs are high and because tariffs have typically insulated the markets from each other. Therefore, each joint venture functions in its own world. Pricing can be set at the level of the joint venture, because one joint venture cannot invade the market of another.

Each joint venture serves its own local market. Markets differ from each other in significant ways, so the marketing policy decisions are made at the local level. Only a modest part of the total cost of manufacturing the trailer is represented by components bought from Trailmobile. The interdependencies are limited, decision making can be delegated to the level of the joint venture, and conflicts can be minimized.

Disadvantages of joint ventures. Many governments that require joint venture formation are inexperienced in foreign direct investment. They enact laws that are hard to understand and even harder to obey. In some instances, only some portions of the joint venture legislation are made public. Other regulations are communicated "as necessary." This creates the specter of a government official showing up to proclaim that the enterprise is violating a law that it did not know existed.

Major problems can arise in maintaining the relationship. Many domestic partnerships turn out to be unhappy. Little wonder, then, that seven out of ten joint ventures fall short of expectations or are disbanded. Typically, the reasons involve conflicts of interest, problems with disclosure of sensitive information, and disagreements over sharing the profits. Lack of communication before, during, and after the formation of the venture is a major culprit.

Sometimes managers are more interested in launching the venture than in actually running it. During the heady planning phase, when all things seem possible, it's fun. The nitty-gritty of day-to-day execution is another thing entirely.

Post-mortems on failed joint ventures frequently show that the parties gave surprisingly little consideration to some of the possible areas of disagreement, covering a range of business decisions reflecting management

How One CEO Sees Joint Ventures[5]

"The key to our strategy has been to use the joint venture as our entree to a region," said Anthony J. F. O'Reilly, CEO of Heinz, in 1988. "A joint venture offers the twin advantages of familiarity and facilities.

"Obviously, an established business has greater familiarity with the political, economic and social environment of its home market. The pioneering spirit can take an investment only so far. Rather than plant our flag and hope for the best, we believe it far more prudent to seek an experienced and knowledgeable partner in each region we enter. That partner may be a successful private business or it may be the host government.

"The facilities of an existing enterprise offer us an important financial advantage in the early stage of an overseas venture. Because so many developing countries find their foreign currency in short supply, they may have difficulty importing material and equipment to build a plant. That bottleneck may be avoided by finding a factory with equipment and infrastructure in place."

Before Heinz starts courting a prospective partner, the company measures the potential mate against the following criteria. Heinz looks for a company:

- whose field is, or is closely related to, the food business.

- staffed by nationals and not reliant on expatriates.

- of sufficient size to serve as a continental base for expansion within the country and the region.

- that is not heavily dependent on imported raw materials.

- that is not dependent on exports and has ready markets for its products within its own country.

- with good profit potential to justify the risk.

---

style, company culture, strategy, accounting, research and development, and human resources. For example, the joint venture identifies a particular market as a profitable target, only to run afoul of the fact that one of the partners has already developed plans for serving this market, plans that would involve competing against its own joint venture.

This last-mentioned difficulty underscores a curious point. Company A forms a joint venture after dealing with stresses, strains, and conflicting impulses within its own ranks. But Company A assumes that Company B, the partner, is miraculously free from such conflicts.

Profit accumulation and distribution are prime causes of discontent. If one partner supplies the joint venture with a product, that partner will prefer that any profits accrue at its headquarters rather than at the joint venture. Such a position will not be greeted with enthusiasm by the other party. When it comes time to divide the profits, one partner might insist on a high payout of dividends because of financial needs, whereas the other prefers to plow back into a growing operation.

Overcoming the disadvantages.   In any alliance, rule one is to find the right partner. That is emphatically true in forming a joint venture. Partners should have a commonality of orientation and goals and should bring relevant and complementary strengths to the joint venture. The tie-up makes little sense if the expertise of both partners is in the same area, for example, if both have production experience but neither has distribution know-how. Unfortunately, this is not an uncommon misalliance. Company A, being strong in a certain area, appreciates and admires the similar strength of Company B.

The joint venture agreement must be negotiated with great care. As we point out in Chapter 6, ambiguities are time bombs. There is a greater possibility of misunderstanding at the negotiation stage between companies in different countries because of differences in tradition, language, and culture. In these negotiations, extensive provisions must be made for contingencies. Subjects like profit accumulation, distribution, and market orientation must be addressed in sufficient detail to cover all the reasonable possibilities. Otherwise, they might surface as serious bones of contention.

The joint venture agreement, although comparable to a marriage contract, should contain (as good marriage contracts do) the elements of a divorce contract. That means a commonsense acknowledgement that it might not work out and a plan for dissolving the agreement and allocating profits and cost. Finally, joint ventures operate in dynamic business environments and therefore must be able to adjust to changing market conditions. The agreement should provide for changes in the original concept so the venture can grow and flourish.

Strategic Alliances: A Tool for the 21st Century[6]

When Michael Thiemann, vice president for new product development at San Diego–based HNC Inc., went shopping in Japan at the outset

Ya Fang Calling[7]

Does this phrase have a ring to it? "Ya Fang," or Exquisite Fragrance, is the Mandarin name for Avon, which opened its first office in Guangzhou in 1990. In doing so, Avon realized the dream of Western companies since the 19th century: tapping into the world's largest consumer market.

Avon operates a joint venture with the Guangzhou Cosmetics Factory. As the first company—foreign or Chinese—authorized to sell directly to Chinese consumers, it has met with phenomenal success.

At first, Avon executives had reservations, wondering if Chinese women would welcome or even understand the concept of direct sales. But China's Avon ladies, selling a mix of make-up and skin-care products similar to those sold in the West and knocking on doors in just about the same way, chalked up astonishing results. During the first month of sales, the stock for half a year was sold.

This success story highlights several points about international marketing's tumultuous development and hints at some principles that might offer some guidance for the future.

Avon's executives were right to ponder, very carefully, whether the new concept would fly in China. Cultural difference is a powerful and enigmatic factor. International marketers are well advised to approach foreign markets with the utmost attention to the culture and what it might do to the venture. In this case, Avon's research turned up enough positive evidence to justify the risk. But there was still a chance that it might not have panned out.

Another facet of the Avon story is the universality of entrepreneurship. Avon tapped into the entrepreneurial spirit. Avon sales representatives in China are willing to take the risk of working on commission, and risk is the central theme of entrepreneurship.

Money is, after all, a great motivator. Avon's Chinese representatives were able to greatly increase their incomes. In February 1991, the top saleswoman earned more than 30,000 yuan (about $5,600) in commission alone, 200 times the average income of a Chinese worker. After training almost 3,600 representatives, Avon had to slow recruitment because the local factory was unable to keep up with demand.

Another theme sounded by the Ya Fang story is the importance of joint ventures and other forms of advanced international marketing activities and direct investment. Export is still the avenue to profitable business abroad. At the end of the road, however, there is likely to be a closer form of involvement in the market and the society.

---

of the 1990s, he was not looking for electronics or samurai swords. Thiemann wanted partners for his $14 million firm so that HNC could extend its neural-network technology into new markets.

After nine months, Thiemann had secured three agreements. One was with Sumitomo Heavy Industries, a major steelmaker, to apply HNC's image-processing system to apple sorting. A production agreement with another steelmaker served to develop a sophisticated chip. A venture with a large Japanese leasing firm was designed to create a new credit analysis program based on HNC's artificial intelligence capabilities.

HNC is "one example of U.S. firms, mostly high-tech start-ups, seeking partnerships with Japanese companies. Such alliances can secure new markets, profits, and applications without loss of equity."

Many firms are creating nonequity strategic alliances. These can include nonexclusive distribution or licensing deals. Boston-based Avid Technology, a maker of video-editing systems, established a distribution agreement in Japan in 1990. One year later, sales in Japan amounted to almost a fifth of Avid's total sales. PeerLogic, a San Francisco-based firm specializing in advanced communications software, signed a licensing agreement with Chori Joho System Co. PeerLogic's president said, "This is not just a licensing agreement, it's a relationship between our two companies. The better they do with our technology, the better we do."

These stories illustrate two points: strategic alliances don't have to involve a lot of money, and small firms can form strategic alliances for international marketing just as large ones do.

New Kinds of Alliances for a New Era

Given the growth of global competition, the considerable investment required for technological progress, and the resulting high risk of failure, corporations are increasingly seeking to join forces to boost capabilities and spread the risk.

A strategic alliance is more than the traditional customer-vendor relationship but less than a merger or acquisition. These alliances take forms ranging from information cooperation in the market development area to joint ownership of worldwide operations. For example, Texas Instruments made agreements with companies including IBM, Hyundai, Fujitsu, Alcatel, and L. M. Ericsson using such terms as "joint development agreement," "cooperative technical effort," "joint program for development," "alternative sourcing agreement," and "design/exchange agreement for cooperative development and exchange of technical data."

There are plenty of reasons why such agreements are being used by more and more companies of all types. Market development is one common focus. In Japan, Motorola is sharing chip designs and manufacturing facilities with Toshiba to gain greater access to the Japanese market.

Some alliances are aimed at defending home markets. With no orders coming in for nuclear power plants, Bechtel Group teamed up with Germany's Siemens to service existing U.S. plants.

Another focus is spreading the cost and risk inherent in production and development efforts. Texas Instruments teamed up with Hitachi to develop the next generation of memory chips. The costs of developing new jet engines are so vast that they force aerospace companies into collaboration: one such consortium was formed by United Technologies' Pratt & Whitney division, Britain's Rolls Royce, Motoren-und-Turbinen Union from Germany, Fiat of Italy, and Japanese Aero Engines (made up of Ishikawajima Heavy Industries and Kawasaki Heavy Industries).

Some alliances are formed to block and co-opt competitors. For example, Caterpillar formed a heavy-equipment joint venture with Mitsubishi. Its strategic purpose was to strike back at its main rival, Komatsu, in its home market.

These last examples are matings of the behemoths. However, as we have shown, small firms as well as big ones can take advantage of the concept.

By now the joint venture, in all its myriad forms, is a well-tested technique, available to all sizes and varieties of companies.

Government Consortia

One particular form of strategic alliance is characterized by government support or even subsidization. Such pairings are the result of escalating cost combined with a government desire to develop or maintain leadership in a given sector.

To combat the high costs and risks of research and development, research consortia have emerged in the United States, Japan, and Europe. Since 1984, well over 100 consortia have been registered in the United States. In 1984, the United States passed a law allowing domestic and foreign firms to participate in joint basic research efforts free from anti-trust action. These consortia pool their resources to conduct research on such frontiers as artificial intelligence.

The Europeans have at least five mega-projects to develop new technologies, registered under the names EUREKA, ESPRIT, BRITE, RACE, and COMET. The Japanese consortia have worked on producing the world's highest-capacity memory chip and advanced computer technologies. On the manufacturing side, the formation of Airbus Industrie secured European production of commercial jets. The consortium, backed by France's Aerospatiale, Germany's Messerschmitt Bölkow Blohm, British Aerospace, and Spain's Construciones Aeronauticas, has become a formidable global competitor.

Management Contracts

Management contracts are a major form of international participation. The management contract permits the international use of corporate resources and can also be an acceptable response to government owner-ship restrictions.

This is a flexible tool, useful to international marketers in various ways. When full ownership or a joint venture is impossible, a company can still participate in a venture through a management contract. If the situation changes in a country, for whatever reason, and a company must relinquish its share of an enterprise, it can still be a player through use of a management contract.

The company might even use a contract to exert a measure of control over the other entity. Say, for example, that a firm is compelled to relinquish its manufacturing process to a foreign company if it wants to participate in a certain market. However, the product still needs international distribution. A contract serves to keep a strong hold on the operation by ensuring that all the distribution channels remain firmly controlled.

The management contract is not, however, merely a defensive ploy, to be used when other forms of participation are impossible. The contract can, for example, overcome the barrier of lack of expertise. This is particularly true when an outside party has specialized knowledge that is crucial to international marketing success, whether in distribution technology, marketing know-how, or worldwide contacts. Some companies have independent entities that specialize in delivering management services. For example, the French airline UTA manages the operations of Air Zaire by handling the accounting system, setting salary and customer-service levels, and building and running training programs.

Looked at from this point of view, the management contract gives a company a chance to sell its know-how as well as its products or services. A technique or system the company has created for its own use becomes a profit center in international business.

Often a management contract is the critical element in the success of a project. For example, a bank can be persuaded to fund a project because a contract assures expertise in an area the bank previously found deficient. Indeed, financial institutions sometimes even specify such an arrangement as a condition for lending money.

The turnkey operation is a specialized form of management contract permitting a client to acquire a completely operational system, together with the skills investment necessary to allow unassisted maintenance and operation of the system after its completion. The client's life is made simple; there is no need to search for contractors and subcontractors, cope with scheduling conflicts, etc. All the burdens are baled up in one package and shouldered by the other party—for a price.

Benefits of Management Contracts

For the supplier, a management contract is a way of participating in an international venture without risking equity capital. The supplier, in spite of not putting up money, can nevertheless obtain a significant amount of operational control. Clearly, being on the inside represents a strategic advantage in influencing decisions in a number of areas that may be of long-term importance to the enterprise, for example, in design specification or sourcing. Existing know-how, which has been built with significant investment, can be commercialized.

There are human resources benefits. Let's say the company loses a significant amount of domestic business. Instead of laying off experienced people who will be needed again when things pick up, the company can employ these people profitably in fulfilling management contracts at home and abroad.

In countries whose economies are increasingly service-based, service knowledge and comparative advantage should be used internationally. Management contracts permit a firm to do so.

Management contracts have clear benefits for the client. They can provide organizational skills that are not available locally, expertise that is immediately available, and support services that would be difficult to replicate locally. At the same time, the outside involvement is distinctly limited. When a turnkey operation goes on line, for example, the system will be totally owned, controlled, and operated by the customer. Many governments look favorably on management contracts as a useful alternative to foreign direct investment and the resulting loss of control to foreigners.

For both sides, this approach can be an ideal solution. A firm that is excluded from foreign marketing by a lack of expertise can look for a contractual partner to fill the void. Another firm can inventory the skills it has built up over the years, asking, "What have we got that we can sell internationally?" The resulting marriage may not be made in heaven, but each party brings something precious to the other.

Drawbacks of Management Contracts

From the client's perspective, the main drawbacks to consider are the risks of overdependence and the loss of control. For example, if the management contractor maintains all international relationships, little if any expertise can be passed on to the local operation. Instead of a gradual transfer of skills leading to increased independence, the client relies more and more on the performance of the contractor.

For contractors, the major risks to consider are (1) the effects of the loss or termination of a contract and the resulting personnel problems and (2) a bid made without fully calculating actual expenses. Winning a management contract can be a Pyrrhic victory, with expense more than outweighing income.

Check Points

✓ Large and small firms can expand globally through foreign direct investment or management contracts.

✓ Levels of involvement vary from full ownership to joint ventures.

✓ In a joint venture, the partners should complement each other's strengths.

✓ Strategic alliances enable partners to join forces to progress toward technology development and competitiveness.

✓ Management contracts offer a means of international involvement without equity participation.

CHAPTER
13

WHO'S AT THE WHEEL?
Controlling Foreign Operations

The eyes of some marketers glaze over when confronted with the subject of organizational structure. That attitude can be fatal. Even when a company makes a product that would sell profitably in a foreign market, the venture can run into serious trouble if the structure and the *modus operandi* are wrong. If problems are not corrected, the venture can flounder.

The structural challenge posed by international operations involves two issues: What kind of organization provides the best framework for developing worldwide strategies and maintaining flexibility in individual markets and operations? And, how much and what kind of control should be exercised from headquarters? Typically, companies fall into three categories.

1. Those with little or no formal recognition of international activities.

2. International divisions.

3. Global organizations.

Alert companies mix and match, adapting structure to situation. One cardinal sin, however, is to try to handle an increasingly complex international marketing effort with too primitive a structure.

Companies without a Formal International Operation

Obviously, when a company starts to fill a few orders from abroad it does not set up a full-fledged international marketing department.

207

Transactions are handled on a case-by-case basis. Domestic operations takes responsibility for the transactions.

This early period is a learning experience. The company can use the occasional international transaction to start learning about the world. If an unsolicited order comes in from a foreign country, follow up with a letter, fax, or phone call. What's behind the order? How did the customer hear about the product? What are the applications in the foreign country? Follow up again after the customer has received the product. How did the product fare in the new environment? What did people like about it? What did they dislike?

The sketchy information you are likely to receive is by no means a substitute for primary research, which the firm will undertake only when it begins to think seriously about going global. But the facts behind foreign transactions can be interesting and suggestive and might lead to further moves to explore new possibilities.

Management, too, should demonstrate its interest in the unusual event of a foreign sale. It's a chance to get people thinking about new opportunities. Even at this early stage, a good asset to look out for within your company is a manager who seems to have a flair for handling overseas inquiries. Take an inventory of existing skills. Who has visited the country in question? Who knows anything about it? Who speaks the language?

Your first steps beyond taking occasional orders is to explore the waters. You may, as we discussed earlier, choose to bring in the help of an outside export management company. This is a relatively low-risk move. The firm is not adding a department, and the function is being handled by experts. The downside is that the firm doesn't accumulate any experience with international marketing.

Alternatively you can, quite early, set up your own export department, staffing it with one or more seasoned individuals to take full responsibility for international activities. At this phase, the new operation is likely to be a subdepartment of marketing, rather than have equal ranking.

A good first-stage solution for many companies is to work through an outside exporting group but at the same time to set up an embryonic department. The new operation is in a learning mode, becoming familiar with the nuts and bolts of international marketing and getting some firsthand experience in target markets.

There are a number of important advantages in making the new operation a subdepartment of marketing. Although cultural differences have a profound effect on the way marketing is conducted abroad, the fundamentals remain the same. The firm's marketing firepower should be a resource, not a rival, for the fledgling department. The realpolitik of corporate infighting might make a new, independent export operation highly vulnerable in struggles for budget and talent. A brand-new group

THE INTERNATIONAL DIVISION

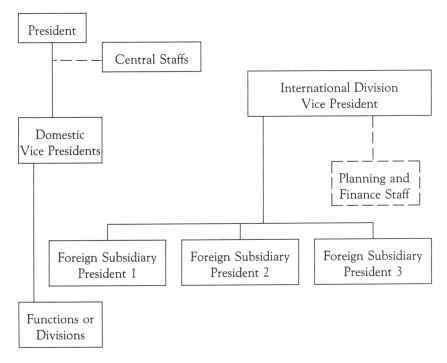

making a small contribution to the bottom line runs the risk of being throttled at birth if it is not given a certain amount of nurturing, protection, and visible sponsorship by top management.

As the firm becomes more involved in foreign markets, the export department structure is likely to become obsolete. The firm, following the dominant trend, is apt to move into joint ventures or direct foreign investment. At this point it is time to establish an international division.

The International Division

The international division centralizes, in one entity (with or without separate incorporation) all the responsibility for international activity. It concentrates international expertise, information channels concerning foreign market opportunities, and authority over international activities. Manufacturing and related functions remain within the domestic divisions. This is the case even when the company begins to manufacture products exclusively designed for sale abroad.

The international division will be competing for production, human resources, research, and a variety of corporate services. The infighting that can easily be harmful to the entire organization. To help keep these dire effects to a minimum, the corporation needs to coordinate between domestic and international operations. One way to achieve good coordination between potentially adversarial divisions is to bring people together, allow them to get to know each other, and to maintain an atmosphere in which they make contributions to each other. Many corporations require and encourage frequent interaction between domestic and international personnel to discuss common challenges in areas such as product planning and strategic planning.

The domestic and international operations will have trouble working together even with the best of intentions. For one thing, they're apt to be set up differently. For example, at Loctite Corporation domestic operations are typically organized along product or functional lines, whereas international divisions are geographically organized. This is why the company makes special efforts to assure maximum coordination.

The international division approach works best in firms with few products that do not vary significantly in terms of their environmental sensitivity, and when international sales and profits are still small compared with those of the domestic divisions. In the evolutionary cycle toward full global participation, the international division represents adolescence. Companies will outgrow their international divisions as their international sales grow in significance, diversity, and complexity. This has been especially true in European multinationals, which have typically outgrown this phase because of the relatively small size of their domestic markets.

Size in itself is not a limitation on the use of the international division structure. Some of the world's largest corporations rely on international divisions, which they feel is the best arrangement for the company's global involvement.

Global Organizations

Successful corporate growth in the 21st century will mean growth into multinational status. This need not imply growth to gargantuan size. It means, rather, that the normal pattern will project the company into involvement with the world. Obviously, there will continue to be firms operating successfully as domestic entities. But we have passed the era when growth was expected to stop at the water's edge.

The organizational evolution of the company will have to keep pace with its marketing evolution, or there will be big trouble. When a firm goes from regional to national, management assumes that its structure must reflect that growth. In the same way, management will have to resist the temptation to stick with a superannuated international division setup too long.

As noted, European firms, with their small domestic territories, are far less likely to succumb to this temptation. N.V. Philips, for example, would never have grown to its present size by relying on the Dutch market or by gearing its structure to Dutch operations.

There are six basic types of global structures.

1. Global product structure.

2. Global area structure.

3. Global functional structure.

4. Global customer structure.

5. Mixed (or hybrid) structure.

6. Matrix structure.

Global Product Structure

Most multinationals have opted for the product structure. This approach gives worldwide responsibility to strategic business units for the marketing of their product lines. Most consumer product firms use some form of product structure, mainly because of the diversity of their product lines. One of the major benefits is improved cost-efficiency through centralized manufacturing facilities. This is crucial in industries in which competitive position is determined by world market share, which in turn is often shaped by the degree to which manufacturing is rationalized.

Consolidation and plant closings almost invariably accompany the switch to a global product structure. When deciding to adopt a global product structure, be prepared to lay off employees (perhaps many), close some operations, and take a lot of heat. A good example is Black & Decker, which, in the mid-1980s, rationalized many of its operations in its worldwide competitive struggle against Makita, the Japanese power-tool manufacturer. Similarly, Goodyear's 1988 reorganization made the company into a single global organization with a complete business team approach for tires and general products.

Cost efficiency, in the face of international competition, is a paramount benefit. Companies find other benefits in the increased ability to balance the functional inputs needed to develop a product and the ability to react quickly to product-related problems in the marketplace. Even smaller brands receive individual attention. Product-specific attention is a key factor in world marketing, because products vary in

TYPICAL STRUCTURES FOR GLOBAL ORGANIZATIONS[1]

THE GLOBAL PRODUCT STRUCTURE

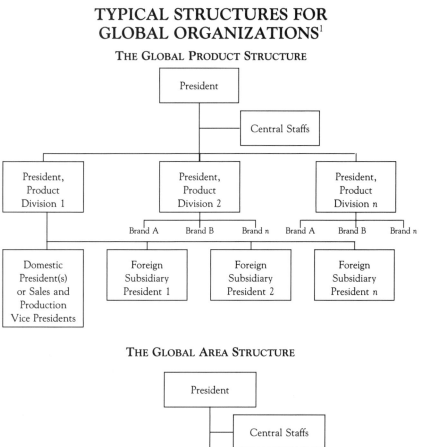

THE GLOBAL AREA STRUCTURE

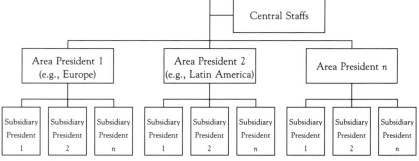

their applications in different markets. Under other structures, variations tend to get lost in the shuffle.

The product structure also has its downside. It fragments international experience within the firm. With all its inadequacies, the international division does constitute a central pool of international experience. Now that pool no longer exists. The product structure assumes that managers will have enough regional experience to make good decisions.

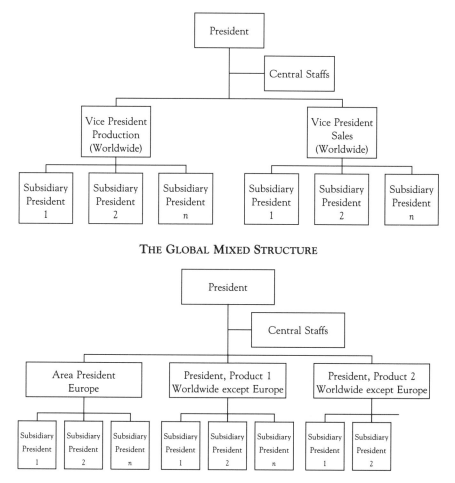

THE GLOBAL FUNCTIONAL STRUCTURE

THE GLOBAL MIXED STRUCTURE

The need to develop a wealth of managers with international know-how is essential. Another is coordination. Globally as well as domestically, when you have a number of product groups operating in the same markets you risk confusing and expensive overlap and duplication of basic tasks. One way to handle this is to use the traditional approach of setting up special staff functions like market research and charging them out to the divisions as needed.

Because product managers are responsible for domestic as well as foreign markets, it's important to give them a global outlook. A gifted and experienced product manager, given the larger responsibility, might offer lip service to competing aggressively in all markets but actually focus only on the larger markets, especially the domestic ones.

THE GLOBAL MATRIX STRUCTURE AT N. V. PHILIPS

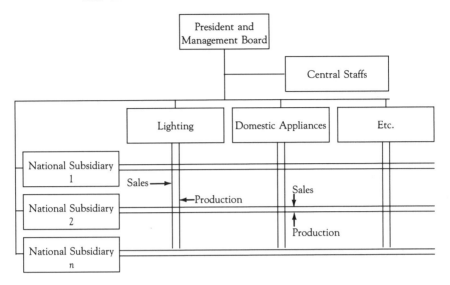

Global Area Structure

Second most common is the area structure, under which the firm is organized on the basis of geographical areas.

The area approach, of all the global approaches, is the one that follows the classic marketing concept most closely, because individual areas and markets are given concentrated attention. It's flexible. If market conditions with respect to product acceptance and operating conditions are likely to vary, the area structure is the right choice.

Companies opting for the area structure typically have relatively narrow product lines with similar uses and end-users. A lot of expertise is needed in adapting the product and its marketing to local market conditions.

As with the product setup, overlap can be a problem. To avoid duplication of effort in product management and in functional areas, staff specialists might be needed. In this case, some staff specialists should be experts in product categories.

Inevitably, area divisions tend to build walls around each other and fail to share essential information. So coordination is a major concern and must be built into the structure.

The global area structure is sometimes the optimum mode of organization. In other cases, it is the stop before the final structural destination. If the company expands in terms of product lines, and if end markets begin to diversify, the area structure becomes inappropriate to current and future needs, especially if continued growth is projected.

Global Functional Structure

This is the simplest structure to administer, because it emphasizes the basic tasks of the firm (e.g., manufacturing, sales, R&D).

This approach works best when products and customers are relatively few and simple. Coordination is typically the key problem, so it is necessary to create staff functions to interact between the functional areas. Otherwise, the company's marketing and regional expertise will not be exploited to the fullest extent.

The process structure is a variation of this approach. It uses processes as a basis for structure. This is common in the energy and mining industries, in which one corporate entity is in charge of exploration worldwide and another handles the actual mining operations.

Global Customer Structure

If the customer groups served by the company are different, a firm might prefer the customer structure. A company whose customer segments are relatively homogenous domestically will find that there is far greater diversity among customers in world markets: consumers versus businesses versus governments. Selling and servicing these various groups requires concentrating specialists in particular divisions. The product is the same, but the buying processes of the various customer groups will differ. The most obvious example is government buying, characterized by bidding, in which price plays a larger role than when businesses are the buyers.

Global Mixed Structure

The answer might be a mixed, or hybrid, organization, combining two or more organizational dimensions. A mixed structure permits the focus to be directed to products, areas, or functions as needed. It might be noted that "as needed" covers matters of tradition and internal politics as well as pure management practice. A corporation might have outgrown the international division stage and encountered ferocious battles among entrenched interests for dominance of the new global structure. Theory and logic dictate one structure; say, a product structure. But powerful opposition cannot be overcome altogether. The optimum resolution might be a mixed organization that responds to the real-world corporate situation and also provides a custom-made structure to maximize the company's strengths and shield its weaknesses in the range of new situations the firm encounters in the world.

The mixed structure is likely to be a stop on the road rather than the end goal. It sometimes occurs in a transition period after a merger or acquisition, when two different structures are being fitted together. It also

IBM Wants It Both Ways, Organizationally[2]

The old ways of thinking don't apply any more in company structure. As IBM thrashed around in the throes of its gargantuan troubles, observers wondered whether the company's new chairman, Louis V. Gerstner, Jr., would choose to continue down the path of centralization or decide to decentralize IBM.

It turned out that Gerstner would try to go down both roads at the same time. As the *Wall Street Journal* reported, he put studies about how to break up the company on the back burner and brushed off "pleas to break up IBM's one-stop-shopping sales force into teams of product specialists."

At the same time, Gerstner set out to encourage IBM's product groups to act as if they were decentralized by behaving more like entrepreneurs and to match up, head to head, against the niche rivals bedevilling the computer giant. "There's a ditch on both sides of the road," Gerstner told shareholders. "We ought to be able to drive down the middle of the road."

One of the new chairman's first major decisions concerned "how to organize IBM's sprawling army of blue-suited salespeople. By geography, as is done now? Or by product, as Microsoft's Bill Gates and numerous others have urged, the better to compete against other one-product companies."

Win or lose, Gerstner's efforts to have it both ways are a manifestation of the new, more fluid approach to organizing companies for the world market.

comes about because of a unique customer group or product line (such as military hardware) that must be handled differently from other customer groups or lines.

Whatever shape the mixed structure finally evolves into, it must evolve into something more coherent, because, in the long term, coordination and control across such structures are difficult, expensive, and inefficient.

Global Matrix Structure

Many multinationals have adopted the matrix structure, because they find it to be the best way to plan, organize, and control interdependent businesses, critical resources, strategies, and geographic regions. Eastman Kodak shifted from a functional organization to a matrix system based on business units. Business is driven by a worldwide business unit (e.g., photographic products or commercial and information systems) and implemented by a geographic unit (e.g., Europe or Latin America). The geographic units, along with their country subsidiaries, serve as the "glue" between autonomous product operations. Matrix managers have product, functional, and resource managers reporting to them. The organization is a constellation of multidisciplinary teams working within a well-defined area. The essence of the matrix approach is team-building and multiple command.

The matrix structure sets up a mechanism for cooperation among country managers, business managers, and functional managers on a worldwide basis, through enhanced communication, control, and attention to balance in the organization. Because communication and control across borders and cultural boundaries are among the most vexing problems for multinationals, the matrix approach is hitting the hot buttons of management thinkers as they envision the shape of the worldwide organization in the 21st century.

The matrices vary according to the number of dimensions needed. For example, Dow Chemical's matrix is three-dimensional, consisting of six geographic areas, three major functions (marketing, manufacturing, and research), and more than 70 products. By providing for cooperation among business managers, functional managers, and strategy managers, the matrix approach helps to slice through enormous organizational complexities.

But matrices are delicate mechanisms. They require sensitive, well-trained middle managers who can cope with the problems of reporting to two bosses—for example, a product line manager and an area manager. Take the case of 3M. Every management unit has some sort of multidimensional reporting relationship, which may cross functional, regional, or operational lines. On a regional basis, group managers in Europe, for example, report *administratively* to a vice president of operations for Europe. *Functionally*, however, they report to group vice presidents at headquarters in Minneapolis–St. Paul.

Many executives and companies have trouble with the concept of the matrix structure. The dual reporting channels are easy causes of conflict. Complex issues are forced into a two-dimensional decision framework. Even minor issues get blown out of proportion and have to be resolved through committee discussion.

No matter what the corporate structure, it's best if managers solve problems among themselves through formal and informal discussion. Here lies a weakness of the matrix approach. The matrix, with its inherent complexity, tends to increase the physical and psychic distances over which disagreements must be resolved. The matrixed

ABB: The Matrix Approach in Action

ABB (Asea Brown Boveri) is a global organization of staggering proportions. From the Zurich headquarters of this $25 billion electrical engineering giant, Swedish, German, and Swiss managers shuffle assets around the globe, keep the books in U.S. dollars, and conduct most of their business in English. However, the ABB companies throughout the world tailor ABB's products (turbines, transformers, high-speed trains, robots, etc.) and methods to local markets so successfully that ABB looks like an established domestic player everywhere it operates.

To a considerable extent, this can be attributed to the company's use of the matrix approach. At the top of the organization sit the CEO and executive committee, responsible for global strategy and performance. The executive committee comprises Swedes, Swiss, Germans, and Americans. Several members of the executive committee are based outside Zurich, and their meetings are held around the world.

Reporting to the executive committee are leaders of the 50 or so business areas (BAs), located worldwide, into which the company's products and services are divided. The BAs are grouped into eight business segments, for which different members of the executive committee are responsible. For example, the "industry" segment, which sells components, systems, and software to automate industrial processes, has five BAs, including metallurgy, drives, and process engineering.

Each BA has a leader responsible for optimizing the business on a global basis. The BA leader devises a global strategy, advocates and defends it, holds installations around the world to cost and quality standards, allocates export markets to each installation, and shares expertise by rotating people across borders, creating mixed-nationality teams to solve problems, and building a culture of trust and communication.

The BA leader for power transformers, who works out of Mannheim, Germany, is responsible for 25 factories in 16 countries. The BA leader for electric metering is based in North Carolina. Country organizations are sometimes assigned as worldwide centers of excellence for a particular product category. For example, ABB Stromberg in Finland for electric drives, a category in which it is recognized as a world leader.

Alongside the BA structure sits a country structure. ABB's operations in the developed world are organized as national enterprises, with presidents, balance sheets, income statements, and career ladders. In Germany, for example, ABB Aktiengesellschaft, ABB's national company, employs 36,000 people and generates annual revenues of more than $4 billion. The managing director of ABB Germany plays a role comparable to that of a traditional German CEO, reporting to a supervisory board whose members include German bank representatives and trade union officials. The company produces financial statements comparable to those turned out by any other German company and participates in the German apprenticeship program.

The BA structure meets the national structure at the level of ABB's member companies. Wherever possible, ABB creates separate companies to do the work of the 50 business areas in different countries. For example, ABB does not merely sell industrial robots in Norway. Norway has an ABB robotics company charged with manufacturing robots, selling to and servicing domestic customers, and exporting to markets allocated by the BA leader.

There are more than 1,100 such local companies around the world. Their presidents report to two bosses: the BA leader, usually located outside the country, and the president of the national company of which the local company is a subsidiary. At this intersection, ABB's "glocal" structure becomes a reality.

---

company might not be able to react fast enough to changing conditions in a world where competition requires quick decisions. To those schooled in the traditional approaches to company organization, the matrix can be jarring. It abounds in the kinds of dual reporting relationships and functional overlaps that the conventional organization chart strives to eliminate.

Having acknowledged its potential weaknesses, however, we should note that the matrix structure is a creative means of building organizations with the fluidity and resourcefulness to balance the factors involved in competing successfully in the global arena. Management education and training will increasingly help executives to work within matrix organizations. This will happen because the matrix structure, with its various combinations and permutations, probably allows a corporation to best meet the challenges of global markets: to be global and local, big and small, to optimize business globally while maximizing performance in every country of operation.

Where the Decisions Are Made

Organization structures themselves do not indicate where the authority for decision making and control rests within the organization.

Firms are typically neither wholly centralized nor wholly decentralized. Functions like finance have always nestled at central headquarters and are, for the most part, likely to continue to do so. However, as companies go global, certain other functions will be decentralized to some extent.

Research and development, especially basic research, is typically centralized in location and decision making. However, the realities of global operation (such as government pressure) have compelled some companies to set up R&D functions on a regional or local basis. The burgeoning communications revolution now makes decentralized R&D practical. When scientists are in constant touch using a worldwide electronic network, the need for them to work under the same roof is considerably reduced. And the challenge of marketing in a variety of selling climates makes it more important that research be sensitive to national and regional differences. Also, spreadout R&D functions are likely to tap a worldwide pool of talent, enhancing the overall strength of the function.

Variations in decision making are fundamentally based on marketing realities, which dictate a blend of centralization and decentralization. For example, Corning Glass's television tube marketing strategy requires global decision making for pricing and local decision making for service and delivery. In other companies, pricing is subject to local decision. The key is flexibility.

The management on the spot knows its market best and can react to changes quickly. A structure that allows maximum flexibility gives full play to local feel for the territory. It also reduces problems of motivation and acceptance. Operations in foreign countries will give half-hearted support to edicts handed down from some Mount Olympus halfway around the globe. When the local decision makers are also the implementers of the strategy, they are much more likely to do the job wholeheartedly.

So decentralization is a prevailing tendency when a firm moves into international marketing. However, single-minded pursuit of decentralization is not the answer. Many multinationals, faced with global competitive threats and opportunities, have adopted global strategy formulation, which by definition requires some degree of centralization.

What has emerged is what we might call coordinated decentralization. This means that overall corporate strategy is provided from headquarters, but subsidiaries are free to implement it within the range established in consultation between headquarters and the subsidiaries.

On the whole, within the typical global organization, subsidiary companies enjoy high degrees of autonomy as long as they meet their profit targets. For example, North American Philips Corporation, a

THE NETWORKED GLOBAL ORGANIZATION[3]

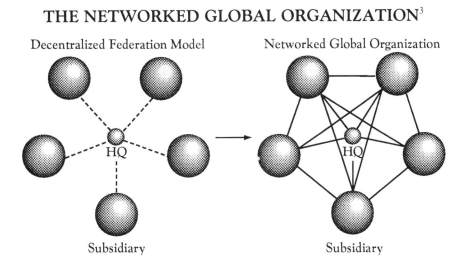

Decentralized Federation Model   Networked Global Organization

Subsidiary   Subsidiary

separate entity of the Dutch N.V. Philips, enjoys independent status in terms of local policy setting and management practice, but it is nevertheless within the parent company's planning and control system.

The firm's country of origin and the political history of the area can have an effect on organizational structure and decision making. For example, Swiss-based Nestlé, with only two percent of its sales in the small domestic market, has traditionally had a highly decentralized organization. European history throughout the 20th century, including two world wars, has often forced subsidiaries of European-based companies to act independently in order to survive.

In a sense, European firms have been forced by geography, demographics, and history to become decentralized. They have an advantage over companies in other areas of the world with a more centralized approach. As a company's stake in the world markets becomes larger, as a greater share of its business and its potential shift abroad, the company's structure must change to reflect the new situation. Some companies will be too slow to adjust to this need.

The "Glocal" Organization

A company that has acknowledged that the future lies in international marketing should not assume that an ideal structure can be found and adopted permanently. The matrix structure is proving to be a viable approach, but it is not the last word. For example, N.V. Philips still has its basic matrix structure, yet major changes have affected internal relations. The basic change has been from a decentralized federation model to a networked global organization.

The word *glocal* has been coined to describe this approach. Companies adopting it have incorporated the following three dimensions into their organizations:

1. The development and communication of a clear corporate vision

2. The effective management of human resources tools to broaden individual perspectives and develop identification with corporate goals

3. The integration of individual thinking and activities into the broader corporate agenda

The first dimension relates to a clear and consistent long-term corporate mission that guides individuals wherever they work in the organization. The second relates to developing global managers who can find opportunities in spite of the cultural differences and challenges and to creating a global perspective among country managers. The third dimension tackles the "not-invented-here" syndrome to co-opt possibly isolated, even adversarial, managers into the corporate agenda.

Here the emphasis is on people: developing managers for the new global arena, giving them a clear mission, and striving for the highest possible degree of cooperation. The challenges managers face in the world arena are numerous and tough. The company's organizational approach can't eliminate those difficulties, but it can ease them. At the very least, the structure should not make things harder for managers.

The network structure reduces the problems of duplication of effort, inefficiency, and resistance to ideas developed elsewhere by giving subsidiaries the latitude, encouragement, and tools to pursue local business development within the framework of the global strategy. Headquarters is encouraged to consider each unit as a source of ideas, skills, capabilities, and knowledge.

And this brings us to a key element of the network approach. The subsidiary is not just an adapter and implementer, it is a contributor and partner in the development and execution of worldwide strategies. Efficient plants can be converted into international production centers, innovative R&D units can become centers of excellence (and thus role models), and effective subsidiary groups can be given a leadership role in developing new strategy for the entire organization.

One tool for implementing this approach is international teams of managers who meet regularly to develop strategy. Although final direction comes from headquarters, the input has included information on local conditions, and the implementation of the strategy is enhanced because local managers were involved from the beginning. This approach works even in cases that, offhand, would seem impossible because of market differences. Both Procter & Gamble and Henkel have successfully introduced pan-European brands for which strategy was developed by European strategy teams consisting of local managers and staff personnel to smooth eventual implementation and to avoid long and disruptive discussions about the fit of a new product to individual markets.

The network approach is not so much structure as it is procedure. It requires a change in management mindset. It is a way of thinking that spreads the decision making and strategic functioning of the firm.

Keeping Close to World Subsidiaries

Country organizations should be treated as a source of supply just as much as a source of demand. Quite often, however, headquarters sees itself as the originator of key decisions and see country organizations as the implementers and adapters of global strategy.

This is an understandable perception. On paper, country organizations and headquarters relationship resembles that between branch offices and the home office. Headquarters calls the shots and the subsidiaries around the world follow. Furthermore, there is a tendency to treat all country organizations as if they were the same.

These two misperceptions are harmful. They add up to a skewed vision that limits use of the firm's resources and deprives country managers of the ability to make key contributions to the success of the international marketing effort.

Global marketing works best when there is a healthy two-way flow of ideas between the outposts and headquarters, and when the managers on the spot are able to influence strategy as well as implement it. The role of each country organization should be tailor-made, depending on the strategic importance of the particular market, the competences of its organization, and the special circumstances of the host country.

We can sort the roles played by country organizations into three categories: strategic leaders, contributors, and implementors.

A strategic leader might be a highly competent international subsidiary located in a strategically critical market. The country organization serves as a partner with headquarters in developing and implementing strategy. Procter & Gamble's Eurobrand teams, which analyze opportunities for greater product and marketing program standardization, are chaired by a brand manager from a "lead country."

A contributor is a country organization with a distinctive competence and a notable track record in, say, product development. Increasingly, country organizations are the source of new products. IBM's breakthrough in superconductivity research (one of the firm's successes during a bad spell) was generated in its Zurich lab. P&G's liquid Tide, made with a fabric-softening compound, was developed in Europe.

This is as it should be. The country organizations are the natural breeders of product ideas. As global marketing grows, there is no reason why as many ideas (or more) should not come from the country organizations as from headquarters.

The critical mass for the international marketing effort is provided by implementors. These country organizations exist in smaller, less-developed countries in which corporate commitment for market development is not as great as in places with a high strategic profile. Most international marketing entities are implementors. Indeed, if those outposts classed as strategic leaders and contributors are not implementors as well, they will not pull their weight. Implementors provide the opportunity to capture and retain economies of scale and scope that are the basis for a global strategy.

There is a phenomenon known as "the black hole" that is a situation that the international marketer has to work out of. The black hole might be, perhaps, a transitional phase that the company went into to emulate or forestall competition. The black hole is a benefit in the short run, but it is not where the marketer wants to be permanently.

For example, in strategically important markets such as the European Community, local presence is considered necessary for maintaining the company's overall global competitiveness and, in some cases, to anticipate competitive moves in other markets. So the black hole can be a kind of strategic gambit. One way to exit the black hole is to enter into strategic alliances. AT&T, which had long restricted itself to the domestic market, needed to go global fast. Some of the alliances it formed were with Philips in telecommunications and Olivetti in computers and office automation. In some cases, firms use their presence in a major market as an observation post to keep up with developments before executing a major thrust for entry.

The relationship between headquarters and the country organization varies. In dealing with strategic leaders and contributors, controls are likely to be loose, with the outpost blazing its own trail and headquarters providing support. With implementors, the reins will be held tighter, with headquarters making sure that strategies are implemented with appropriate tactics and that policy directions are followed.

Loose or tight, it is imperative that country organizations have enough operating independence to meet local needs and to provide motivation to the country manager. Even the smallest and least important of country organizations should have more latitude and provide more input to strategy than, say, a subordinate domestic branch. It is not just an operating entity but also a staff resource, a kind of in-house consulting cadre that feeds back information about what's going on in the country and in neighboring countries and delivers ideas about what will sell and how it can best be sold.

As large and small companies become multinational, the conventional notions of central headquarters and strategy-executing subordinates is blurring. The 21st-century organization will still produce centralized corporate policy, but, to a greater extent, that policy will be formed by ideas constantly circulating around the globe.

Controlling the International Organization

Most organizations find that, no matter what mode of control they use, they must display more administrative flexibility in international management than in domestic operations. Control systems do not always evolve in the way that the company envisions. Shifts can, for example, be triggered by changing political situations, new market conditions, or growth in importance of the international activity. Initially, Hoover's U.S. headquarters had strong control capability. As Hoover's European operation grew, however, the subsidiary assumed an increasing role in overall corporate planning and control.

In designing a control system, a key question is: What is the object of the control? Typically, there are two: output and behavior. Output control involves measuring *what* the subsidiary does, through balance sheets, sales data, product-line growth, performance reviews of personnel, etc. Behavior focuses on *how* the subsidiary does those things.

The classic alternatives are bureaucratic (formalized) control and cultural control. Bureaucratic controls consist of a limited and explicit set of rules and regulations. Cultural controls are much less explicit; they come about as the result of shared beliefs and expectations among the members of the organization.

Bureaucratic (Formalized) Control

The elements of bureaucratic control are (1) an international budget and planning system, (2) the reporting system, and (3) policy manuals. As in the domestic sphere, the international marketing operation must cope with the pervasive dichotomy of time between budgets and plans. Because the international marketing budget is, for accounting purposes, tied to the overall corporate budget, the budgetary period is typically one year. Long-range plans, on the other hand, can extend from two up to ten years.

Functional reports required by multinationals typically include the following:

- Balance sheet

- Profit and loss statement

- Production output

- Market share

- Cash and credit statement

- Inventory levels

- Sales per product

- Performance review of personnel

- Report on local economic and political conditions

The incidence of these reports varies widely. Balance sheets are in far greater use, for example, than performance reviews.

Reports can become boring and burdensome for those who have to fill them out. This antipathy to reporting can become magnified in distant stations. It's important to motivate employees by showing them that their reports make a difference. Preparers of reports should be involved, at least to some extent, in their ultimate use. If this is not feasible, at least headquarters ought to feed back information about the results and consequences of the reports. If there are few (or no) results or consequences, then maybe the report should be revised or scrapped.

North American multinationals rely heavily on manuals for all major functions. In this regard they are far more formalized than their Japanese and European counterparts. The manuals cover functions like personnel policies for recruitment, training, motivation, and dismissal.

Cultural Control

In countries other than the United States, less emphasis is placed on formal controls, which are often viewed as rigid and too quantitative. The emphasis is on corporate values and culture. Evaluations are based on the extent to which an individual or entity fits in.

Personal interaction is central to the process of cultural control. Substantial resources must be spent to train the individual to share the corporate culture, that is, "the way we do things here at the company." At Matsushita, for example, managers spend a substantial portion of their first months in what the company calls "cultural and spiritual training." They study the company credo, the "Seven Spirits of Matsushita," and the philosophy of the founder, Konosuke Matsushita. They then learn how to translate these internalized lessons into daily behavior and operating decisions.

Although this kind of orientation is identified with Japan, many Western companies have similar programs. Philips runs "organization cohesion training" and Unilever has its own special brand of indoctrination.

Employee turnover is the enemy of cultural control. Cultural control depends on the assumption that key people can be infused with the company's viewpoint and approach so thoroughly that they can function effectively and harmoniously without a lot of bureaucratic direction. It takes time and money to select and develop such people. If the manager who is the instrument of cultural control quits and goes to another company, this brand of control loses cost-effectiveness.

Japan has been the bastion of cultural control because of the famous "lifetime employment" offered to personnel. When Japan ran into economic riptides at the beginning of the 1990s, the tradition of lifetime employment began to seem somewhat less unshakable. Nevertheless, Japanese firms, as well as firms from other Pacific Rim countries and from Europe, will continue to keep key people on the payroll for longer periods than typical U.S. companies.

A healthy dose of cultural control can be a big plus in running the international operation. Bureaucratic control is difficult over the boundaries of countries and cultures. One result of this fact of life is likely to be the increased use of employment contracts for people involved in the overseas effort.

A contract with a term of, say, five years is a strong (although not foolproof) assurance that a manager will be around long enough to make it worthwhile to indoctrinate and work with him or her through cultural control. Contracts are also being written to safeguard specific trade secrets (patents, formulas, inventions, strategies, etc.) and also to relate to "the broader area of knowledge that a manager acquires about his company's structure, objectives, plans, philosophy, ways of doing business, and points of vulnerability."[4]

Companies exercise cultural control in their selection of managers for foreign operations. When a U.S. firm gives a top job in Europe to an American who has been with the company for a long time, it is placing its chips on the cultural square. One of the notable advantages of using such people is that they have already internalized the norms and values of the company. What they must do now is to absorb the foreign culture. When foreign nationals are hired, they are assumed to know the territory but must be guided through bureaucratic means: manuals, directives from headquarters, etc.

Another reason for choosing non-nationals is to avoid parochialism. For example, in 1992 only four of 3M's 53 managing directors of overseas subsidiaries were local nationals. The company's experience is that non-nationals tend to run a country operation with a more global view. The non-nationals are not, of course, uniformly American; increasingly, they are foreign nationals from other countries.

In some cases, the company finds it advisable to use headquarters personnel to ensure uniformity in decision making. For instance, for the position of financial officer, Volvo prefers to use a home-country national.

Expatriate managers are used in subsidiaries not only to further uniformity of control, but also to initiate change. When the expatriate corps is small, headquarters can exercise control through other means. Nationals who are hired to run the company's operation in a particular country are put through training programs often held at headquarters.

The indoctrination period should be long enough to get the job done. In many cases it will be longer than domestic training. For instance, a Chinese executive selected to run Loctite's operation in China spent two years at the country's headquarters before taking over in Beijing.

Follow-through is important. No matter how good the indoctrination, the executive in the foreign country can lose touch and motivation through isolation. Visits to subsidiaries by headquarters teams promote a sense of belonging, keep the subsidiary's staff up to date on what's happening in the company, and reinforce the benefits of the indoctrination period.

Mixing Quantitative and Qualitative Controls

Corporations rarely use one pure control mechanism. Both quantitative (bureaucratic) and qualitative (cultural) controls are used. The mix varies from firm to firm. Some companies place high value on detailed performance measures. Others—perhaps newer, less structured organizations—don't rely as much on formal mechanisms.

An optimum control system for foreign subsidiaries is likely to emphasize cultural controls to the extent possible. Bureaucratic measures (manuals, plans, etc.) serve as a skeleton to be fleshed out by training, orientation, and continuing acculturation. The words and numbers on paper or in the memory bank are points of reference, laying out the straightaways and turns of the track. How to run on the track is a matter of cultural control.

Designing the Control System

Controls should be tailor-made to the function and the people involved in it. So most multinationals use a variety of control systems in dealing with their subsidiaries. The basic ingredients of each headquarters/outpost relationship are the same, but the mix changes according to circumstances.

However, controls are not always logical. One researcher has hypothesized that manufacturing subsidiaries are controlled more intensively than sales subsidiaries because production more readily lends itself to centralized direction, and technicians and engineers adhere more firmly to standards and regulations than do salespeople. Parkinson's Law states that work expands to fill the time allotted to it. A variation of the law might say that controls expand to the degree that they can be applied.

In their international operations, U.S.-based multinational corporations emphasize obtaining quantitative data. This allows headquarters to make standardized comparisons against established benchmarks. It also allows for cross-comparisons between different corporate units.

Numbers and percentages in comparative columns are comforting. They convey a feeling of solidity. But this feeling can be deceptive. Even in domestic operations, comparing one unit against another often leads headquarters to draw mistaken inferences and make bad decisions. In the larger international sphere, the risk of comparing apples with oranges is magnified.

In the international environment, new dimensions such as inflation, differing rates of taxation, and exchange-rate fluctuations distort the performance evaluation of any given individual or organizational unit. For the global corporation, measurement of whether a business unit in a particular country is earning a superior return on investment relative to risk might be irrelevant in gauging the contribution an investment makes worldwide or to the long-term results of the firm.

Formalized control systems tend to reward or punish on the basis of performance measurements. This is not always useful, even when the measurements are accurate and the comparisons can be made with reasonable precision. It can be a real drawback when the data used for comparison are not reliable. Standardizing the information received from subsidiaries around the globe can be difficult if the environment fluctuates and requires frequent and major adaptations. Further complicating the issue is the fact that, although quantitative information is collected monthly, or at least quarterly, environmental data might be available only annually or "now and then."

To those at headquarters who design the control system, the familiar quantitative measurements often seem more real than the alien environmental facts about the special circumstances affecting the performance of the subsidiary. Even worse, the subsidiary managers who cite environmental factors are sometimes put down as making excuses. If they can't measure up to the tried-and-true yardsticks, then they are just not cutting it.

Control is essential and the control system must be acceptable to headquarters as well as to the organization and individuals abroad. Above all, the system must provide data that are relevant to the task. Familiarity should not be a paramount criterion in judging a control element. The fact that it has been around a while doesn't mean it should be used perpetually in all circumstances. If anything, controls that have

Control Characteristics of Global Marketers

	Dominant Organizational Concept	Planning and Control
American Cyanamid Company (U.S.)	Product divisions with global responsibility	Heavy reliance on strategic planning under guidance of Corporate Planning and Development Department; plans prepared by designated business units; accompanied by annual profit plan; investment priority matrix to facilitate allocation of funds
Ciba-Geigy Limited (Switzerland)	Product divisions with global responsibility, but gradual strengthening of key regional organizations	Moderate reliance on strategic planning by global product divisions; gradual build-up of the role of key regional companies planning; operational plans and capital budgets by country organizations, with product divisions playing the more active role
Dow Chemical Company (U.S.)	Decentralized into five regional companies; central coordination through World Headquarters Group	Coordination of geographic regions through World Headquarters Group, particularly the Corporate Product Department; strategic planning at the corporate level on a product basis and in the operating units on a regional basis; operational plans and capital budgets by geographic region; control function at the corporate level

	Dominant Organizational Concept	Planning and Control
General Electric Company (U.S.)	Product-oriented strategic business units worldwide	Heavy reliance on strategic planning under guidance of Corporate Planning and Development Department; plans prepared by designated SBUs; investment priority matrix to facilitate allocation of funds
Imperial Chemical Industries Limited (U.K.)	Product divisions with global responsibility, but gradual strengthening of regional organizations	Coordination of planning through Central Planning Department; strategic planning and operational planning at the divisional and regional levels; tight financial reporting and control by headquarters
Nestlé S.A. (Switzerland)	Decentralized regional and country organizations	Increasing emphasis on strategic planning, with formation of Central Planning and Information Services Department; annual plans (budgets) by each major company; tight financial reporting and control by headquarters
N. V. Philips (The Netherlands)	Product divisions with global responsibility, but gradual strengthening of geographic organizations; U.S. company financially and legally separate from parent	Moderate to heavy reliance on strategic planning by planning units in product divisions, selected national organizations, and Central Planning Department; operational plans by division and national organizations, with initiative from the former; monthly review of performance

	Dominant Organizational Concept	Planning and Control
Rhône-Poulenc S.A. (France)	Product divisions with global responsibility, but major country organizations retain special status	Moderate reliance on strategic planning by Central Strategy and Planning Department; in addition, strategic planning at the operational level, primarily by product divisions; operational plans and capital budgets by divisions and country organizations; monthly review of performance
Solvay & Cie S.A. (Belgium)	Product divisions with global responsibility, but national and subsidiary organizations allowed to exercise a reasonable degree of autonomy	Increasing emphasis on strategic planning, indicated by formation of Central Planning Department; operational plans and capital budget by country organizations

been around so long that they are taken for granted should be rigorously reexamined.

Nor is uniformity a reliable guide. Perhaps it's overly harsh to quote Emerson's observation that "A foolish consistency is the hobgoblin of little minds," but consistency becomes a harmful luxury when it is achieved at the expense of effective control. And in international marketing, the effectiveness of the control system can be sabotaged by excessive consistency.

Trade-offs are the key. In designing a control system, management must balance the costs of establishing and maintaining the system with benefits to be gained. There are substantial costs associated with cultural controls. Personal interaction, use of expatriates, and training programs are all quite expensive. They are so expensive and the risks— such as turnover of key employees—are so high, that the company's top management often simply rejects the idea and sticks with the more familiar bureaucratic approach.

But the cost of a program that doesn't work must also be considered. The expenses of a cultural control system are justified by the creation of a worldwide information system as well as an improved control system. If controls are erroneous or too time-consuming, they can slow or misguide the strategy implementation process and thus the overall capability of the firm.

We are at a stage in which the competition for international markets is a race, something like the great Oklahoma land rush. Competitors are vying to stake and hold their claims. A control system that impedes progress is worse than just an administrative problem. It can lead to losing opportunities that can never be regained and to increasing threats from competitive forces.

In addition, time spent on reporting takes away from other tasks. The people staffing the foreign outposts of the company have their hands full. When they spend too much time on irksome controls, especially when they don't believe in those controls, their jobs are made harder.

The impact of the environment must be taken into account in designing controls. First, the system should measure only dimensions over which the organization or the unit has control. Rewards or sanctions might make sense at headquarters because they relate to overall corporate performance, but they are pointless if no influence can be exerted over the dimension measured.

Control systems should harmonize with local regulations and customs. This must not be carried too far. In some cases, corporate controls have to take precedence over local customs; for example, when a subsidiary operates in markets where unauthorized facilitating payments are a common business practice. To adjust the reporting system to officially countenance such activities would be folly indeed.

When a company goes global, it does well to design its control mechanism from scratch, rather than simply to extend what already exists to the subsidiaries abroad.

It's Tough to Keep a Global Grip

It's always difficult to build and run a control system that generates the kind of information needed for good planning and decision making while allowing latitude for initiative and creativity. When the company goes international, the job is much harder. With an increase in local (government) demands for a share in the control of businesses, controls become even more cumbersome and tedious, especially if the multinational company is a minority partner. Even in a merger, such as the one between ASEA and Brown Boveri, or in a new entity formed by two companies, such as when Toyota and GM formed NUMMI, the backgrounds of the partners might be sufficiently different to cause problems in terms of controls. The table on pages 230–32 provides an overview of the key organizational and control approaches used by leading corporations around the world.

Controls Have Consequences

One nagging problem facing atomic physicists is that, in delicate experiments, the use of measurements affects the outcome of the experiment. So they strive to devise ways to find out what is going on without interfering in what is going on.

Corporations face a similar problem in controlling foreign operations. Headquarters needs information. Headquarters must exert some control, especially over money. But the information must not be gathered, or the control exerted, in ways that hurt performance. The danger of this happening with overseas subsidiaries is greater than with domestic operations, for at least two reasons. The foreign subsidiary works in an environment that is not fully understood at headquarters. And the negative effect on the outpost often festers undetected because of its remoteness from the center of power.

Check Points

✔ Companies of all sizes and types are becoming multinationals and must adopt appropriate controls.

✔ The three categories of control structure are the following:

1. Little formal recognition of foreign operations

2. International division

3. Global organization

✔ The fledgling foreign operation must be fostered and protected while it is weak and vulnerable.

✔ The six basic modes of global structure are the following:

1. Product

2. Area

3. Function

4. Customer

5. Mixed

6. Matrix

✔ The matrix structure, a new approach, entails complexity and difficulty but can provide the necessary strength and flexibility.

✔ Whatever the structure, the tendency is toward decentralization.

✔ Country organizations should be given wide latitude.

✔ The four types of country organization are the following:

1. Strategic leader

2. Contributor

3. Implementor

4. Black hole

✔ The Japanese emphasis on cultural rather than bureaucratic control style has proven itself in world competition.

GETTING THE WORD OUT

Global Promotional Strategies, Policies, and Ploys

There is no single right way to win customers in foreign markets. Qantas abandoned its symbol, the koala bear, in late 1991 for a more sophisticated image in its first global campaign. The $35 million campaign ran on television in the United States, Japan, New Zealand, Singapore, Hong Kong, and Thailand and in print in 25 countries. It carried the tag line "The Spirit of Australia." Two of the five TV spots featured Australian scenery; the others focused on quality and service, aircraft maintenance, and business-class facilities. In the mid-1980s, 70 percent of Qantas passengers were from Australia; five years later that had dwindled to 30 percent. Cute as the koala is, Qantas and its agency decided that business travelers needed other persuaders.

Gillette opted for a global advertising campaign to introduce its Sensor Shaver simultaneously in 19 countries throughout North America and Europe. Every commercial in every country used the theme, "Gillette, the best a man can get," accompanied by images of strong, energetic men and a whisker-clipping diagram. Commercials underwent changes to fit local circumstances, some of them quite subtle. For instance, to get the theme across in France, the phrase *la perfection au masculin* was used. Roughly translated, this means "perfection, male-style." The rather cumbersome locution was necessary because the word *perfection* in French takes the feminine article *la*, which, used by itself, would belie the macho theme. Language is not only a barrier; it is sometimes a trap.

237

Nike created a worldwide advertising program at corporate headquarters, tailored to each overseas market. The baseball and football player Bo Jackson featured in the commercials was seen playing other games, like tennis and basketball, while wearing Nike shoes. A recognizable player from each sport exclaimed that "Bo knows" the sport. Overseas, the campaign teamed Jackson up with well-known foreign athletes, including cricket celebrity Ian Botham and soccer star Ian Rush.

Reebok chose a strategy opposite to that of its rival, Nike, in creating different, localized commercials for many country markets, sometimes using different advertising themes. For the most part, Reebok's ads featured actors and athletes famous in each country, promoting the company's shoes in campaigns devised locally. A typical U.K. advertisement shows a British athlete praising the performance and reliability of Reebok's tennis or running shoes. Some country operations chose to use Reebok's U.S. campaign. For example, a TV commercial featuring pop singer Paula Abdul singing about "Reebok life-style" ran in Japan and other Far Eastern markets.

Hewlett-Packard (HP) is different from most high-tech firms in that it does not formally centralize advertising strategy or implementation. Most high-tech firms centralize advertising because they assume that professionals all over the world speak the same scientific language, and the firms want the message to be consistent. HP delegates most product-related advertising decisions to its overseas affiliates. However, when devising local advertising campaigns, business units are constrained by companywide identity and design standards, as well as by their budgets, which are approved at headquarters. HP encourages general managers to be guided by local market characteristics, business trends, and cultural preferences in planning their advertising programs. The resulting advertisements for HP products in other countries usually bear little resemblance to those created in the United States, except when simultaneous worldwide campaigns are underway.

So some companies keep a tight grip on the promotional reins at headquarters, and others allow more freedom. However, all must be wary of language and cultural differences, and all must base strategic decisions on an intimate knowledge of the environments in which their promotions will be received. Effective promotional principles still apply, but sometimes they pass through the looking glass.

Basic Marketing with an International Flavor

The basic principles of good marketing apply anywhere in the world. However, in international marketing these principles undergo changes.

How well marketers handle those changes can spell victory or defeat in the global arena.

The Target Audience

Planning any promotional campaign begins with the target audience. Global marketers face multiple audiences. They have to look beyond customers. It is necessary to communicate the message to any or all of the following publics: suppliers, intermediaries, government, the local community, bankers and creditors, media organizations, and shareholders. Each can be reached with an appropriate set of promotional tools.

Take, for example, the public relations tools that fall under the heading of "special events." Exxon sponsored an exhibition of Colombian art in the United States. The acclaim garnered by the show led the Colombian government to award Exxon its highest decoration. This helped Exxon to secure its market position as well as to create a favorable public image throughout South America.

Multiple audiences. Some campaigns are targeted at multiple audiences. For example, British Airways' "Manhattan Landing" campaign (in which Manhattan Island takes to the air and lands in London) was directed not only at international business travelers but also at employees, the travel industry, and potential stockholders (the campaign coincided with the privatization of the airline).

If a campaign can be targeted at multiple audiences, its cost-effectiveness grows. So many marketers use research to seek audience similarities. Grey Advertising checks for commonalities in variables such as economic expectations, demographics, income, and education. Consumer needs and wants are scanned for common features. The sidebar on the next page illustrates an example of how a medium signals an important commonality.

Commonality: worthwhile but risky. The search for commonality often runs into snags. Tang, marketed in the United States as an orange juice substitute, was repositioned in France as a refreshment drink, because the French rarely drink orange juice at breakfast. In the Philippines, Tang could be marketed as a premium drink, whereas in Brazil it was a low-priced item.

Audience similarity is more readily found in business markets than in consumer markets; in either case, it is well worth pursuing. However, marketers must guard against the tendency to find commonalities where they don't really exist, and to stick too long with an approach based on market similarity when it is not working.

Reaching the Elusive Youth Market

MTV has emerged as a significant global force, with more than 110 million households in 37 countries subscribing to its services. The reason for MTV's success and scope is that it leaps political and cultural boundaries to offer programming that reflects the tastes and life-styles of young people.

According to *Music Week*, Britain's leading music trade paper, MTV is "the best bet to succeed as a pan-European thematic channel, with its aim to be in every household in Europe by the mid-1990s."[1] Since its viewers are largely from the elusive but much-sought-after 16–34 age group, MTV has become an entree to the youth market for world marketers like Wrangler, Wrigley's, Braun, Britvic, Pepsi, Pentax, and many others.

MTV USA runs 24 hours a day on cable in (as of 1991) 56 million U.S. homes. MTV Europe reaches 26 countries, 24 hours a day. MTV Japan reaches 18 million homes in the Greater Tokyo area. MTV Australia, a joint venture between Viacom International and the Nine Network, reaches more than 8 million homes in Australia. MTV Internacional is a one-hour weekly Spanish-language show featuring a mix of Spanish- and English-language videos, interviews, entertainment news, and on-location specials, broadcast in the United States and various Latin American countries. MTV Brazil was launched in 1990 following a licensing agreement with the Abril Group, Brazil's leading magazine publisher. It runs on stations in Rio and São Paulo.

Campaign objectives. Nothing is more vital to the planning of international promotional campaigns than the establishment of clearly defined, measurable objectives. These objectives can be divided into overall global and regional objectives as well as local objectives. Compaq, for example, set as its worldwide objective to consistently rank number two for business PCs. For this to happen, Compaq's international sales would have to represent 50 percent of total sales. Such objectives offer the general guidelines and control needed for broad-based campaigns.

The objectives set at the local level are more specific. They establish measurable targets for individual markets. These objectives may be product- or service-related or related to the corporation itself. Typical goals are to increase awareness, enhance image, or improve share in a particular market. Whatever the objectives, they should be measurable. Typically, local objectives grow out of interaction between headquarters and country organizations. Basic guidelines are initiated at headquarters; local organizations set the country-specific goals. These goals are subject to headquarters' approval to ensure consistency. Although some campaigns, especially those extending widely across the globe, have more headquarters involvement than usual, local input is vital, especially for good implementation.

Budgeting for International Promotion

The promotional budget links established objectives with media, message, and control decisions. Ideally, the budget would be set as a pure response to the objectives. In the real world, of course, it doesn't work this way. Resources have to be allocated, and, lamentably, they are not always allocated on the basis of pure merit. Squeaky wheels are greased; long-established thinking holds sway past the point at which it should be decisive. There is infighting, sniping, and forced trade-offs. Internationally minded marketers who try to push innovation encounter considerable inertia.

In funding international promotion, most marketers use the objective-task method. Nicolaose Synodinos, Charles F. Keown and Lawrence W. Jacobs studied leading brand advertisers in 15 countries. Here's how they broke down in their preferred method of promotional budgeting.

When headquarters retains final budget approval, the budget becomes a control mechanism. However, headquarters decision makers should clearly understand the cost and market realities in order to make rational decisions.

INTERNATIONAL PROMOTION BUDGETING[2]

Method	Percentage Using
Objective and task	64
Percentage of sales	48
Executive judgment	33
All you can afford	12
Matched competitors	12
Same as last year plus a little more	9
Same as last year	3
Other	10

Note: The total exceeds 100% because respondents checked all budgeting methods that they used.

Media Strategy

In any promotional campaign, target audience characteristics, campaign objectives, and the budget are the three main legs on which rests the choice among media vehicles and the development of a media schedule. In international marketing there are some special considerations, including the availability of the media in a given market, the product or service itself, and media habits of the intended audience.

Media Availability

Media spending varies dramatically around the world. The United States spends more money on advertising than all the other major advertising nations combined. Some countries—Peru, Venezuela, and Costa Rica, for example—have traditionally concentrated a very high percentage of advertising in television. In countries where commercial television and radio have been unavailable or in limited use, the percentage devoted to print soars: Oman (100 percent), Norway (97 percent), and Sweden (96 percent). Radio accounts for more than 20 percent of total measured media in only a few countries, such as Trinidad and Tobago, Nepal, and Mexico. In a 1987 survey, outdoor/transit advertising accounted for 48 percent of Bolivia's media spending, as against 1.6 percent under this category in the United States. Cinema advertising is important in countries such as India and Nigeria. In China, the prevailing advertising technique for decades has been 7,000 outdoor boards and posters found outside factories, all of them carrying handpainted advertisements.

All this is changing as the world changes. The reach of television is making it increasingly difficult for countries to limit it. Nevertheless, in going worldwide, the marketer must reassess the media situation in each market, and, if necessary, tailor the message to the media available.

Dealing with advertising limits. Marketers who are accustomed to a great deal of latitude in choosing advertising media are sometimes unpleasantly surprised when they look over the choices available in foreign markets. In recent years, global promotional efforts have been afflicted with conflicting international regulations. Some notable regulations involve limits on the amount of TV time available for advertising. These limits have ranged from complete prohibition (Sweden) to the practice of holding advertising to 15 to 20 minutes per day in blocks of 3 to 5 minutes. Germany is one country that has used such an approach.

France and Italy limit the percentage of revenues that the state monopoly broadcasting systems can derive from advertising. U.S. computer manufacturers, vying for more advertising time in the fast-growing European market, have had to wait as long as 18 months for allocation of air time.

This means that marketers often cannot use television as a tactical medium for new-product introductions. Television, as the spearhead of intrusive media, is the marketer's weapon of choice for most product insertions. Marketers venturing into this new arena must learn how to wield unfamiliar weapons.

Strict separation between programs and commercials is almost a universal requirement. Restrictions on comparative product claims are generally much tougher abroad than in the United States. For example, Germany bans the use of superlatives like "best."

Most European nations try to control advertising entering their borders and, until recently, they have been fairly successful. That's changing, and the change is significant for marketers. Take, for example, the strategic broadcast importance of tiny Luxembourg. When Belgium barred commercials on the state-run stations, advertisers placed their ads on the Luxembourg station. Radio Luxembourg has traditionally been used to beam messages throughout Europe. By the end of the 1990s, approximately half of the homes in Europe will have access to additional TV broadcasts through either cable or satellite. Television will no longer be restricted by national boundaries.

The implications for global marketers are significant. The viewer's choice will be greatly expanded. Government-run channels will have to compete with state channels from neighboring countries, private channels, and pan-European channels.

There will be considerably more advertising time available on European television, but there will also be more complexities for marketers to cope with as they try to make effective buys. Then there is the additional problem of making sure that advertising works not only within markets but across countries as well. This has major implications for other areas of marketing, such as branding and positioning.

Product Influences

International marketers and advertising agencies are currently frustrated by wildly differing restrictions on how products can be advertised. Agencies have had to produce several separate versions to comply with various national regulations. This is galling to marketers. They might groan at the necessity for changing advertisements to suit varying cultures, but this at least has a rational function. Making a whole new flight of commercials strictly to conform to local regulations seems like a waste.

Government restraints will not soon disappear, even as the EC concept takes hold. But the trend will be toward standardizing regulations. The emphasis of the regulating bodies, however, will still come down heavily on the side of consumer protection against the wiles of the advertisers.

The amount of regulation of promotion varies by product. Certain products are subject to special rules. In Western Europe, alcohol and tobacco are the most heavily regulated products in terms of promotion. In the United Kingdom, a real person cannot be shown applying an underarm deodorant. (Hence the spate of commercials showing animated figures using these products.) What is and is not allowed reflects the culture of the country that makes the rules. Explicit advertisements for contraceptives are commonplace in Sweden, to a degree that is rarely equaled in other countries.

Audience Characteristics

The paramount principle in media is to reach the target audience with a minimum of waste. Amoco Oil Company wanted to launch a corporate image campaign in the People's Republic of China, in the hope of receiving drilling contracts. It was not hard to identify the target market: all decision makers working for the government. The selection of appropriate media proved to be equally simple. Most of those overseeing petroleum exploration were readers of the vertical trade publications: *International Industrial Review, Petroleum Production,* and *Offshore Petroleum.*

The problem of media selection is usually far tougher. However, the Amoco example underscores the importance of looking first for the common denominator. Media strategists who are going global need data on (1) media distribution (i.e., the number of copies of the print medium or the number of sets for broadcast), (2) media audiences, and (3) advertising exposure.

For instance, an advertiser interested in using television in Brazil would need to know that the music show "Cassino de Chacrinha" averages a 25 rating and a 50 audience share for the 4:00 p.m. to 6:00 p.m. time slot. In markets where more sophisticated market research services are available, marketers can obtain data on advertising perception and consumer response.

However, *caveat emptor* must be the eternal rule in international promotion. There are numerous examples of advertisers delightedly welcoming precise circulation and broadcast coverage figures, only to learn that the numbers are fabricated.

Global Media

Media vehicles that have target audiences on at least three continents and for which the media buying takes place through a central office are considered to be global media. Global media have traditionally been publications that, in addition to the worldwide edition, offer the option of regional editions. For example, *Time* provides more than 130 editions, enabling advertisers to reach a particular country, continent, or the world. Other global publications include the *Wall Street Journal, Reader's Digest, International Herald Tribune,* and *National Geographic.*

Advertising in global media has been dominated by major consumer categories, particularly airlines, financial services, automobiles, communications, data processing, and tobacco. AT&T, IBM, and General Motors loom large in use of global media.

In weighing global media, media buyers consider the three most important characteristics to be targetability, client-compatible editorial, and editorial quality.

In broadcast media, pan-regional radio stations have been joined in Europe by television. The pan-European satellite channels, such as Sky Channel and Super Channel, were conceived from the very beginning as advertising media.

Many are skeptical about the potential of these channels, at least in the short run, because of the difficulty of developing effective cross-cultural messages in Europe's still highly nationalistic markets. Pan-European channels have been forced to cut back, while native-language satellite channels like Tele 5 in France and RTL Plus in Germany have increased their viewership. British Satellite Broadcasting—competing directly with U.K. networks ITV and the BBC—estimates that it will have 10 million viewers and ad revenues of $1.7 billion by the turn of the century.

While pan-European channels struggle, certain cable channels will continue to do well. These include cable systems that cater to universal segments with converging tastes, like MTV or the Children's Channel.

The Promotional Message

The principles for effective advertising are the same as in the domestic marketplace. However, some things that are easy to do domestically become difficult when advertising ventures abroad.

Gauging Consumer Motivations

Creative people must have a clear idea of the characteristics of the audience. They need to know what the consumer is really buying. Consumer motivations will vary, depending on the following factors.

The diffusion of the product or service into the market. For example, to penetrate Third World markets with computers is difficult because few potential customers know how to type.

The criteria by which the customer will evaluate the product. These vary, as Campbell soup learned in Italy and Brazil when it advertised the time-saving qualities of its products. It turned out that women in those countries felt inadequate if they did not make soup from scratch.

Positioning. For example, Parker Pen's high-class image around the world does not pay off where the pen market is more or less a commodity business. Working from the opposite end, some marketers have given a commodity product an exclusive image and made the public pay for it, as was done with Perrier's positioning in the United States as a premium mineral water.

One good situation for message strategy is to have a world brand: a product that is manufactured, packaged, and positioned the same everywhere.

Advertising to multiple markets is a tightrope act, requiring balance between conveying the message and allowing for local nuances. Global ideas can be localized by various means: adopting a modular approach, localizing international symbols, or using international advertising agencies.

Marketers can develop a menu of multiple broadcast and print ads from which country organizations can choose the most appropriate for their operations. For example, the "Membership Has Its Privileges" campaign of American Express, which ran in 24 countries on television and three more in print, was adjusted in some markets to make sure that "privileges" did not convey a snob or class appeal, especially in places with a strong caste or class system.

Product-Related Regulations

Product-related regulations affect advertising messages. When General Mills Toy Group's European subsidiary launched a product line related to G.I. Joe–type soldiers and war toys, it had to develop two TV commercials, a general version for most European countries and another for countries that bar advertisements for products with military or violent themes. In the commercials running in Germany, Holland, and Belgium, jeeps replaced the toy tanks and guns were removed from the hands of toy soldiers. Other countries, such as the United Kingdom, did not allow children to appear in advertisements.

Marketers often decide to localize their international symbols. Pepsi used Tina Turner and other stars who are famous around the world. In some versions, local stars were included.

Global marketers have to be careful about offending customers or incurring censorship. For example, even though importers of perfumes

Developing a World Brand

When Xerox's leading position in photocopying started to erode in the mid-1970s, the company wanted to develop one comprehensive plan to combat competition, stop the sales decline, and restore its leadership position.

Various entities of the corporation worked to develop a new line. Fuji Xerox developed two copiers, the 1020 and the 1035, for the low-volume segment. Rank Xerox came up with the 1045 for the middle-volume segment. Xerox U.S. designed the 1075 for the high-volume market.

With the products ready for global introduction, Xerox needed a comprehensive communications program, with a single, powerful message instantly understood anywhere, to convey the endurance of its products. Xerox chose as its symbol the marathon.

The program combined international and local media. An umbrella campaign in English-language print media (such as the international editions of *Time, Newsweek, Business Week,* and *Fortune,* and the European and Far Eastern editions of the *Wall Street Journal* and *Herald Tribune*) was supported by advertising in local languages.

Xerox also used two media aimed at business travelers: a high-visibility poster campaign in major airports and a two-minute, editorial-style commercial shown before movies on international flights.

To reinforce the advertising program, Xerox sponsored marathon races around the world, combining the PR technique of special events with advertising. World-class runners such as Grete Waitz and Rob de Castella agreed to run in six races a year wearing the Xerox logo.

The effort paid off in sales. Although many factors contributed to favorable results, the marathon campaign was vital to the essential job of generating speedy awareness of the new line of products.

---

into Saudi Arabia want to use the same campaigns used in Europe, they occasionally have to make adjustments. A European ad for Drakkar Noir, a perfume for men, shows a man's hand clutching a perfume bottle and a woman's hand seizing his bare forearm. In the Saudi Arabian version, the man's arm is clothed in a dark suit sleeve and the woman's finger is merely brushing his hand.

The use of one agency or just a few enhances consistency and coordination, especially when the marketer's operations are decentralized. It also makes it easier to exchange ideas and to achieve wider use of a new idea or a worthwhile application.

The Language Puzzle

Culture, economic variables, and life-styles impel modifications of advertising. Of the cultural variables, language is the most apparent in its influence on promotional campaigns. The European Union alone has nine major native languages, along with minor languages, dialects, and languages spoken by the millions of people from outside Europe. Advertisers in the Arab world sometimes find to their dismay that the voices in a TV commercial speak in the wrong Arabic dialect.

The challenge of language is often strongest when the advertiser is trying to translate a theme. Coca-Cola's "Can't Beat the Feeling" is the equivalent of "I Feel Coke" in Japan, "Unique Sensation" in Italy, and "The Feeling of Life" in Chile. In Germany, where no translation really worked, the original English was used.

One way of getting around the language barrier is to have no copy or very little copy and to use innovative approaches, such as pantomime. For example, many advertising professionals worry about the best ways to dub commercials into other languages rather than about developing a worldwide visual language that is widely understandable and that transcends cultural barriers. Cartoon producers have shown that this can be done; powerful images, shrewdly aimed at basic human feelings, don't need words. Any kind of symbolism will naturally require adequate copy testing to determine how the target market perceives the message.

The stage of economic development may differentiate the message from one market to another. In a developed market the aim might be to persuade buyers to ignore alternatives. In a developing market people might need a purely informative campaign. Campaigns must also recognize life-style differences in regions that are demographically quite similar. For example, N. W. Ayer's Bahamas tourism campaign for the European market emphasizes clean water, beaches, and air. In Germany, however, the campaign focuses on sports activities. In the United Kingdom, it features humor.

While graphics are central to a new universalism in advertising usage—somewhat similar to the international language of road signs—copy is still the core of the message. Copywriters will, increasingly, be fluent in several languages, rather than relying on translators, who are apt to lose much of the flavor of the original. Polyglot copywriting is the wave of the future. Tomorrow's creative types will speak in tongues—several of them.

Watch Your Language—Even When It's English

How do you like this advertising theme?

NOTHING SUCKS LIKE AN ELECTROLUX

It works for Electrolux vacuum cleaners in the United Kingdom. You can imagine the reaction to a space advertisement with this headline in the United States.

George Bernard Shaw's dictum that Great Britain and the United States are two countries separated by a common language does not grow any less true with the years. English-speaking countries communicate instantaneously with each other, all around the world, via broadcast and fiber optics. But, paradoxically, the faster the communication method the greater the risk of misunderstanding.

In the old days, managers in the United States and United Kingdom wrote letters to each other. They dictated their thoughts to secretaries. Good secretaries bailed their bosses out of trouble by putting abrasive material into more diplomatic language, by questioning obscure points, and by looking things up when they weren't clear.

The message was being passed through a human filter, often a person with the language expertise to make it sharper, more effective, and less risky.

For rapid communication, people talk on the telephone. Here there is no filter, nobody to question the ambiguous use of a word or to straighten out a misleading implication. But, of course, on the phone there is give and take, a chance to ask questions and to clear up misunderstandings.

Today e-mail, fax, and a constellation of instant transmission media combine the speed of telephoning with the permanence of print. Safeguards are sacrificed for speed. There is no filter, nor is there the give and take of the phone.

When people around the world communicate with each other across language barriers, they're aware of the dangers. But sometimes those who speak (or think they speak) the same language run into trouble. An American talks about "tabling a proposal," meaning delaying a decision, but the British counterpart under-stands the expression as meaning a decision is imminent. If the British promise something "by the end of the day" it doesn't mean within 24 hours, but rather when the job is done. A British executive reports that negotiations "bombed"; the American thinks "disas-ter!" But the British use of "bombed" means success.

When you move into global marketing, you will of course be con-scious of the language factor. However, when English is the "com-mon" language of the countries involved, you might assume that the language barrier is minimal or nonexistent. That can be a big mistake. When you're communicating with someone in the United Kingdom or Australia—or even Canada—the cultural context in which the words are exchanged can lead to differences in meaning just as great as if the other party's primary tongue were Arabic or Swahili. The insidious thing is that, if you're dealing with Arabic you know there's a danger. English can give you a false sense of security.

Unique market conditions require localized approaches. Although IBM has used global campaigns (the Little Tramp, for example), it has also used major local campaigns in Japan and Europe for specific pur-poses. In Japan, it used a popular TV star in poster and outdoor-board ads to tell viewers, "Friends, the time is ripe" (for buying an IBM 5550 personal computer). The campaign was intended to bolster the idea that the machine was a class act from America. At the same time, IBM was trying to overcome a problem in Europe of being perceived as "too American." Stressing that IBM is actually a "European company," a campaign told of IBM's large factories, research facilities, and tax-paying subsidiaries in the EU.

The Campaign Approach

Most international marketers eschew the in-house approach, preferring to rely on the outside expertise of advertising agencies and other promo-tions-related companies like media buyers and specialty marketing firms. There are two basic decisions:

• What type of outside services shall we use?

• Who will make the decisions?

Advertising Agencies

A list of the world's top 50 advertising agencies and agency groups shows that 22 are based in the United States, 14 in Japan, and the rest in the United Kingdom, France, Australia, South Korea, and Italy. Whereas Japanese agencies tend to have few operations outside their home country, American and European agencies have been expanding worldwide.

Agencies form world groups for better coverage. WPP Group includes such entities as Ogilvy & Mather; J. Walter Thompson; Brouillard Communications; Scali, McCabe, Sloves; Fallon McElligot; and the Martin Agency. Smaller advertising agencies are teaming up with affiliates in foreign markets.

For many, the concept of the global campaign is now inseparable from global marketing. Agencies with networks too small to compete have become prime takeover targets in the drive to create worldwide mega-agencies.

Not everyone has implicit faith in size. There are many believers in the proposition that local, mid-sized agencies will more than hold their own in the face of global competition because they will be able to develop local solutions while networking with affiliates in other countries to do the necessary jobs.

Although the notion of half a dozen huge agencies placing most international advertising is exaggerated, global marketing is the new wave and is having a strong impact on advertising. In the 1980s, the major multinational agencies increased their share of the advertising market from 14 percent to more than 20 percent. There have been major realignments of client-agency relationships. The sidebar highlights some examples of the new approach at work in Western Europe.

As new markets emerge, agencies will vie to establish a presence in them. For example, DDB Needham, which had been serving its clients in the Chinese market from Hong Kong, has now formed a joint venture with the Chinese government.

Conflict is a major concern arising from the growth of mega-agencies. With only a few agencies to choose from, you may find yourself with the same agency as your main competitors. The mega-agencies meet this concern by structuring their companies as rigidly watertight agency networks (such as the Interpublic Group) under the umbrella of a holding group. Following that logic, Procter & Gamble, a client of Saatchi & Saatchi Advertising Worldwide, and Colgate-Palmolive, a client of Ted Bates, should not have been perturbed when Saatchi & Saatchi purchased Ted Bates. However, Colgate-Palmolive took its business to another agency.

Supportive government regulations are helping local agencies survive the onslaught of globalization. In Peru, for instance, a law mandates that any commercial aired on Peruvian television must be 100 percent nationally produced.

Local agencies are forging ties with foreign agencies for better coverage

Approaching Europe with New Ideas

Johnson & Johnson's $35 million rollout of its Silhouette feminine hygiene products approached Europe as a single market, rather than as a collection of distinct countries. Saatchi & Saatchi coordinated the effort.

When Backer Spielvogel Bates Worldwide announced the merger of its Ted Bates Ltd. and Dorland offices in London, the reason was to strengthen Bates' European network through the presence of a London office.

United Pictures International—the export marketing organization for Paramount, Universal, and MGM/UA studios in the United States—fired an assortment of advertising agencies in national European markets and named Young & Rubicam to handle $30 million in billings for film promotion.

To implement a pan-regional strategy, Whirlpool hired Publicis-FCB International. In testing pan-European slogans, Publicis found that Austrian consumers resist products with overly American appeal more than others. It also learned that although most Europeans associate innovation and technology with Germany, the French do not. After rejecting several slogans, as well as a proposal to do a British ad for northern Europe and a French ad for southern Europe, the agency reached a neutral solution: "Whirlpool Brings Quality to Life."

and client service, thus becoming part of the global trend while remaining independent. However, the local agencies find themselves making fewer decisions as the trend toward centralization continues.

The fear of conflict should not loom largest in the eyes of marketers looking for agencies for international campaigns. While a competitor might be handled by another group under the same vast umbrella, this does not mean the advertising team will do any less than its best. If anything, the rivalry to succeed is likely to be more intense between advertisers within the same world organization.

How Can You Assure High-Quality Advertising?

Globalization inevitably spurs a trend toward greater centralization. However, that trend should not be followed unquestioningly. The important question is not who makes the decisions but how to assure high-quality advertising at the local level.

Multinational corporations are, increasingly, favoring an interactive approach using coordinated decentralization, striving for common strategy but flexible execution. The approach has six steps:

1. *Strategy and Objectives*
   Subsidiaries develop tentative strategies and objectives subject to home office review.

2. *Individual Market Input*
   Subsidiaries develop individual advertising campaigns subject to home office review.

3. *Testing*
   Execute and test creative work subject to home office review.

4. *Campaign review*
   Develop creative work to presentation standards subject to home office review.

5. *Budget Approval*

6. *Campaign Implementation*

The approach maintains strong central control while capitalizing on the strengths of the local entities. A good example of this approach was Eastman Kodak's launch of its Ektaprint copier-duplicator line in 11 separate markets in Europe. For economic and organizational reasons, Kodak did not want to deal with different campaigns. It wanted the same advertising graphics in each country, accompanied by the theme "First name in photography, last word in copying." Translations varied, but the campaign was identifiable from one country to another. A single agency directed the campaign. This was more economical than campaigns in each country would have been. The campaign was unified and identifiable throughout Europe. The benefit of association of Kodak's paramount position in photography with its line of copiers was fully exploited.

Agencies are adapting to centrally run client operations. Many accounts are now handled by a lead agency, usually in the country where the client is based. More and more agencies are assigning a strong international supervisor to global accounts. This supervisor can override local agencies and make personnel changes. For example, McCann-Erickson set up a global advertising unit of 25 professionals in New York to develop worldwide campaigns.

Does International Advertising Really Work?

The advertising industry in the United States and other Western countries has developed a multitude of techniques designed to measure advertising effectiveness, ranging from pretesting of copy appeal to posttesting of recognition and retention of the message. Some advertising people would feel lost without this research.

Things are radically different in other areas of the world. Very often, syndicated services such as A. C. Nielsen are not available. Testing is quite expensive, and might not be considered cost-effective, especially in smaller markets. Compared to costs in the United States, the costs of research in the international market are higher in relation to the overall advertising expenditure.

The biggest challenge to advertising research comes from the increase in global and regional campaigns. Comprehensive and reliable measures of campaigns for a mass European market, for example, are difficult because audience measurement techniques and analyses differ from country to country. Advertisers are pushing for universally accepted parameters to compare audiences in one country to those in another. This is a laudable goal, but it will be difficult to achieve.

At one time there was little or no research done to measure advertising effectiveness. Advertisers were still able to create ads that sold. In international marketing, advertisers and marketers will have to accept the fact that they have gone back to that earlier time. It's more important to do the research needed to measure the markets and gauge the selling environment than to test advertising effectiveness after the advertisements run.

Other Promotional Elements

Personal Selling

Personal selling can be truly international. Big companies like Boeing, Northrop, United Technologies, and many others send salespeople around the world from their domestic bases. However, most personal selling is done by subsidiaries, with varying degrees of headquarters involvement.

Eastman Kodak developed a line-of-business approach to allow for standardized strategy throughout a region. In Europe, one person is placed in charge of the entire copier-duplicator program in each country. That person is responsible for all sales and service within the country. Typically, each customer is served by three people: a sales representative, a service representative, and a customer service person, who acts as liaison between sales and service.

Training of the multinational sales force usually takes place in the national markets, but headquarters have a voice in the training methods used. When Kodak introduced the Ektaprint line, most European marketing personnel had to be recruited from outside the company and trained. Sales managers and a select group of sales trainers were sent to headquarters in Rochester, New York, for six weeks of training. Back in Europe, they set up programs for individual countries. To ensure continuity, all the U.S. training materials were translated into the languages of the individual countries. To maintain a unified program and overcome language barriers, Kodak created a service language consisting of 1,200 words commonly found in technical information.

Foreign countries entering the Japanese market face challenges in establishing a sales force. The first problem is recruitment. Well-established local companies have an edge in attracting people. This is one more factor leading to the choice of joint ventures or distribution agreements in penetrating the Japanese market.

Sales Promotion

As they look for selling approaches that leap the boundaries of culture and untangle the knots of language, many marketers are increasing the use of sales promotion as a support for advertising and, in certain cases, an alternative to advertising. The appeal of sales promotion grows out of several roots. As media advertising gets more expensive and more cluttered, sales promotion offers itself as cheaper and simpler. With sales promotion it can be easier to target customers. And, since it is so difficult to measure the effectiveness of international advertising, marketers like the ease of measuring the effectiveness of some promotions. For example, coupon returns provide a clear measure of how well the tactic is working.

General Foods used sales promotion to sell Tang, the presweetened powder juice substitute, in Latin America. One promotion involved trading Tang pouches for free popsicles from Kibon, General Foods' Brazilian subsidiary. Kibon also placed coupons for groceries in Tang pouches. In Puerto Rico, the company ran Tang sweepstakes. In Argentina, in-store sampling featured women in orange Tang dresses pouring samples from Tang pitchers. The decorative pitchers became a hit throughout Latin America. Heavy trade promotion included trade shows and exhibits, trade discounts, and cooperative advertising.

For sales promotion abroad to be effective, the local retailer population must be fully on board. When A. C. Nielsen tried to introduce cents-off coupons in Chile, the nation's supermarket union told its members not to accept the coupons. The main complaint was that an intermediary, like Nielsen, would unnecessarily raise costs and thus consumers would have to pay higher prices. Also, some critics believed that coupons would limit the ability of Chileans to bargain for their purchases.

Sales promotion tools are subject to regulations that vary from country to country. Austria and Germany have maintained a near-total ban on premiums. The United Kingdom places major restrictions on competitions. Japan restricts competitions, premiums, and gifts.

A particular level of incentive might be permissible in one market but illegal in another. The Scandinavian countries present great difficulties, because every promotion has to be approved by a government body. In France, a gift could not be worth more than 4 percent of the retail value of the product being promoted (subject to a maximum of 10 francs). The maximum prize in the Netherlands was pegged at 250 guilders, making some promotions virtually impossible. The German prohibition on requirement of proof of purchase as a condition of entry in competitions put a damper on contests.

Some restrictions are being relaxed, but there continue to be plenty of conflicting regulations, making truly global promotions rare. However, multinational promotions do work. They are best suited to products spanning cultural divides: soft drinks, liquor, airlines, credit cards, jeans. The promotions are funded centrally but implemented differently in each market. For example, 7–UP's multiterritory Music Machine promotion carried a common theme: youth-oriented rock music. The promotion offered gifts such as videos and audiotapes. One way in which it adapted itself, country by country, was through the sponsorship of local radio shows featuring locally popular artists.

Public Relations

Public relations is becoming more important in international marketing. One reason is that, when a company ventures for the first time into a foreign country, it runs the risk of being perceived as an alien entity and shunned. The challenge is to project the image of an acceptable corporate culture, even before getting down to the nitty-gritty of selling products or services.

In the 1980s, non-U.S. marketers were far more active than U.S. firms in trying to boost their global identities. They recognized that the effort was necessary in order to compete against firms with strong local identities. Failure to respond to this need can cripple marketing programs that would succeed otherwise.

Image Building

One big mistake a firm can make when it goes into the international marketplace is to assume that its domestic image is transferable.

Some companies take it for granted that they are perceived abroad much as they are perceived at home. Other organizations avoid that mistake, but they fall into another trap. Acknowledging that they are not well known in foreign countries, they set out to promote the tried-and-true domestic image, using just about the same techniques as they use domestically.

Conner Peripherals, Inc., a fast-track Silicon Valley disk-drive manufacturer, managed to penetrate the tough Japanese market in the 1990s. Writing in *Business Marketing,* Kate Bertrand describes how Conner conceived and executed an image-shaping campaign for Japan.[3] In mid-1990 the company kicked off the effort with a space advertisement headlined "Unique Ideas Are Often the Most Enduring." The artwork was a photo of handmade chopsticks with a Japanese maple leaf. The copy was low-key, using a softer sell than Conner uses in Western markets. The president of Conner's ad agency said, "Subtle messages often work better. In the States we tend to hit each other on the head with a two-by-four. In Japan it's not that way. They feel you're bragging and wonder what's wrong with your product." Conner ran a Southeast Asian version of this campaign using different images, for example, Chinese bone chopsticks.

The Conner campaign was designed to build awareness and preference for the drive maker among Japanese OEMs. The medium used to get the message out is space advertising, but the advertising is deployed on behalf of a traditional public relations strategy: the engineering of favorable perception among the members of a highly segmented target audience.

In the United States, public relations is becoming more powerful as a marketing tool. In their book *Power Public Relations,* Leonard Saffir and John Tarrant analyze the "coming of age" of PR: its use of sophisticated research, its growing function as a heavyweight element of integrated marketing programs, and even its occasional role as a substitute for advertising.[4]

The full power of modern public relations techniques has not yet been exploited by many marketers and advertising agencies. They still have a mindset that relegates PR to a distinctly subordinate role: sending out releases, trying to keep unfavorable news out of the media, and so on. That mindset is fading. Greater proportions of marketing budgets are being allocated to public relations to do specific marketing jobs previously done by advertising.

One reason for this is advertising overexposure. We live in an age in which generations have grown up discounting, dismissing, and distrusting advertising. At the same time, we see material in the "free" media (including the print and TV tabloids) achieving a high degree of credibility. Effective public relations can do a tremendous job of engineering perception, and it can be more cost-effective than advertising.

European Consumers Change Their Buying Habits[5]

Whirlpool Corporation is posting higher profits and bigger market share in Europe. Whirlpool's acquisition of the European appliance business of Philips Electronics NV was a major move in the company's aggressive expansion abroad. In 1993, Whirlpool's European shipments rose about five percent, even as the overall European appliance market was flat or declining.

Currently Europe has a collection of 200 appliance brand names, many of them popular in just one country. Whirlpool's strategy is to stand out with strong pan-European brands. Hank Bowman, president of Whirlpool Europe BV, spotlights an important development: "Research tells that the trends, preferences and biases of consumers, country to country, are reducing as opposed to increasing." Although regional preferences will remain, the company sees a chance to take advantage of the move toward a less fractured Europe.

When Whirlpool first entered Europe, it used a dual Philips/Whirlpool brand. Now the company is going it alone, silencing skeptics who thought Europeans wouldn't buy the new American name. According to Andrew Haskins, electronics analyst at London's James Capel and Co., Whirlpool connotes quality to consumers: "Philips had a strong brand name, and Whirlpool has been able to build on that quite considerably."

With the growth of international marketing, there are new and interesting ways to use public relations. The need for PR is intensified by the fact that in vast areas of the world now opening up, advertising is practically unknown, and, to the extent that it is known, it is shunned.

When the Berlin Wall came down, marketers geared up to sell to millions of new consumers. They used all the elements of modern marketing. But at least one of those elements did not work the way it was expected to. In our work in the Eastern European region, we found that many citizens of these newly emerging market economies deeply distrust the ad campaigns of Western firms.

Saffir and Tarrant observe that these consumers "have had forty years of anti-advertising conditioning." The East Germans, and others in the former Eastern Bloc nations, "resist advertising simply because they perceive it as advertising. The quality of the ads does not matter because the target audience is not letting the message get over the threshold."

One area in which top-notch modern public relations can be used to good effect is the always touchy area of image. Countries around the world might want the things the West can offer, but the people in those countries often carry a high level of resentment against the source countries. At a time when companies will start making a lot of money abroad (sometimes more than they make at home), executives realize that they must cultivate community relations in the target countries.

When resentment is left to fester (even though the sales within the country are good), the needle on the danger gauge rises toward the red. If something goes wrong, if there is a crisis with a product or a plant, then the company is engulfed by the raging flood of negative feeling before it can even begin to react. The cultivation of a favorable image for good community relations should be a planned, long-term policy, not an assortment of piecemeal efforts or a spasmodic reaction to a crisis.

Good community relations is a matter of vision, serious commitment, and real contribution to the host culture. These good things are then molded by skillful public relations into an effective image-maintenance campaign. No amount of PR maneuvering can create the image if the substance is not there.

IBM strives to be among the most admired companies in its host countries. In Thailand, for example, IBM provides equipment and personnel to universities and donates money to the nation's wildlife fund and environmental protection agency. In 1986, IBM won the Garuda Award, which recognizes significant contributions to Thailand's social and economic development. The winning of such recognition can be of immeasurable help in fostering an image that will stand up through the ups and downs of politics and economics.

Ford Motor Company carries on active community relations programs in 30 countries hosting Ford manufacturing, assembly, or sales facilities. The community affairs department at Ford's world headquarters in Dearborn, Michigan, has functional responsibility for all corporate community relations around the globe. However, as a practical matter, managers at each overseas facility have the day-to-day job of cultivating and maintaining close ties with the local community. Headquarters serves as a resource. Among other aids, each operation receives the *Community Relations Handbook,* a 100-plus page guide to community involvement that is updated annually.

Firms that are beginning to do business in countries around the world have a golden opportunity to do things that establish and maintain good relations. The other side of the coin is that firms that are newly arrived on the scene abroad are vulnerable to public relations blunders that can have serious and long-lasting repercussions.

Many countries have reduced (in some cases, sharply reduced) government funding of social services. Community health, child care, recreation, and athletic facilities have been privatized or are simply no longer funded. The citizens who relied on these services are cast adrift. Nobody is picking up the slack. The society does not have a tradition of handling such matters through private efforts.

Here's where the marketing newcomer can make a substantial contribution. It's not just a matter of money. The incoming company has an organization and community relations experience and expertise that can be brought to bear on local problems.

Governments in Europe are welcoming private-sector programs to provide job training for inner-city youths. Many U.S. companies have some experience in helping with inner-city problems in the United States, but they might not be aware that such problems plague cities in other lands as well.

European countries are grappling with the agonizing dilemmas posed by the massive movements of people across borders. The trend, especially in Germany and France, is toward tightening up on immigration. But changes in laws don't solve the problems of meeting the needs of immigrants who are already on the scene and of those who come in illegally.

Eastern Europe has a tremendous pollution problem. The "green" movement has achieved considerable strength throughout Europe. The incoming company might have ideas, techniques, or technology that help to alleviate the ecological problems. Some European governments are rethinking the more extreme "green" regulations that establish expensive recycling programs and specifications relating to packaging. Although certain of the more stringent requirements might be relaxed, the environment will continue to be a major preoccupation in these areas, and if incoming companies can help, they will make themselves more welcome.

First, Do No Harm

An important part of the Hippocratic Oath is frequently rendered as, "First, do no harm." Whatever the success of the therapy, the doctor should at least not make the patient worse. A company that begins a marketing program in a foreign country will not be able to solve the country's problems. But at least the marketer can avoid being perceived as indifferent to those problems or actually making the problems worse. For example, a company builds a small plant to manufacture goods to be sold in the host country. The plant emits a vapor that looks like smoke but is actually a harmless residue. The people who see the "smoke" will believe that something bad is being pumped into the air. The company produces scientific analyses and explanations that satisfy the regulatory bodies of the host country. But people still think there is poison coming out of that stack. A good deal of damage to the company's image has been done.

So the basic community relations job, even if nothing else is done, is to appear aware of the community's concerns, sensitive to them, and ready and willing to help with them. Sometimes this is just a matter of saying "We care." But with all the other chores involved in opening up the market, "We care" often gets lost in the shuffle.

Bring in the PR Pros at the Beginning

When a firm has targeted a country for a marketing effort, it makes sense to have a plan for PR/community relations right from the start. All too often the community relations campaign is damage control. Things go wrong; the company realizes, "We have a problem"; and a drive is mounted, at considerable expense, to fix it.

The place to start is with the basic research that preceded the decision to begin the international marketing effort in this particular place. (Chapter 4 on primary research lays out the questions to be answered about demographics, politics, culture, attitudes, etc.) This research can be the foundation for a sound community relations/ public relations program. Who handles those responsibilities for the company? Is there an in-house capability? Does the company use outside PR counsel? Whatever the situation, it makes sense at this early stage to bring in one or more PR professionals and ask them to make some comments and suggestions about the company's image in the host country.

These professionals are unlikely to be able to put together a detailed program. They don't know enough about the situation on the ground. But their experience and the basics of their discipline will enable them to ask some fundamental questions and lay out some broad parameters.

Building and maintaining the company's image abroad need not involve an elaborate and high-priced program. If such a program is deemed necessary, the company will want to bring in an agency based in the target country. For most firms the program will consist, first of all, in making sure that all employees in the host community are briefed on local attitudes and problems. Knowledgeable trainers should conduct role-playing of what to do and say in certain situations. The operation need not have special PR persons attached to it. However, the managers should be prepared to handle community relations functions. Indeed, they should be instructed that the community relations dimension is an important facet of the job. Home office management should demonstrate its concern for community relations by monitoring the program.

Check Points

✓ International marketers must address multiple audiences.

✓ Visual language looms large in addressing various foreign markets.

✓ Media can be difficult to evaluate.

✓ Many countries limit broadcast advertising.

✓ Language and cultural variations make it necessary to be extra-cautious in using copy in multiple markets.

✓ As global marketing grows, so do mega-agencies.

✓ Client conflict is no longer the issue it once was.

✓ Promotion is an important adjunct to advertising in international marketing.

✓ Promotion in international marketing often takes up a larger proportion of the total budget in relation to advertising than is the case domestically.

✓ The trend is toward harmonization of strategy while allowing for flexibility at the local level.

✓ Regulation of promotion efforts varies widely from country to country.

✓ Many multinationals are realigning their accounts worldwide to streamline promotion and achieve a global approach.

✓ Personal selling tends to be localized, with decisions about recruitment, training, motivation, and evaluation made locally, under general guidance from headquarters.

- ✔ Public relations becomes more important because corporations must often establish a favorable image before selling their products.

- ✔ Where advertising is restricted or impractical, promotional efforts, and particularly PR, can be highly effective selling tools.

15

REMARKABLE, RISKY, AND REWARDING
Global Marketing into the 21st Century

As the year 1994 dawned, the Dudson Group factory in Stoke-on-Trent, England, was turning out fine china for customers all over the world: "fruit bowls for a Canadian restaurant, soup dishes for roadside stops on Italy's *autostrada,* teacups for the Belgian railway, dinner plates for a Singapore hotel."[1]

The firm was not selling much in the United States, because of the 36 percent tariff the United States was imposing on tableware for restaurants and hotels. However, the General Agreement on Tariffs and Trade (GATT) will change all that. The British firm, along with millions of other companies worldwide, was facing an expanded global market: the chance for success beyond anything experienced in the past. At the same time, the British firm and its myriad counterparts were facing vastly increased competition, coming from all corners of the world.

Welcome to the exciting, risky, and immensely rewarding new realities of worldwide business. Marketing is a new game, on a global field. And we're all in the game, whether we like it or not. The *Wall Street Journal* quotes Joe Richardson II, head of a furniture and wood products company in Sheboygan Falls, Wisconsin:

> There's a great misimpression that it's only the big guys interested in a world market. That's baloney. In 20 years, doing business in the world economy for us will be as accepted as doing business in St. Louis and San Francisco.[2]

Building business ties with other countries is, increasingly, a primary national objective. Edward N. Luttwak, a director at the Center for Strategic and International Studies in Washington, believes that world power will, from now on, be exercised through economic diplomacy. Luttwak says that the United States is headed for Third World status if it does not master the contours of the new global marketplace.[3]

As international trade grows in importance, U.S. businesses will be able to look to the federal government as an ally rather than as a suspicious second-guesser. Businesses in other countries—Germany, the United Kingdom, Japan—have already been receiving substantial government help in opening new international markets.

Marketing executives can be proud in the knowledge that as they pursue the goal of legitimate profit abroad, they are also furthering the cause of a peaceful and smoothly functioning world. The world today confronts a massive threat from the growing friction between cultures. Samuel P. Huntington, professor of government and director of the Olin Institute for Strategic Studies at Harvard, wrote that:

Cultural characteristics and differences are less mutable and less easily compromised and resolved than political and economic ones. In the former Soviet Union, Communists can become democrats, the rich can become poor and the poor rich, but Russians cannot become Estonians . . . economic regionalism is increasing. Successful economic regionalism will reinforce civilization consciousness.[4]

It would be foolish to celebrate international trade as a panacea for all the world's ills. Nevertheless, it is apparent that the inevitable surge of international marketing is likely to make the world a better place to live in for a great many of its people. So international marketing can be beneficial in ways that reach far beyond profitable business growth. But first you have to be equipped to handle it.

A Volatile Global Scene

Every day's news brings fresh evidence of the profound changes shaking the world as we have known it. The Japanese Goliath stumbles, displays astonishing weakness, begins to open its doors to a variety of products from different parts of the world. The Pacific region, once viewed as monolithic by many Western observers, segments itself in distinctive ways. Korea and Japan are joined by other "tigers," such as Singapore and Hong Kong, among the ranks of highly developed economies. The tigers, in turn, establish operations in less-developed Asian countries because of lower costs. Korea is dethroned as the champion sneaker manufacturer, because it can no longer compete with the lower-wage

Worldwide Thirst for Usable Water Fuels Marketing Opportunities[5]

The 21st century presents the earth with stark challenges. One is the looming shortage of water. As governments and corporations worldwide seek ways to desalinate sea water and to make brackish water usable, many companies and individuals will find opportunities—if they look for them.

Paul Green is Publisher and Editorial Director of *The International Desalination & Water Reuse Quarterly* based in Westport, CT. The magazine is an example of the new breed of publications which focus in depth on particular business and governmental issues and circulate around the globe. Green says, "In the Mideast, in Japan, in many parts of the world, water is an endangered resource. Techniques like electrodialysis and reverse osmosis are being used to provide water that is fit for industry and for living. And companies of all kinds are finding new markets in the field."

Makers of all kinds of products—pumps, pipes, valves, filters, fiberglass vessels, etc.—never thought of themselves as being in the pure water business. But now they are getting involved in water treatment projects in the United Kingdom, China, Japan, Saudi Arabia, and other countries.

In the 21st century, international marketing will, increasingly, converge with international movements to keep the earth viable.

---

economy of Indonesia. Lured by the magic of vast numbers, marketers explore the virtually limitless potential of China.

U.S. companies that had previously considered only Japan and Germany as profitable foreign markets now find to their surprise that Latin America is a vibrant and growing complex of markets. Anheuser-Busch buys a substantial stake in a Mexican brewer. Headlines proclaim that "Many U.S. Businesses Entering Mexico Are Small, Entrepreneurial."

Ford commits $6 billion to perfect a "world car" the Mondeo. The discount phenomenon hits Europe. Even as zealots on both sides try to destroy the vulnerable buds of peace between Israelis and Arabs, businesspeople from the opposing camps make the first tentative moves toward trading with each other.

KPMG Peat Marwick runs a two-page spread in the *Wall Street Journal* headlined "Go Global, But Not Without a Map," and beginning:

As your business inevitably becomes more global (whether you've targeted the world or the world has targeted you), success will depend more and more on your knowledge of far-flung markets.[6]

Yes, success will depend on your knowledge of far-flung markets. But that's not the only thing you need. Success also depends on your ability to develop the personal skills and resources you need to qualify as a player in the international marketing arena.

Management Training and Self-Preparation

Men and women who are already embarked on marketing careers, or who are considering marketing careers, can equip themselves fully for success only by acquiring a working grasp of international marketing. Today and tomorrow, the marketing career is a world career.

Learning languages is an obvious step. Learning about other cultures is important. However, preparation for world marketing goes beyond these matters. It involves reexamining one's business education. And it involves decisions about the size and nature of the companies you go to work for.

Career Preparation for Going Global

Management education in Europe and Japan has, in a number of significant respects, been equipping students better for international business than has been the case in the United States. This lack is one reason for the critical scrutiny now being directed toward some of the most important centers for management preparation in the United States.

Like it or not, the global market is now a reality. U.S. graduate schools will speed the rate of their international orientation. Students considering institutions at which to pursue the MBA should take a close look at the weight and quality of the curriculum devoted to preparing managers for the world arena.

It makes sense to look abroad for graduate training. Some foreign universities specialize in developing international managers. INSEAD in France, the London Business School, the University of Western Ontario in Canada, IMEDE in Switzerland, and the Stockholm School of Economics are only a few examples of such universities. Many organizations are able to help students who are interested in studying abroad or in gathering foreign work experience. Apart from universities, various nonprofit institutions can provide information and assistance.

Working for a Big Company

The "big versus small" argument will go on forever. Is it better to go to work as a manager in a giant corporation or in a small company? Both decisions have their merits.

Business Schools Hit Hard Times Amid Doubt over Value of MBA[7]

The number of MBAs has been declining. "There's a growing realization that an MBA is not a ticket to the gravy train," said the director of the organization that accredits graduate schools of business.

Tracy Ott, a New York marketing consultant who was attending NYU's graduate business school part time and wondering whether to go full time, stated, "There is a question of whether going to business school is a good investment. . . . The big question I have is, are MBAs really learning what students need for the 90s?"

One area in which the graduate schools have not been on the cutting edge is international business. They are moving slowly toward a wider embrace of the world in their recruiting and their curricula. At Columbia, recruiting trips now extend to Hong Kong and principal Japanese cities. The curriculum has been revised to place more emphasis on international affairs.

Most U.S. corporations have been, if anything, even slower to acknowledge and prepare for the coalescing world market looming just over the horizon. There is a deep-rooted tendency to view international business as a kind of Jurassic Park, full of strange monsters and strange perils.

The American Society for Training and Development deplores U.S. managerial unpreparedness in an era of increasing globalization of markets.

Denise S. Wallace, a co-author of the training society's article on the subject, said that U.S. managers, "because of their educational background, lack experience and diversity that many of their offshore counterparts have." Wallace commented that U.S. managers need "organizational expatriate experiences along with knowledge of languages, cultures and foreign business systems.

"Continuous change and chaos will be the dominant influences. The global leader needs a cosmopolitan perspective that comes from traveling and working abroad. He or she needs a knowledge of international relations and must be sensitive to diversity of beliefs and social forces. Yet such leaders must be grounded in their own skills."

An earlier study of leading managers of major corporations showed that 96 percent agreed that, over the coming five years, their companies' ability to compete internationally was essential to long-term success. Yet few companies had managers who boasted language skills or the rudiments of knowledge of the countries in which they hoped to do business.

For the manager who wants training and hands-on experience abroad, a multinational seems like a natural choice. The huge corporations, after all, already do business internationally. Not that young managers walk into companies like Procter & Gamble or PepsiCo and get overseas assignments. Usually the new employee is expected to become thoroughly familiar with the company's internal operations before being considered for an international position. There's a lot riding on it from the corporation's point of view. For one thing, it's expensive to send a U.S. executive to a foreign country; the first-year cost will run, typically, to three times base salary.

Traditionally, U.S. corporations send a manager abroad to reflect the corporate spirit, to be tightly wed to the corporate culture, and to be able to communicate well with local people and the home office. As an intermediary, the expatriate must be empathetic, understanding, and yet fully prepared to implement the goals set by headquarters.

This attitude reflects the Father (or Mother) Knows Best approach, which has for a long time been the hallmark of U.S. business dealings with the rest of the world. That approach, inevitably, is changing. To be successful in a foreign country, the marketer will, logically, approach the task in the same general way that domestic markets are approached—listening to what the consumers want and then applying ingenuity to supplying it, rather than trying to dictate what the consumer wants. That doesn't work domestically, and it doesn't work internationally.

In recent years some managers in multinational corporations have been reluctant to take overseas assignments. The foreign stint is seen as a possible trap. The executive's heart is not set on making it big abroad. The preferred career path winds back to corporate headquarters, and sometimes that path runs into pitfalls.

Often the timing of a return is decided by the length of an expatriate's tour of duty abroad or by the conclusion of a foreign project, with little regard to where or how the employee will fit in back home.

Making matters worse, executives who work abroad sometimes develop grand and unrealistic expectations. Typically they run their own operations overseas. Their housing supplements, overseas benefits, and other perks support a luxurious life-style. One U.S. executive who had worked for three years in an Asian country said, "It's a surreal kind of experience. You appear to be more important than you are." Abroad, the executive had supervised 50 people. Returning to New York, he found himself in much the same job he had had previously, except that now he was supervising four people.[8]

General Electric, which sends many managers to foreign assignments, has adopted several strategies to make reentry easier. To start with, GE usually picks its best people for these assignments, on the theory that various divisions will be highly interested in these managers when they return. GE division managers often commit to hiring expatriates back to specific jobs before they go abroad.

A survey of more than 400 North American executives, conducted by Nancy Adler, a management professor at McGill University in Montreal, showed that nearly all had expected the foreign assignments they were undertaking to benefit their careers. However, more than half said the experience turned out to be a detriment.

Another survey, by the executive search giant Korn/Ferry, found that 20 percent of returning expatriates at 34 U.S. multinationals were undergoing reentry stress so severe that they were considering quitting their jobs.

Unhappiness about foreign assignments sends ripples through the company. "When expats come home and report bad experiences, it discourages other people from going abroad," says Stephen Kobrin, a professor of international management at the University of Pennsylvania's Wharton School.

Foreign experience is valued more highly in U.S. multinationals that get half or more of their sales overseas. Herein lies an important point. As long as overseas marketing is a negligible part of the typical company's operation, overseas assignments will be simply side trips off the main career path. Even if you do well, many executives reason, it doesn't impress anyone because the amounts of money involved are proportionately small, and the skills used in achieving success abroad are not as effective in the "big leagues" of domestic competition.

The picture is changing. As foreign business becomes more of a priority, managers who perform well overseas are reaping the rewards. This development was highlighted when Procter & Gamble (where foreign operations were once neglected) selected Edwin Artzt to be CEO. Artzt's great achievement had been the revamping of P&G's overseas business.

The core cultures of big companies, especially those in which tradition has been very strong, tend to change slowly. The change often comes from an external stimulus. Even though a giant corporation is doing a substantial amount of its business abroad, and even though the company's long-range plans involve even more international involvement, a pronounced domestic mindset often prevails that values experience at home over experience abroad.

The young manager who sees that there is a great future in international marketing can accomplish a lot and learn a lot while working with a multinational. An eagerness to grasp overseas assignments, when contemporaries shy away from them, can help in getting the choice postings abroad. And the trend is running toward ultimate acceptance of foreign managerial achievement as being equal in value to the domestic brand.

The experience of working abroad for a big company can be greatly rewarding, but two potential drawbacks remain: reentry woes (comparable to the "bends" suffered by divers who return to the surface too quickly) and the inbred preference (diminishing but still strong) among some top managements for executives with domestic experience.

Working for a Small or Medium-Sized Firm

For a long time, huge companies, with all their drawbacks, were the only places where someone interested in international marketing could gain experience. Most smaller firms simply did not get involved in foreign sales. Now, medium-sized and even small firms are developing an international outlook. Usually they are involved in export.

The managerial tasks include evaluating potential foreign customers, preparing quotes, and dealing with shipping and transportation. Now, chores like shipping and transportation may seem mundane assignments, but they are key elements in the logistical infrastructure of overseas business. The manager who understands them will have a great advantage when it comes time to build and run an enlarged foreign operation.

One difference between the multinationals and smaller companies is that, with the giants, the manager involved in foreign business is likely to do more traveling. Smaller firms with limited budgets tend to try to reach out to the world from home base. The export manager will only occasionally visit foreign markets to discuss strategy with foreign distributors. Most of the work is done by mail, telex, fax, and telephone. The hours are long because of the need to reach contacts overseas, for example, during business hours in Hong Kong.

However, because small and medium-sized companies often are newcomers in the international arena, a new employee will be in on the ground floor. The possibilities for implementing creative business methods are much greater than they would be in a firm steeped in long tradition. The contribution made by the successful export operation will be visible in the company's growing export volume.

Alternatively, international work in a smaller firm can involve importing: finding new, low-cost sources for products in demand in the domestic market. Decisions must often be based on limited information because smaller firms don't have the research amenities of the giants. The import manager is beset with many uncertainties. There are numerous frustrations. Things do not work out as planned. Shipments are delayed, letters of credit are canceled, and products almost never arrive in exactly the form anticipated. Yet the problems are always new. Each day is a fresh challenge. Those who survive are tough enough for any international venture.

As a training ground for international marketing, there is probably no better place than a smaller firm. Ideally, the person with some experience can find work with an export-trading or export-management company, resolving other people's problems. In such a job the international arena is the center ring, not a sideshow. You learn the nitty-gritty of international marketing, you sharpen the instincts needed to make good, fast decisions based on less-than-complete information, and you develop a feel for the cultural differences that contribute a healthy portion of risk.

Going into Business for Yourself

Executives who have acquired experience in international marketing will be in increasing demand. Many companies are in dire need of help for their international marketing efforts and are quite prepared to part with a portion of profits to receive it. As the competitive pressure to move into world business grows, the demand for people with savvy in the area will grow with it.

This development favors those who choose to hang up a consultant's shingle or to establish a trading firm. It takes in-depth knowledge and broad experience to run a trading company or serve as a consultant in the field.

Specialized services that might be offered by a consultant include international market research, international strategic planning, or even full-service assistance in international market entry or international marketing negotiations.

The up-front costs in offering such a service are substantial. They are not covered by turnover; they have to be covered by profits. The work can be arduous and the risks can be high, but the rewards are there. An international marketing expert will typically bill at an hourly rate of $250–300 for experienced principals and more than $100 for staff. When international travel is required, overseas activities are often billed at a daily rate of $2,000 plus expenses. Expenses can add up quickly to a substantial amount.

Besides lending one's expertise to others, there is the alternative of

Learning Affluence[9]

Consumers in advanced nations are learning how to be affluent. Take this example of an affluent person living in Asia: he wears Ferragamo-designed shirts and Hermes ties, sports a Rolex or Cartier watch, carries a Louis Vuitton attaché case, writes with a Montblanc pen, drives to work in his flashy BMW, charges with his American Express card, and flies Singapore Airlines. He uses Giorgio Armani aftershave and buys Poison for his girlfriend. As a career woman, she has a wardrobe filled with Christian Dior and Nina Ricci, a dressing table crowded with makeup and skin care from Guerlain, YSL, and Estee Lauder, shoes from Bruno Magli. She wears Chanel No. 5 and jewelry from Tiffany. They both listen to Beethoven's Ninth on the Sony CD player in her Mazda sports car.

---

trading on one's own. This is truly the high trapeze act of international marketing. Risk can be limitless; so can income. Consultants and owners of trading firms work at a higher risk than employees, but with the chance for higher rewards.

Multicultural Management Training

Knowledge is one essential ingredient of success in international marketing. Experience is a second ingredient. A third is sensitivity to cultural nuances.

The *Wall Street Journal* describes how BP Oil Europe, a Brussels-based unit of British Petroleum Co., is manifesting its conviction that this is an important training area. The company has put more than 250 of its managers through courses conducted by Bob Waisfisz, a Dutchman whose firm, based in The Hague, offers seminars in multicultural management.

Some companies are setting up their own in-house multicultural training programs. Motorola, Inc. has opened a special center for cultural training at its Schaumburg, Illinois, headquarters. The company is putting hundreds of managers through short courses there, conducted by Fons Trompenaars. The center is run by Rs Moorthy, a Malaysian, who declares the goal is to make Motorola managers "transculturally competent."

Many companies dispute the need for this kind of training. To some

Multicultural Management Seminars[10]

The growth of international business is creating a yawning need for training that helps executives to bridge the cultural gap. That need is being filled.

Companies get into international marketing these days without spending a lot of time in preparation. They do some things right. They gather the relevant facts about the target market. They adapt their products to suit the challenge. Everything appears to be "go," but the venture keeps running into problems. A training official at the Management Centre Europe in Brussels says, "The missing element is the human factor."

Management Centre Europe is one of the centers for cultural orientation springing up in Europe and other points around the globe. The seminars go beyond a simple introduction to coping with the differing customs and attitudes of various countries. The objective is to change attitudes and challenge biases—to give marketing executives a workable system for coming to terms with a wide range of people with different values and for solving problems caused by cultural differences.

The focus is on mindset, not skills. Multicultural management, says Fons Trompenaars, a Dutch trainer, is "a question of attitude, an openness to human variety, not a question of knowledge." Here's an example of how Trompenaars works. He divides a class of managers into two groups. Four of the managers are designated as "international experts in building paper towers." All the other managers become residents of the mythical nation of Derdia.

The experts leave the room to learn how to make paper towers and to get ready to train the Derdians in that discipline. Trompenaars tells the Derdians about their strange customs. Holding out a hand to someone means "Please go away." When Derdians wish to indicate disagreement with something, they say yes and nod their heads. Derdian women will not use paper or scissors when men are present. Derdian men never use a pencil or ruler in front of women.

Now the "experts" try to establish lines of communication with the Derdians. An expert asks the Derdians to sit. "Yes," they reply, remaining standing. The experts confer. "They didn't understand us," says one. Here, of course, we are at the center of the issue.

More to the point, the expert might have said, "We didn't understand them."

Persisting, the experts try to explain things to the Derdians. They speak very slowly, as if to small children. When a Derdian shows familiarity with the workings of scissors, a trainer exclaims, "Good boy!" At the end of the session, the tower is unbuilt. The game ends; the participants hold a critique. "They treated us like idiots," says a Derdian.

As the interest in multicultural training increases, the approaches to it will proliferate. The programs will, essentially, be devoted to revamping the mindset that makes people misunderstand and undervalue the abilities of people from other parts of the world. "No culture is better or worse than another," says Knud Christensen, a Danish personnel manager at BP Oil Europe. "They're just different. We have to understand that."

---

extent that's part of the mindset. David Howell, a culture trainer in Ashley, England, comments on American and English impatience in doing business abroad. "Americans say, 'If there is a buck in it, we'll do business with them.' But people in other parts of the world say, 'Unless we like you, we won't do business together.' "[11]

However it happens, ingrained Western attitudes and practices will have to be modified as the companies go after more business abroad. The company that moves decisively to multiculturalize its management corps will have a competitive advantage.

Some organizations offer a kind of training buffet table to executives. Within reason, people are allowed to choose the programs they will attend and the courses they will take at company expense. Managers who are permitted such choices should consider multicultural training. It stamps the manager as someone who ought to be considered for overseas assignments. And it will help to prepare the manager to take full advantage of the opening in international marketing if and when it comes.

Companies, even smaller companies, should consider introducing multiculturalism into the training and development menu. All too often, training programs go on year after year, covering pretty much the same ground, without reference to the company's changing situation or the new realities of the competitive environment. Periodically all training ought to be reviewed, subjected to questions like these:

- What is the purpose of this program?

- In what ways should the trainees be different at the end of the program?

• Is the program working?

• Does the program suit the company's present needs?

• Does the training mix conform proportionately to the overall mix of company needs and involvements?

• What significant moves is the company likely to make in the future?

• Is the training program preparing us for that move?

• What changes in training should be made to get us ready for the future?

When the management training arrangement is reviewed in the context of a possible expansion of the company's international marketing efforts, the firm might decide to emphasize multicultural management, as well as the languages, laws, and demographics of possible target countries. In fact, even if a company does not go global, multiculturalism is by no means wasted.

Adventuring into the New World

International marketing is the great business adventure of our time. It's competitive, risky, and full of unknowns. For those who are able to meet the challenges of the global arena, the excitement and the satisfaction of accomplishment will be matched by the rewards in business success.

This book is a primer on a sophisticated and complex topic. You have become acquainted with the outlines of international marketing in these pages. To be a winner, you will want to move ahead, preparing yourself and your organization for doing business in the world. You don't have to do it on your own. Help is available for the asking.

You can get rich by succeeding in international marketing. And, at the same time, your success is contributing to the peaceful growth and survival of the planet and its peoples. We wish you the best of luck.

Appendix 1   Sources

This book contains hundreds of quotations, citations, and cases. To the extent possible, sources have been indicated in the chapter-by-chapter references below.

Publications. We have drawn on a wide range of printed sources, including newspapers and general magazines, professional journals, company publications and releases, government publications, and books, some general and some specialized.

Interviews. The authors have been able to speak with company executives, government officials, professionals, and educators. Authors Czinkota and Ronkainen travel widely, advising companies and governments, and lecturing in symposia throughout the world. These occasions provide the added benefit of up-to-the-minute contact with developments in international business.

Governments. We have been able to use material from the trade-related government bureaus of established world powers and developing countries.

Correspondence. In certain cases, text material is based upon correspondence (corporate, government, private) that the authors have been permitted to use.

References
Chapter 1

1. "Whirlpool Makes a Splash," *International Management* 23 (December 1991): 59–61; "Whirlpool Plots the Invasion of Europe," *Business Week* September 5, 1988, 70–72.

2. Gail E. Shares, John Templeman, Robert Neff, and Stanley Reed, "Think Small: Export Lessons to Be Learned from Germany's Mid-size Companies," *Business Week* November 4, 1991, 58–65; William J. Holstein, "Why Johann Can Export but Johnny Can't," *Business Week* November 4, 1991, 64.

3. Laurie Hays, "Some Americans Take the Steppes in Stride," *Wall Street Journal* January 23, 1992, B1, B2.

4. *Wall Street Journal* October 11, 1993.

Chapter 2

1. S. Tamer Cavusgil, "Guidelines for Export Market Research," *Business Horizons* 28 (November–December 1985): 29. Copyright by the Foundation for the School of Business at Indiana University. Reprinted by permission.

2. "Western Firms Poll Eastern Europeans to Discern Tastes of Nascent Consumers," *Wall Street Journal* April 27, 1992, B1.

3. Vinay Kothari, "Researching for Export Marketing," in *Export Promotion: The Public and Private Sector Interaction,* ed. M. Czinkota (New York: Praeger Publishers, 1983), 169–172.

Chapter 3

1. *Wall Street Journal* May 27, 1991.

2. *Wall Street Journal* October 24, 1991.

3. Johnny K. Johansson and Ikujiro Nonaka, "Market Research the Japanese Way," *Harvard Business Review* 65 (May–June 1987): 16–22.

4. Lothar G. Winter and Charles R. Prohaska, "Methodological Problems in the Comparative Analysis of International Marketing Systems," *Journal of the Academy of Marketing Science* 11 (Fall 1993): 429.

5. As quoted in Christopher Madison, "Kissinger Firm Hopes to Make Its Mark as Risk Advisors to Corporate Chiefs," *National Journal* June 22, 1985, 1452–1456.

Chapter 4

1. "Sizing Up the Customers' Needs," *Export Today* 5 (February 1989): 32–33.

2. "Exporting Pays Off," *Business America* August 23, 1993, 20.

3. Dan Koeppel, "From War Torn Beirut, Peppermint Chiclets," *Adweek's Marketing Week* 30 (1989): 24.

4. *Wall Street Journal* May 18, 1993.

5. Bill of Lading, Shipper's Export Declaration forms: reprinted from Michael R. Czinkota and Ilkka Ronkainen, *International Marketing* 3rd edition (The Dryden Press/Harcourt Brace Jovanovich College Publishers, 1993): 424–25.

Chapter 5

1. John Tarrant, *Drucker: The Man Who Invented the Corporate Society* (Cahners Books, 1976).

2. "Dominos, Pizza Hut Make Run for the Border, Continue Their War," *Marketing News* November 11, 1991, 5.

3. "Exporting Pays Off," *Business America* February 25, 1991, 35.

Chapter 6

1. John Tarrant, *Drucker: The Man Who Invented the Corporate Society* (Cahners Books, 1976).

2. Michael R. Czinkota and Ilkka Ronkainen, *International Marketing* 3rd edition (The Dryden Press/Harcourt Brace Jovanovich College Publishers, 1993): 360–61.

3. "America: The Export Edge," *Export Today* 5 (February 1989): 5–19.

Chapter 7

1. *Wall Street Journal* May 12, 1988.

2. "Do Round-Toed Boots Contribute to Trade Gap?" *Journal of Commerce* April 5, 1989, 1A, 12A.

3. "Exporting Pays Off," *Business America* February 25, 1991.

4. Michael Czinkota and Jon Woronoff, *Unlocking Japan's Markets* (Probus Publishing, 1991): 174.

5. Ibid., 177.

Chapter 8

1. Michael R. Czinkota and Ilkka Ronkainen, *International Marketing* 3rd edition (The Dryden Press/Harcourt Brace Jovanovich College Publishers, 1993): 334–35.

2. "The Corporate Shell Game," *Newsweek* April 15, 1991, 48–49; "Worldwide Tax Authorities Promise Increased Scrutiny of Transfer Pricing," *Business International Money Report* February 22, 1988, 72; "Smaller Bill Seen in Texaco Dispute," *New York Times* January 19, 1988, D2.

3. Gregory L. Miles, "Exporters' New Bully Stick," *International Business* December 1993, 46.

4. S. Tamer Cavusgil, "Unraveling the Mystique of Export Pricing," *Business Horizons* May–June 1988, 55–59.

5. "An Exporter Complains: Low-Value Cargo Equals Low-Priority Service," *Distribution* October 1991, 36.

6. Helmut Becker, "Pricing: An International Marketing Challenge," in *International Marketing Strategy,* eds. Hans Thorelli and Helmut Becker (New York: Pergamon Press, 1980): 215. Reprinted with permission.

Chapter 9

1. Chase Manhattan Bank, *Dynamics of Trade Finance* (New York: Chase Manhattan Bank, 1984): 5.

2. Clemens P. Work, Sarah Peterson, and Hidehiro Tanakadate, "Two Air Disasters, Two Cultures, Two Remedies," *U.S. News and World Report* August 26, 1985, 25–26.

3. Richard Loth, American Export Group International Services.

Chapter 10

1. The authors acknowledge the assistance of Robert J. Kaiser of the Export-Import Bank of the United States and Louis G. Guadagnoli in the preparation of this section.

2. "Japan's Hands-On Foreign Aid," *Washington Post* January 13, 1991, H1, H4; Kenan B. Jarboe, Robert R. Miller, and John A. Alic, "Project Financing: The Case of the International Construction Industry," in *Trade Finance: Current Issues and Developments,* ed. Michael Czinkota (Washington D.C.: Government Printing Office, 1988): 86–92; D. Barchard, "Ozal Model Sets Pattern For the Future," *Financial Times* December 18, 1986, 6; and L. Ingrassia, "How Japan Sealed Deal to Build Bridge Spanning the Bosporus," *Wall Street Journal* May 29, 1985, 1.

Chapter 11

1. *German Tribune* June 12, 1988.

2. Abla Adel-Latif, *Journal of World Trade* October, 1990.

Chapter 12

1. *Wall Street Journal* October 12, 1993.

2. Janet Guyon, "Czechs Play a Tough Game of Monopoly," *Wall Street Journal* October 12, 1993.

3. Richard H. Holton, "Making International Joint Ventures Work," paper presented at the seminar on the management of headquarters/subsidiary relationships in transnational corporations, Stockholm School of Economics, June 2–4, 1980, 4.

4. Ibid., 5.

5. Anthony J. F. O'Reilly, "Establishing Successful Joint Ventures in Developing Nations: A CEO's Perspective," *Columbia Journal of World Business* 23 (Spring 1988).

6. Peter Fuchs, "Strategic Alliances," *Business Tokyo* (April 1991).

7. Lena H. Sun, "Avon Rings a Bell in China," *Washington Post* June 29, 1991, C1, C3; "The Avon Lady Comes Knocking on Chinese Doors," *Singapore Straits Times* May 29, 1991, 5.

Chapter 13

1. Michael R. Czinkota and Ilkka Ronkainen, *International Marketing* 3rd edition (The Dryden Press/Harcourt Brace Jovanovich College Publishers, 1993): 692–701.

2. *Wall Street Journal* July 26, 1993.

3. Thomas Gross, Ernie Turner, and Lars Cederholm, "Building Teams for Global Operations," *Management Review* (June 1987): 340.

4. John Tarrant, *Perks and Parachutes: Negotiating Your Executive Employment Contract* (Stonesong Press/Simon & Schuster, 1985).

Chapter 14

1. Press releases from MTV Europe, January–February 1991.

2. Nicolas G. Synodinos, Charles F. McKeown, and Laurence W. Jacobs, "International Advertising Practices," *Journal of Advertising Research* 29 (April–May 1989): 43–50.

3. *Business Marketing* December, 1991.

4. Leonard Saffir and John Tarrant, *Power Public Relations* (NTC Publishing Group, 1993).

5. Robert L. Rose, "Whirlpool is Expanding in Europe Despite the Slump," *Wall Street Journal* January 27, 1994, B4.

Chapter 15

1. *Wall Street Journal* December 7, 1993.

2. Lawrence Ingrassia and Asra Q. Nomani, "Trading Up: Firms Far and Wide Are Looking to GATT for Competitive Edge," *Wall Street Journal* December 7, 1993.

3. Edward N. Luttwak, *The Endangered American Dream* (Simon & Schuster, 1993).

4. Samuel P. Huntington, "The Coming Clash of Civilizations Or, the West Against the Rest," *New York Times* June 6, 1993.

5. John Tarrant, interview with Paul Green, *Desalination and Water Reuse*.

6. *Wall Street Journal* September 20, 1993.

7. "Business Schools Hit Hard Times Amid Doubt Over Value of MBA," *New York Times* May 12, 1993; Elizabeth M. Fowler, "Education for Global Awareness," *New York Times* April 25, 1989.

8. Thomas F. O'Boyle, "Little Benefits to Careers Seen in Foreign Stints," *Wall Street Journal* December 11, 1989.

9. Adapted from John Naisbitt, *Global Paradox* (Morrow & Co., 1994): 31.

10. Bob Hagerty, "Trainers Help Expatriate Employees Build Bridges to Different Cultures," *Wall Street Journal* June 14, 1993.

11. Ibid.

Appendix 2   Sample Contracts

Counterpurchase contract with the USSR

Concerning the cooperation in the erection of a complex for the production of polyester fibers, polyester threads and their raw materials in the USSR, and the delivery of chemicals and cotton entered into by the Ministry for Foreign Trade of the USSR, Moscow, as the party of the first part and the firms [NAMES] as the parties of the second part.

WITNESSETH

Article 1

1.1 The parties to this agreement shall cooperate in erecting a complex for the production of polyester fibers, polyester threads, and their raw materials in the USSR, comprising:

	Capacity in Tons/Year
Polyester Fibers	35,000
Polyethylene Terephthalate (Granulate)	57,000
Polyester Threads	24,000
Polyester Threads	28,000
Polyester Fibers	50,000
Polyester Fibers	50,000

1.2 The firms listed below shall submit technical and commercial offers for the licensing, transfer of technical documentation for the delivery of the complete equipment (hereinafter called "equipment") and the granting of services on the facilities listed under numeral 1.1, not later than by the deadline listed below, to V/O "Techmashimport" Moscow:

(a) [GENERAL CONTRACTOR FIRM'S NAME] for the facilities

(b) [ENGINEERING FIRM'S NAME] according to the know-how of
[TECHNOLOGY LICENSOR'S NAME] for the facilities:

Polyester Fibers	35,000 tons/year	April 15, 19--
Polyethylene		
Terephthalate		
(Granulate)	57,000 "	June 15, 19--
Polyester Threads	24,000 "	June 15, 19--
Polyester Threads	28,000 "	July 15, 19--
Polyester Fibers	50,000 "	July 1, 19--
Polyester Fibers	50,000 "	Sept. 1, 19--

Article 2

2.1 V/O "Techmashimport" and the firms mentioned under numeral 1.2 shall,
if they agree on reciprocally acceptable technical and commercial terms, conclude
agreements about the licensing and transfer of the technical documentation
(including the projection documentation), delivery of the equipment and the performance of services, including supervision of the erection, start of the operation
of the facilities and training of Soviet technical personnel for which the corres-
ponding firms shall present offers as per numeral 1.2.

V/O "Techmashimport" and the firms mentioned above shall agree on the method
of the conclusion of the agreements, including their sequence.

The technical documentation and equipment to be furnished by the suppliers for
the facilities listed in numeral 1.1. shall be on the level of world engineering
standards in the area involved, which will assure the production of products with
a high value.

The warranty conditions and the liability of said suppliers for meeting the responsibilities assumed by them shall be determined in agreements to be concluded
between V/O "Techmashimport" and the said firms.

2.2 V/O "Techmashimport" has the right to request offers on licensing, transfer
of technical documentation, delivery of equipment and performance of services
for the facilities listed in numeral 1 at all times from any third party firms. If
comparable offers from any third party firms prove to be more favorable for
V/O "Techmashimport," the aforementioned suppliers shall improve the conditions of their offers. If during the negotiations no agreement is reached about
reciprocally acceptable technical and commercial terms, V/O "Techmashimport" may conclude agreements with third party firms.

Article 3

3.1 The parties to the agreement rely on the premises that the purchase of the licenses, technical documentations, equipment and services listed under article 1 of this agreement will be effected on the condition of the granting of long-term, project-bound *bank loans* for *85%* of the contractual amounts, 15% of the contractual values being paid in cash. It is further assumed that the detailed terms of these loans shall be set forth in the agreement(s) between the Foreign Trade Bank of the USSR and the banks of the [WEST EUROPEAN COUNTRY]. If it should turn out that it is impossible to obtain bank loans, both sides shall search for other forms of credit.

3.2 The parties to the agreement further assume that under the licensing, delivery of technical documentation and equipment, and under the performance of services from countries with which the USSR maintains loan agreements on a government level, the financing of such operations shall take place under the terms of the credit agreements concluded on government levels.

3.3 The parties to the agreement are obligated to promote the credit negotiations. The supplier firms of the [WEST EUROPEAN COUNTRY] shall use their influence so that the loans will be made available by the banks at the best possible terms.

Credit negotiations shall be conducted as rapidly as possible. Such discussions shall be attended on the one hand by representatives of the Ministry for Foreign Trade of the USSR and the Bank for Foreign Trade of the USSR and on the other hand, the [WEST EUROPEAN COUNTRY] banks and the supplier firms, in order to reach an agreement about the essential terms of the loan contracts to be entered into.

Article 4

4.1 The buyers, [NAMES OF THREE WEST EUROPEAN BUYERS], shall conclude at the same time long-term agreements with the vendors V/O "Sojuzchimexport" and/or V/O "Exportljon," Moscow, concerning the supply of chemicals and cotton from the USSR, if they agree on reciprocally acceptable terms.

The total value of these agreements shall correspond with the entire value payable by V/O "Techmashimport" in foreign exchange to the supplier firms according to the agreements covering licenses, technical documentation, equipment and services, including interest on loans.

4.2 The vendors and buyers listed under numeral 4.1 shall sell and/or purchase the following products and quantities:

BUYER	PRODUCT	QUANTITIES IN 1000 TONS/YEAR	START OF DELIVERIES
[BUYER A]	DMT	20	19--
	Para-Xylol	20	Will be agreed on by the end of 198-
	Methanol	30	19--
[BUYER B]	Methanol	40	19--
	Ortho Xylol	20	Will be agreed on by the end of 198-
	Acetic Acid	10	19--
[BUYER C]	Cotton	30	19-- (19--; 19,000 tons)

4.3 The parties to the agreement assume thereby that in view of the expected price trends, the full value will have to be reached not later than 12 years effective with the beginning of the deliveries as set forth under numeral 4.1.

If the *full value* cited in numeral 4.1 is reached earlier than at the aforementioned deadline, the obligations of the parties to the agreement concerning the sale and/ or purchase of the products are considered as having been met.

If it becomes obvious that the total value cited in numeral 4.1 for all contracts cannot be reached within the time limit quoted in said numeral, the buyer(s) unable to attain the total value cited in its (their) *individual contract* shall try to reach an agreement in time with V/O "Sojuzchimexport" and/or V/O "Exportljon" about increasing the scope of the delivery of the goods according to numeral 4.2 and/or about an extension of the above time limit by reciprocal accord. If the Soviet foreign trade associations can offer other products, this question may be decided on by mutual agreement between the contracting parties.

Article 5

5.1 The prices for the chemicals mentioned in article 4 of this agreement shall be determined by the parties to the contract per metric ton net, CIF West European basic ports.

The prices shall be determined for a period of 6 months, in each case 2 months prior to the start of such a period (or for other periods to be agreed on between the parties to the contract), on the basis of the world market prices which are determined on the basis of the following documents:

—Agreements in effect on export and import transactions, except transactions of the vendor with RGW countries and transactions of the buyer with his branches and under barter transactions;

—Inquiries and quotation of the firms;

—Customs statistics of the countries into which said chemicals will be exported;

—Publications (newspapers, magazines, etc.) reproducing the trends of market development for these products;

—Other representative and objective data on the market situation of these products.

5.2 The prices for cotton shall be determined by V/O "Exportljon" and [BUYER C] per metric ton net CIF West European basic ports for periods to be agreed on on the basis of world market quotations. V/O "Exportljon" and [BUYER C] shall premise themselves in their agreements on prices for cotton on the principle of cooperation, reciprocal benefit and competitive conditions according to the international commercial practice for cotton.

Article 6

6.1 The agreements about the delivery of equipment according to article 2 and the long-term agreements about the delivery of chemicals and cotton according to article 4 shall become effective simultaneously, with the premise that the agreements about the delivery of chemicals and cotton according to article 4 shall be concluded prior to or simultaneously with the contracts on the delivery of equipment according to article 2.

A tie-in of the sale of Soviet products with the purchase of licenses, technical documentation, equipment and services by V/O "Techmashimport" can be established only in the agreements between V/O "Sojuzchimexport" and V/O "Exportljon" and the buyer firms involved. The parties to the agreement shall take every possible measure for the agreements to be concluded as soon as possible following the execution of the present contract.

These agreements will become effective only following the resolution of financing problems in connection with the loans to be granted for the licenses, technical documentation, equipment and services to be performed.

6.2 Each contracting partner is liable only for the accomplishment of the obligations it assumes in each individual agreement on the basis of this contract.

Article 7

7.1 In consideration of the high significance of the cooperation of the partners to this contract, under the present agreement, and of the large scope of the reciprocal deliveries of equipment and merchandise on a long-term basis, the parties to the agreement shall engage in joint efforts to take all measures necessary to secure the obligations assumed according to this agreement.

7.2 Any disputes and differences of opinion which could arise out of this agreement shall be solved by way of negotiations between the contracting partners under this agreement. The invocation of any courts (including arbitration courts) by the contracting parties under this agreement is ruled out.

Article 8

Agreements concluded in harmony with the present agreement shall provide for licensing conditions, terms of delivery, including among other matters, scope, prices, delivery dates, terms of payment, warranties, shipping conditions, liability of the contractual partners according to the contracts for compliance with their terms, type of settlement of possible disputes, etc.

Article 9

The present agreement becomes effective as of the date of signing and remains in force until all obligations under the contracts concluded on its basis have been complied with.

This present agreement has been signed on February 20, 19--, in two originals, each original being drawn up in the Russian and [WEST EUROPEAN] languages, in [WEST EUROPEAN CITY], whereby both texts are equally binding.

For the USSR side   For the [WEST EUROPEAN] side

Letter of Undertaking with Indonesia

Standard document provided by the Indonesian Department of Trade to foreign contractors/suppliers bidding on public tenders.

(Letterhead of Tenderer)*

_____, 19--

Department of Trade and Cooperatives
Republic of Indonesia
Directorate General for Foreign Trade
Jalan Abdul Muis 87
Jakarta
INDONESIA

c/o(Insert name of Department, Agency or Corporation
    issuing Tender)

Dear Sirs:

We refer to (describe subject matter of tender and tender number) issued on _____, 19__ by (insert name of Indonesian Department, Agency or Corporation issuing tender) and to our tender document no. _____ submitted on _____ , 19__ in response thereto.

We hereby irrevocably undertake during the period from the date of award of the contract relating to such tender until final acceptance (or equivalent) of our work and services thereunder or until completion of deliveries thereunder, as the case may be:

1. to purchase, or to cause to be purchased by one or more of our affiliated companies in the country or countries** to be confirmed by the Department of Trade and Cooperatives in a letter in the form of Annex A hereto or by third parties located in any other country or countries acceptable to you, agricultural and/or industrial products contained in Books A.1 and A.2, each entitled "List of Indonesian Export Commodities Available for Additional Exports in 1982," published in January 1982 and March 1982, respectively, by the Department of Trade and Cooperatives, and/or such other Indonesian products as you may

---

*This letter should be signed and submitted by the Tenderer. If the Tenderer is a foreign contractor/supplier, this letter should be signed by the foreign contractor/supplier and not by its Indonesian agent, partner or representative, if any.

**The Department of Trade and Cooperatives will normally only confirm the country of nationality of the contractor/supplier. However, depending upon the circumstances of any given contract, other countries may be confirmed by the Department.

approve in writing (hereinafter, collectively, the "Products"), from one or more of the commodity associations or exporters named in Books B.1 and B.2, each entitled "List of Indonesian Commodity Associations and Exporters" published in January 1982 and March 1982, respectively, by the Department of Trade and Cooperatives, and/or from other duly licensed Indonesian exporters (herein, collectively, the "Exporters"), in an amount at least equal to the foreign currency value of all equipment, materials and products pursuant to the term of the above described contract, such value to be agreed with the Department of Trade and Cooperatives and confirmed in a letter in the form of Annex A hereto;

2. to use the Products, or to resell the Products for use, or to cause the Products to be used or resold, in the country or countries to be confirmed as aforesaid, unless with your specific authorization we are permitted to use the Products, or to resell the Products for use, or to cause the Products to be used or resold, in any other country or countries;

3. to purchase the Products, or to cause the Products to be purchased, before the end of the term of the contract relating to the above-described tender and, in any event, to purchase, or to cause to be purchased, at least twenty percent (20%) of the total value of Products to be purchased hereunder within six (6) months after the date of award of such contract; and

4. to submit, or to cause to be submitted, to the Department of Trade and Cooperatives the relevant PEB Form and such other evidence of the shipment of Products purchased pursuant to this undertaking as will permit the Department of Trade and Cooperatives to monitor compliance herewith.

In connection with our irrevocable undertaking contained herein, this will confirm our understanding that:

a. the commercial terms, including those relating to price and delivery, in respect of each purchase of Products from an Exporter shall be negotiated by us or by other purchasers thereof at the time of actual purchase;

b. the amount of each such purchase to be applied towards our obligation hereunder shall be equal to the invoiced purchase price of the Products purchased, excluding, however, any shipping costs included in such invoice and any taxes or custom duties charged in connection therewith;

c. the amount of each such purchase (if measured in a currency other than the currency in which our obligation hereunder is measured) shall be applied against our obligation hereunder at exchange rates (as quoted by Bank Indonesia) prevailing at the date of the Exporter's invoice issued in respect of such purchase;

d. if we or our affiliated companies in the country or countries to be confirmed as aforesaid have traditionally purchased Products from Indonesian exporters, our undertaking contained herein shall be viewed as representing a commitment over and above such traditional level of purchases, it being the spirit and intention of such undertaking that purchases of Products hereunder shall be in addition to such traditional level of purchases; and

e. if the contract relating to the above-described tender should be prematurely terminated, our undertaking contained herein shall also terminate without further obligation on our part.

f. if during the course of performance of our obligations contained herein, we should be of the view that sufficient Products are either not available in Indonesia or are not of suitable export quality or internationally competitive in price, you shall, at our request, review with us the actual circumstances at the time and shall consider, but without obligation, modifying the requirements contained herein, (including, without limitation, an extension of the time during which our obligations contained herein must be satisfied).

If we fail to comply with our undertaking contained herein, we hereby agree to pay you as liquidated damages an amount equal to 50% of the difference between the total value of Products actually purchased pursuant to this undertaking and the foreign currency amount to be confirmed as aforesaid.

In connection with our undertaking contained herein, we hereby represent and warrant to you that (i) we have full power and authority and legal right to enter into this undertaking and to perform and observe the terms and provisions thereof, (ii) we have taken all necessary legal action to authorize, execute and deliver this undertaking, (iii) this undertaking constitutes our legal, valid and binding obligation, and (iv) no law, rule or regulation or contractual or other obligation binding on us is or will be contravened by reason of our execution and delivery of this undertaking or by our performance and observance of the terms and provisions hereof.

This undertaking shall be binding upon our successors.

Very truly yours,

(Name of Tenderer)
By _____
Name:
Title:

Counterpurchase Contract with India

No.MMTC/91-92   Dated:

This Agreement hereinafter referred to as "Countertrade Agreement" is made this _____ day of _____ 1991 between the Minerals & Metals Trading Corporation of India Ltd., New Delhi, represented by their Export Division (hereinafter referred to as "MMTC"), which expression shall unless excluded by or repugnant to the context include its successors and assignors, of the first part and M/s _____, a company established under the laws of and having its Regd. office at _____ and represented by their duly constituted attornies (hereinafter referred to as "Overseas Supplier") of the second part.

AND WHEREAS THE Overseas Supplier has signed a contract with MMTC No. _____ dated _____ (hereinafter referred to as "Import Contract") for supply of _____ valued at US$ _____

AND WHEREAS it was provided in Clause No. __ of the Import Contract that the Overseas Supplier shall purchase or cause to be purchased Indian Goods, Commodities, Services (hereinafter referred to as "Goods") from Indian Companies and export the Goods from India for an amount and within a time period in accordance with the provisions of this Agreement.

NOW THEREFORE IT IS MUTUALLY AGREED TO BETWEEN THE PARTIES HERETO AS FOLLOWS:

DEFINITION OF TERMS
Clause 1

1.1 In this Agreement, unless the context otherwise provides

1.2 Indian Goods, Commodities and Services, means, any goods, commodities, services manufactured/produced within India with the exclusion of Free Trade Zones or Export Promotion Zones, so designated by Appropriate authorities. It shall also include services by Indian companies outside India, the earnings from which is fully repatriated to India. Indian companies means any corporate body established under the law of India, including sole proprietorship.

1.3 Countertrade means purchase and export of goods, commodities and services from India by an Overseas Supplier of a value equivalent to a specified percentage of the value of the import contract, payments for either link of the transaction to be on mutually acceptable terms.

1.4 For the purpose of countertrade under this Agreement, the list of goods can include items listed in Annexure-1 and excludes all items listed in Annexure-2 enclosed.

PURCHASE AND EXPORT
Clause 2

2.1 The Overseas Supplier shall purchase Indian goods, directly or through MMTC, from Indian companies and export them from India in accordance with this Agreement.

2.2 The sum of such purchase of goods and their subsequent export from India under this Agreement shall be in the value of _____ based on the FOB prices of goods so purchased and exported out of India (hereinafter referred to as "Export Obligation").

2.3 Subject to Sub-clause 2.4, the Overseas Supplier shall commence export of goods from India subsequent to the date of the Countertrade Agreement and shall complete such exports up to a total sum as per subclause 2.2, and do so no later than 12 months from the date of the import contract.

2.4 Notwithstanding the provisions in Sub-clause 2.3, if the Overseas Supplier is not able to complete the obligations for exports of Indian Goods as per sub-clause 2.2, within the time period stipulated in Subclause 2.3, they may at the discretion of MMTC for reasons other than force majeure under Clause 8, be granted an extension of the period stipulated in Sub-clause 2.3 based on MMTC's evaluation of the need for granting such an extension which shall not exceed _____ months in total.

2.5 The date of export performance by the Overseas Supplier, as per this Agreement, shall be linked to the dates of the bill of lading of the export.

2.6 The Overseas Supplier may send an enquiry to MMTC for the goods they intend to purchase and export as per this Agreement. Wherever MMTC is able to make an offer directly as principal on competitive terms, MMTC and the Overseas Supplier will enter into separate contracts for each transaction on mutually agreed terms and conditions. Alternatively, the Overseas Supplier may at its option make arrangements for purchases from alternate sources of supply within India. However, such deals must be referred to MMTC immediately upon finalization indicating the export deal finalization date, the goods proposed to be bought, the name of the buyer, the name of the Indian seller, the goods' prices/quantity, the total value, the payment terms, etc., along with the agreement duly signed by the Indian seller in terms of Sub-clause 2.7 for our specific approval before proceeding with the exports. In all such cases, the Overseas Supplier shall indemnify MMTC from all losses, obligations, risks and responsibilities arising out of such arrangement.

2.7 In case of payment on CAD basis, the Indian seller will be required to enter into an agreement with MMTC as per Annexure 6 appended to this Agreement.

2.8 Payments for exports of goods by the Overseas Supplier in terms of this Agreement shall be governed by the "documentation procedure" relating to export documentary credits, as per Annexure 3 appended to this Agreement.

PERFORMANCE BANK GUARANTEE
Clause 3

3.1 The Overseas Supplier shall furnish to MMTC within 15 days of the signing of this Agreement a security deposit in the form of an export performance bank guarantee (hereinafter referred to as "EPBG") as per Annexure 4 attached herewith. The EPBG shall be confirmed by an Indian nationalized bank, having its duly authenticated branch office in Delhi. This security deposit in the form of EPBG shall be for a sum of US $_____ being _____ percent of the value of the export obligation of the Overseas Supplier as per Sub-clause 2.2 of this Agreement. The amount secured herein shall be payable to MMTC on demand, notwithstanding any arbitration proceedings under Clause 11, for any breach of any provisions of this Agreement, on the part of the Overseas Supplier. The validity of this EPBG shall be from the date of the issue up to two months after the stipulated period for completion of the export obligations.

3.2 The validity of the EPBG shall be extended by the Overseas Supplier for a further period up to _____ months in case any extension is granted as per Sub-clause 2.4 of this Agreement.

3.3 MMTC shall release the EPBG after deducting the amount of liquidated damages, if any, due to MMTC under Clause 8 of this Agreement after the export obligations of the Overseas Supplier as per various clauses of this Agreement have been duly fulfilled.

Clause 4

4.1 The Overseas Supplier would have to submit "non negotiable" copies of the various export shipping documents to MMTC as proofs of exports required to be made by him as per Sub-clause 2.2 of this Agreement. These documents must be presented to MMTC within 30 days from the date of B/L in accordance with the documentation procedure as per Annexure 3, otherwise countertrade credit will not be allowed by MMTC.

4.2 Within 15 days from the submission of documents as per Clause 4.1, in case the documents are in order and evidence satisfactory fulfillment of the countertrade obligation, MMTC will issue a certificate confirming the acceptable value of exports as per Annexure 5 attached herein, towards the value accountable towards the fulfillment of the export obligation of the Overseas Supplier.

ASSIGNMENT

Clause 5

5.1 The Overseas Supplier can purchase from India directly or through nominees. Nominees/assignees may be changed on a selective basis, as and when necessary, with mutual written consent of both MMTC and the countertrade obligant. The nominee/assignee cannot sub-assign in full or part the benefits and the obligations so assigned to them by the Overseas supplier to any fourth party nor can they nominate a fourth party to fulfill the obligations so assigned to them as above. The consent for assignment of benefits and obligations of the Overseas Supplier as per this Agreement to a third party(ies) shall be given entirely at the discretion of MMTC and the same shall not relieve the Overseas Supplier from any liabilities or obligations under this Agreement.

Clause 6

6.1 If the import contract is cancelled for any reason whatsoever, the Overseas Supplier's obligation under this contract shall not, to the extent of the value of goods purchased by MMTC under the import contracts, be relieved; PROVIDED ALWAYS that such cancellation shall not prejudice or affect any right of action or remedy which shall have accrued or shall accrue thereafter to MMTC.

Clause 7

7.1 This Agreement shall be deemed to have been completed upon the occurrence of any of the following events:

7.1.1 MMTC releases the EPBG upon fulfillment of export obligations as per Clause 2.2.

7.1.2 The Overseas Supplier has paid the liquidated damages to MMTC as per Clause 8.

7.1.3 The import contract is cancelled for any reason as provided under relevant clauses of the import contract.

Clause 8

8.1   Subject to any extension of time that may be allowed by MMTC under Sub-clause 2.4 of this Agreement, the failure of the Overseas Supplier to fulfill the countertrade obligations as per this Agreement shall be subject to liquidated damages in the following manner:

8.1.1 If only less than 50 percent of the export obligations has been fulfilled within the time period specified under Clause 2 of this Agreement, then 100 percent of the EPBG would be forfeited.

8.1.2 If only 50 percent or more of the export obligations as per Sub-clause 2.2 of this Agreement has been fulfilled within the stipulated time as per Clause 2 of this Agreement, then the encashment of the EPBG would be on a pro-rata basis of the unfulfilled part of the export obligations.

Clause 9

9.1 The Overseas Supplier shall not be liable for any delay due to labor strike, fire, floods, war, riot and any other circumstances beyond its control by reason of Force Majeure and which materially affects the due performance of its export obligations under this Agreement. The Overseas Supplier shall notify the MMTC with documentary proof as soon as any such Force Majeure occurs.

9.2 The Overseas Supplier shall provide MMTC with all the necessary proof of the occurrence of any of the aforementioned events and of their effect on the Overseas Supplier's export obligations, should it wish to apply for an extension of the date of completion of the export obligations under Sub-clause 2.4. Failure to provide MMTC with the necessary proof shall not entitle the Overseas Supplier to make a claim under this clause. MMTC shall be entitled to conduct an investigation into the delay immediately, and if the Overseas Supplier is unable to fulfill its export obligations under this Agreement within the period stipulated in Sub-clause 2.4 by reason of Force Majeure as above, MMTC shall, if it has reasonable grounds for believing the reason given in the notice, extend the period of completion of the export obligations as MMTC thinks fit.

Clause 10

10.1 All export purchases and subsequent exports of goods as per this Agreement shall be subject to the policy, guidelines and procedures laid down by the Government of India from time to time during the time this Agreement is in force.

ARBITRATION

Clause 11

11.1 Any dispute/difference arising out of this Agreement shall be settled in a friendly and amicable manner between the two parties. Should this not be possible, then the procedures under the Indian Arbitration Act will apply. The place of arbitration shall be New Delhi. The arbitrator shall give reasoned award.

Clause 12

12.1 Normally, all export invoicing and Letters of Credit would be in freely convertible U.S. dollars. Should any export be invoiced in any other freely convertible currency, then, for the purpose of assessment of fulfillment under the Agreement, the invoice value would be converted into U.S. dollars at the rate of exchange prevailing between these currencies on the date of the presentation of documents to the bank for payment. The rate of exchange would be as determined by the Reserve Bank of India.

COMMUNICATION

Clause 13

13.1 All communications shall be made to the party at the address first set forth above or communicated in writing by either party to another.

Clause 14

14.1 This Agreement shall be governed and construed in accordance with the laws of India.

14.2 The Overseas Supplier hereby irrevocably submits to the exclusive jurisdiction of the Courts of India.

ADDITIONALITY

Clause 15

The purpose of the Counterpurchase Agreement is to generate additional exports and not to divert existing exports from India.

Additionality is to be seen with reference to the base level of export of the individual Indian exporter. In this regard, exports of the India exporter for a particular commodity and to a particular destination in the base year would be relevant.

An Additionality Certificate is to be furnished by the Indian exporter accordingly.

IN WITNESS WHEREOF, the parties hereto have caused this Agreement to be executed in their respective names and by their only authorized representatives, the day and year first above written.

Signed for and on behalf of
The Minerals & Metals Trading
Corporation of India Ltd.,
New Delhi

Signed for and on behalf of
Overseas Supplier/Countertrade
Obligant

In the presence of
Witness
1.
2.

INDEX

State government, 27-28
Statistics, international, 26
Statistical Abstract of the United States, 26
Statistical Yearbook, 27
Strategic alliance, 200-206, 223-24
Strategic planning, 273
Strategist, marketing, 48
Strategy formulation, 109
Sumitomo, 102
Sumitomo Heavy Industries, 202
Sun Microsystems, 135
Survey methods, 49, 51-53
Switch trading, 178, 188
Syntellect, Inc., 1, 3

Tabak S.A., 195
Target audience, 239, 242, 244-46
Ted Bates, 251, 252
Television, 242-45
Terms of sale, 148
Territory, 63
Testing, 131
Tetra Pak International, 124-25
Texas Instruments, 203
Thompson, J. Walter, 251
3M Corp., 217, 227
Timberland Shoes, 65, 66
Time, 245, 247
Toshiba, 203
Toyota, 49, 127, 231
Toys 'R' Us, 4
Trade association, 28
Trade fair, 68-69
Trade financing, 162-69
Trademark licensing, 93-94
Trading company, 99, 101-4
Trailmobile Company, 198
Training, 276-77
Translation-retranslation approach, 52
Turbo Tek Inc., 125
Turnkey operation, 205

Union Carbide, 59
Unilever, 119, 122, 226
United Nations, 57, 121

United Nations Conference on Trade & Development, 90
United Pictures International, 252
U.S.–Canada Free Trade Arrangement, 193
U.S. Census Bureau International Data Base, 57
U.S. Customs Service, 81
U.S. Dept. of Commerce. *See* Commerce, U.S. Dept. of.
U.S. Dept. of Defense, 98
U.S. Foreign and Commercial Service, 50-51
U.S. government services, 26,33, 50-51, 21
U.S. Supreme Court, 81
U.S. Trade Development Program (TDP), 171
United Technologies, 172, 203, 254
Pratt & Whitney division of, 203
Universal, 252
UTA, 204

Viacom International, 240
Volkswagen AG, 195
Volvo, 228

Wall Street Journal, 43, 83, 155, 194-95, 216, 245, 247 258, 265, 267, 274
Warner-Lambert Inc., 80
Whirlpool Corporation, 2, 252, 258
Wilhelm Zuleeg Company, 6
World Atlas, 27
World Bank Group, 27, 57, 171
World Information Services, 58
World trade clubs, 28
World Traders Data Report, 158
WPP Group, 251
Wrangler, 240
Wrigley s, 240

Xerox, 247

Young & Rubicam, 252

Zeiger, Jeffrey, 8
Zenith Data Systems, 192